P9-CLD-307

A Pocket
Style
Manual

A Pocket Style Manual

Sixth Edition

Diana Hacker

Nancy Sommers
Harvard University

Contributing ESL Specialist
Marcy Carbajal Van Horn
St. Edward's University

Bedford/St. Martin's
Boston ◆ New York

For Bedford/St. Martin's

Executive Editor: Michelle M. Clark
Senior Editors: Mara Weible and Barbara G. Flanagan
Production Editors: Lindsay DiGianvittorio and Rosemary Jaffe
Senior Production Supervisor: Jennifer Peterson
Production Assistant: Laura Winstead
Senior Marketing Manager: Marjorie Adler
Editorial Assistant: Kylie Paul
Copyeditor: Linda McLatchie
Indexer: Ellen Kuhl Repetto
Permissions Manager: Kalina K. Ingham
Senior Art Director: Anna Palchik
Text Design: Claire Seng-Niemoeller
Cover Design: Donna Lee Dennison
Composition: Nesbitt Graphics, Inc.
Printing and Binding: Quad/Graphics Leominster

President: Joan E. Feinberg
Editorial Director: Denise B. Wydra
Editor in Chief: Karen S. Henry
Director of Marketing: Karen R. Soeltz
Director of Production: Susan W. Brown
Associate Director, Editorial Production: Elise S. Kaiser
Managing Editor: Elizabeth M. Schaaf

Library of Congress Control Number: 2011932253

Manufactured in the United States of America.

6   5   4   3

g   f

Distributed outside North America by PALGRAVE MACMILLAN,
Houndmills, Basingstoke, Hampshire RG21 6XS

For information, write: Bedford/St. Martin's, 75 Arlington
Street, Boston, MA 02116 (617-399-4000)

ISBN: 978-0-312-54254-2

Acknowledgments

How to use this book

A Pocket Style Manual is a quick reference for writers and researchers. As a writer, you can turn to it for advice on revising sentences for clarity, grammar, punctuation, and mechanics. As a researcher, you can refer to its tips on finding and evaluating sources and to its color-coded sections on writing MLA, APA, *Chicago*, and CSE papers.

Here are the book's key reference features.

The brief or detailed contents   The brief table of contents inside the front cover can help you identify broad areas of helpful coverage. To target specific sections, check the detailed contents inside the back cover.

The index   If you're not sure which topic to choose from the tables of contents, check the index at the back of the book, which includes user-friendly terms like "*I* vs. *me*" to point to common problems like pronoun case.

Charts and checklists   If you need quick advice on revising a draft or preparing for a writing center visit, you can find key strategies for improving your writing in the charts and checklists throughout the book and at the end of the book, after the index.

MLA, APA, *Chicago*, and CSE papers   Color-coded sections help you focus on the kind of research paper you are writing. You can refer to discipline-specific advice on supporting a thesis, avoiding plagiarism, and integrating sources in MLA, APA, and *Chicago* styles. Directories to documentation models in MLA, APA, *Chicago*, and CSE styles appear on the first pages of each section and in the back of the book.

The glossaries   When in doubt about the correct use of commonly confused or misused words (such as *affect* and *effect*), consult section 47, the glossary of usage. For brief definitions of grammatical terms such as *subordinate clause* or *participial phrase*, turn to section 48.

Web references   Check the bottoms of pages for references to practice exercises or complete model papers on the book's companion Web site (hackerhandbooks.com/pocket). See the next page for more about these free online resources.

How to use the companion Web site

Throughout *A Pocket Style Manual*, you'll find references to models, practice exercises, and additional support at **hackerhandbooks.com/pocket**. The resources listed here are free.

Exercises   Practice online with more than 1,400 interactive grammar and research exercise items with immediate feedback. Unique research exercises help you integrate and document sources and avoid plagiarism.

Model papers   More than thirty models of student writing in five documentation styles provide cross-curricular examples of writing and formatting various types of documents. Model papers are listed by genre and by documentation style.

Revision   Check out papers in progress and models of global and sentence-level revisions.

Research and Documentation Online   Consult guidelines and models for finding and documenting sources in more than thirty academic disciplines.

Multilingual writers and ESL   Check out charts, study help, sample papers, and exercises designed for writers who speak languages in addition to English.

Writing center resources   Make the most of your writing center sessions with revision checklists and helpsheets for common writing, grammar, and research problems.

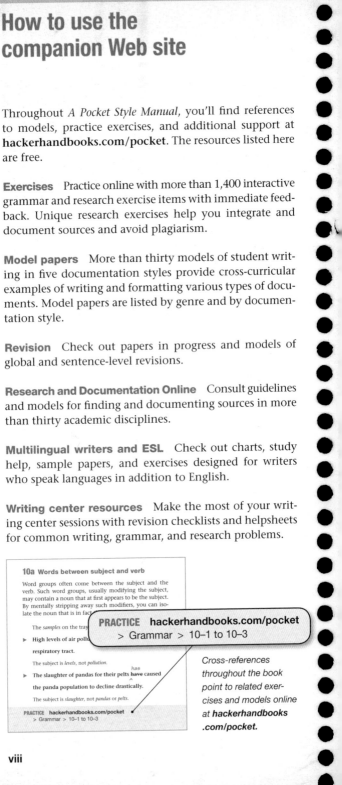

10a Words between subject and verb

Word groups often come between the subject and the verb. Such word groups, usually modifying the subject, may contain a noun that at first appears to be the subject. By mentally stripping away such modifiers, you can isolate the noun that is in fact

The *samples* on the tray

► High levels of air poll

respiratory tract.

The subject is *levels*, not *pollution*.

► The slaughter of pandas for their pelts **has caused** the panda population to decline drastically.

The subject is *slaughter*, not *pandas* or *pelts*.

PRACTICE   hackerhandbooks.com/pocket
  > Grammar > 10–1 to 10–3

PRACTICE   **hackerhandbooks.com/pocket**
> Grammar > 10–1 to 10–3

*Cross-references throughout the book point to related exercises and models online at **hackerhandbooks .com/pocket**.*

Clarity

1 Tighten wordy sentences.

Long sentences are not necessarily wordy, nor are short sentences always concise. A sentence is wordy if it can be tightened without loss of meaning.

1a Redundancies

Redundancies such as *cooperate together*, *yellow in color*, and *basic essentials* are a common source of wordiness. There is no need to say the same thing twice.

▶ Daniel ~~is employed~~ at a private rehabilitation center
  works
  ~~working~~ as a physical therapist.

Modifiers are redundant when their meanings are suggested by other words in the sentence.

▶ Sylvia ~~very hurriedly~~ scribbled her name and

  phone number on the back of a greasy napkin.

1b Empty or inflated phrases

An empty word or phrase can be cut with little or no loss of meaning. An inflated phrase can be reduced to a word or two.

▶ ~~In my opinion,~~ Our current immigration policy is
                    O

  misguided.

                   now.
▶ Funds are limited ~~at this point in time.~~

INFLATED	CONCISE
along the lines of	like
at the present time	now, currently
because of the fact that	because
by means of	by
due to the fact that	because
for the reason that	because
in order to	to
in spite of the fact that	although, though

PRACTICE hackerhandbooks.com/pocket
> Clarity > 1–1 to 1–4

INFLATED	CONCISE
in the event that	if
until such time as	until

1c Needlessly complex structures

In a rough draft, sentence structures are often more complex than they need to be.

▶ Researchers ~~were involved in examining~~ the effect of classical music on unborn babies.
examined

▶ ~~It is imperative that~~ all night managers *must* follow strict procedures when locking the safe.
A

▶ The analyst claimed that because of volatile market conditions she could not ~~make an~~ estimate ~~of~~ the company's future profits.

2 Prefer active verbs.

As a rule, active verbs express meaning more vigorously than their weaker counterparts — forms of the verb *be* or verbs in the passive voice. Forms of *be* (*be, am, is, are, was, were, being, been*) lack vigor because they convey no action. Passive verbs lack strength because their subjects receive the action instead of doing it.

Forms of *be* and passive verbs have legitimate uses, but if an active verb can convey your meaning as effectively, use it.

BE VERB   A surge of power *was* responsible for the destruction of the pumps.

PASSIVE   The pumps *were destroyed* by a surge of power.

ACTIVE   A surge of power *destroyed* the pumps.

2a When to replace *be* verbs

Not every *be* verb needs replacing. The forms of *be* (*be, am, is, are, was, were, being, been*) work well when you want to link a subject to a noun that clearly renames it or to a vivid adjective that describes it: *Orchard House was the home of Louisa May Alcott. The harvest will be bountiful after the summer rains.*

If a *be* verb makes a sentence needlessly wordy, however, consider replacing it. Often a phrase following the verb will contain a word (such as *violation*) that suggests a more vigorous, active verb (*violate*).

▶ Burying nuclear waste in Antarctica would ~~be in~~ *violate*

   ~~violation of~~ an international treaty.

▶ When Rosa Parks ~~was resistant to~~ giving up her *resisted*

   seat on the bus, she became a civil rights hero.

NOTE: When used as helping verbs with present participles to express ongoing action, *be* verbs are fine: *She was swimming when the whistle blew.* (See 11b.)

2b When to replace passive verbs

In the active voice, the subject of the sentence does the action; in the passive, the subject receives the action.

ACTIVE   The committee *reached* a decision.

PASSIVE   A decision *was reached* by the committee.

In passive sentences, the actor (in this case *committee*) frequently does not appear: *A decision was reached.*

In most cases, you will want to emphasize the actor, so you should use the active voice. To replace a passive verb with an active one, make the actor the subject of the sentence.

▶ ~~The~~ debris ~~was removed~~ from the construction site. *The contractor removed the*

▶ ~~The land was stripped of timber before the settlers~~ *The settlers stripped the land of timber before realizing*

   ~~realized~~ the consequences of their actions.

The passive voice is appropriate when you wish to emphasize the receiver of the action or to minimize the importance of the actor. In the following sentence, for example, the writer wished to focus on the tobacco plants, not on the people spraying them: *As the time for harvest approaches, the tobacco plants are sprayed with a chemical to retard the growth of suckers.*

NOTE: Scientific writing often uses the passive voice to emphasize the experiment or the process rather than the researcher: *The solution was heated to the boiling point and then reduced in volume by 50 percent.*

3 Balance parallel ideas.

If two or more ideas are parallel, they should be expressed in parallel grammatical form.

A kiss can be a comma, a question mark, or an
exclamation point.   —Mistinguett

This novel is not to be tossed lightly aside, but to
be hurled with great force.   —Dorothy Parker

3a Items in a series

Balance all items in a series by presenting them in parallel grammatical form.

▶   Cross-training involves a variety of exercises,
    such as running, swimming, and weights.
                                        lifting
    ^

▶   Children who study music also learn confidence,
                         creativity.
    discipline, and ~~they are creative.~~
                    ^

▶   Racing to work, Sam drove down the middle of the
                              ignored
    road, ran one red light, and two stop signs.
                                  ^

3b Paired ideas

When pairing ideas, underscore their connection by expressing them in similar grammatical form. Paired ideas are usually connected in one of three ways: (1) with a coordinating conjunction such as *and*, *but*, or *or*; (2) with a pair of correlative conjunctions such as *either . . . or*, *neither . . . nor*, *not only . . . but also*, or *whether . . . or*; or (3) with a word introducing a comparison, usually *than* or *as*.

▶ Many states are reducing property taxes for home

               extending
  owners and ~~extend~~ financial aid in the form of tax
          ^

  credits to renters.

    The coordinating conjunction *and* connects two *-ing* verb
    forms: *reducing . . . extending*.

▶ Thomas Edison was not only a prolific inventor

  but also ~~was~~ a successful entrepreneur.

    The correlative conjunction *not only . . . but also* connects two
    noun phrases: *a prolific inventor* and *a successful entrepreneur*.

                          to ground
▶ It is easier to speak in abstractions than ~~grounding~~

  one's thoughts in reality.

    The comparative term *than* links two infinitive phrases: *to
    speak . . . to ground*.

NOTE: Repeat function words such as prepositions (*by*, *to*) and subordinating conjunctions (*that*, *because*) to make parallel ideas easier to grasp.

▶ Our study revealed that left-handed students were

  more likely to have trouble with classroom desks
    that
  and rearranging desks for exam periods was useful.
  ^

4   Add needed words.

Do not omit words necessary for grammatical or logical completeness. Readers need to see at a glance how the parts of a sentence are connected.

4a Words in compound structures

In compound structures, words are often omitted for economy: *Tom is a man who means what he says and [who] says what he means.* Such omissions are acceptable as long as the omitted word is common to both parts of the compound structure.

If a sentence defies grammar or idiom because an omitted word is not common to both parts of the compound structure, the word must be put back in.

▶ Some of the regulars are acquaintances whom we *who* see at work or live in our community.

The word *who* must be included because *whom live in our community* is not grammatically correct.

▶ Mayor Davidson never has and never will accept a *accepted* bribe.

Has . . . accept is not grammatically correct.

▶ Many South Pacific tribes still believe and live by *in* ancient laws.

Believe . . . by is not idiomatic English.

4b The word *that*

Add the word *that* if there is any danger of misreading without it.

▶ In his obedience experiments, psychologist Stanley Milgram discovered ordinary people were willing to *that* inflict physical pain on strangers.

Milgram didn't discover people; he discovered that people were willing to inflict pain on strangers.

4c Words in comparisons

Comparisons should be between items that are alike. To compare unlike items is illogical and distracting.

▶ The forests of North America are much more extensive than Europe. *those of*

Comparisons should be complete so that readers will understand what is being compared.

INCOMPLETE   Brand X is less salty.

COMPLETE   Brand X is less salty than Brand Y.

Also, comparisons should leave no ambiguity about meaning. In the following sentence, two interpretations are possible.

AMBIGUOUS   Kai helped me more than my roommate.

CLEAR   Kai helped me more than *he helped* my roommate.

CLEAR   Kai helped me more than my roommate *did*.

5 Eliminate confusing shifts.

5a Shifts in point of view

The point of view of a piece of writing is the perspective from which it is written: first person (*I* or *we*), second person (*you*), or third person (*he, she, it, one,* or *they*). The *I* (or *we*) point of view, which emphasizes the writer, is a good choice for writing based primarily on personal experience. The *you* point of view, which emphasizes the reader, works well for giving advice or explaining how to do something. The third-person point of view, which emphasizes the subject, is appropriate in most academic and professional writing.

Writers who are having difficulty settling on an appropriate point of view sometimes shift confusingly from one to another. The solution is to choose a suitable perspective and then stay with it. (See also 12a.)

▶   Our class practiced rescuing a victim trapped in a
          We   *our*
    wrecked car. ~~You~~ were graded on ~~your~~ speed and
    our   ^   ^
    ~~your~~ skill.
    ^

          You
▶   ~~Travelers~~ need a signed passport for trips abroad.
    ^
    You should also fill out the emergency information

    page in the passport.

5b Shifts in tense

Consistent verb tenses clearly establish the time of the actions being described. When a passage begins in one tense and then shifts without warning and for no reason to another, readers are distracted and confused.

▶ There was no way I could fight the current and
                                                  jumped
  win. Just as I was losing hope, a stranger ~~jumps~~
                       ^
           swam
  off a passing boat and ~~swims~~ toward me.
                    ^

Writers often shift verb tenses when writing about literature. The literary convention is to describe fictional events consistently in the present tense. (See p. 29.)

6 Untangle mixed constructions.

A mixed construction contains sentence parts that do not sensibly fit together. The mismatch may be a matter of grammar or of logic.

6a Mixed grammar

You should not begin with one grammatical plan and then switch without warning to another.

     M
▶ ~~For~~ most drivers who have a blood alcohol level
     ^
  of .05 percent increase their risk of causing an
  accident.

The prepositional phrase beginning with *For* cannot serve as the subject of the verb *increase*. The revision makes *drivers* the subject.

▶ Although the United States is a wealthy nation, ~~but~~
  more than 20 percent of our children live in poverty.

The coordinating conjunction *but* cannot link a subordinate clause (*Although . . .*) with an independent clause (*more than 20 percent . . .*).

6b Illogical connections

A sentence's subject and verb should make sense together.

▶ Under the revised plan, the elderly,/~~who now receive~~ _the double personal exemption for_

  ~~a double personal exemption,~~ will be abolished.

  The exemption, not the elderly, will be abolished.

▶ We decided that ~~Tiffany's welfare~~ would not be _Tiffany_

  safe living with her mother.

  Tiffany, not her welfare, would not be safe.

6c Is when, is where, and reason . . . is because constructions

In formal English, readers sometimes object to _is when_, _is where_, and _reason . . . is because_ constructions on grammatical or logical grounds.

▶ Anorexia nervosa is ~~where people~~ think they are too _a disorder suffered by people who_

  fat and diet to the point of starvation.

  Anorexia nervosa is a disorder, not a place.

▶ ~~The reason~~ ╱The experiment failed ~~is~~ because _T_

  conditions in the lab were not sterile.

7 Repair misplaced and dangling modifiers.

Modifiers should point clearly to the words they modify. As a rule, related words should be kept together.

7a Misplaced words

The most commonly misplaced words are limiting modifiers such as _only_, _even_, _almost_, _nearly_, and _just_. They should appear in front of a verb only if they modify the verb. If they limit the meaning of some other word in the sentence, they should be placed in front of that word.

▶ Lasers ~~only~~ destroy the target, leaving the

> *only*

surrounding healthy tissue intact.

▶ I couldn't ~~even~~ save a dollar out of my paycheck.

> *even*

When the limiting modifier *not* is misplaced, the sentence usually suggests a meaning the writer did not intend.

▶ In the United States in 1860, all black southerners

> *not*

were ~~not~~ slaves.

The original sentence means that no black southerners were slaves. The revision makes the writer's real meaning clear.

7b Misplaced phrases and clauses

Although phrases and clauses can appear at some distance from the words they modify, make sure your meaning is clear. When phrases or clauses are oddly placed, absurd misreadings can result.

▶ ~~There~~ are many pictures of comedians who have

> *On the walls*

performed at Gavin's. ~~on the walls.~~

The comedians weren't performing on the walls; the pictures were on the walls.

▶ The robber was described as a six-foot-tall man

> *170-pound,*

with a mustache. ~~weighing 170 pounds.~~

The robber, not the mustache, weighed 170 pounds.

7c Dangling modifiers

A dangling modifier fails to refer logically to any word in the sentence. Dangling modifiers are usually introductory word groups (such as verbal phrases) that suggest but do not name an actor. When a sentence opens with such a modifier, readers expect the subject of the next clause to name the actor. If it doesn't, the modifier dangles.

DANGLING Upon entering the doctor's office, a skeleton caught my attention.

This sentence suggests — absurdly — that the skeleton entered the doctor's office.

To repair a dangling modifier, you can revise the sentence in one of two ways:

1. Name the actor in the subject of the sentence.
2. Name the actor in the modifier.

▶ Upon entering the doctor's office, a skeleton *I noticed*

~~caught my attention.~~

▶ *As I entered* ~~Upon entering~~ the doctor's office, a skeleton

caught my attention.

You cannot repair a dangling modifier simply by moving it: *A skeleton caught my attention upon entering the doctor's office.* The sentence still suggests that the skeleton entered the doctor's office.

▶ **Wanting to create checks and balances on power,**

the framers of
the Constitution divided the government into three

branches.

The framers (not the Constitution itself) wanted to create checks and balances.

▶ **After completing seminary training,** *women were often denied* **~~women's~~**

access to the priesthood. ~~was often denied.~~

The women (not their access to the priesthood) completed the training. The writer has revised the sentence by making *women* (not *women's access*) the subject.

7d Split infinitives

An infinitive consists of *to* plus a verb: *to think, to dance.* When a modifier appears between its two parts, an infinitive is said to be "split": *to carefully balance.* If a split infinitive is awkward, move the modifier to another position in the sentence.

▶   Cardiologists encourage their patients to

~~more carefully~~ watch their cholesterol levels.∕ *more carefully.*

Attempts to avoid split infinitives sometimes result in awkward sentences. When alternative phrasing sounds unnatural, most experts allow — and even encourage — splitting the infinitive. *We decided to actually enforce the law* is a natural construction in English. *We decided actually to enforce the law* is not.

8   Provide sentence variety.

When a rough draft is filled with too many same-sounding sentences, try to inject some variety — as long as you can do so without sacrificing clarity or ease of reading.

8a Combining choppy sentences

If a series of short sentences sounds choppy, consider combining sentences. Look for opportunities to tuck some of your ideas into subordinate clauses. A subordinate clause, which contains a subject and a verb, begins with a word such as *after, although, because, before, if, since, that, unless, until, when, where, which,* or *who.* (See p. 276.)

▶   We keep our use of insecticides to a minimum.∕
    because we
    ~~We~~ are concerned about the environment.

Also look for opportunities to tuck some of your ideas into phrases, word groups without subjects or verbs (or both).

▶   The Chesapeake and Ohio Canal, ~~is~~ a 184-mile

    waterway constructed in the 1800s.∕ ~~It~~ was a major

    source of transportation for goods during the

    Civil War.

▶ *Enveloped*
~~Sister Consilio was enveloped~~ in a black robe with only
  ^

her face and hands visible~~.~~/, ~~She~~ was an imposing figure.
                              Sister Consilio
                                    ^

When short sentences contain ideas of equal importance, it is often effective to combine them with *and*, *but*,
or *or*.

                                                    and
▶ Shore houses were flooded up to the first floor~~.~~/,
                                                  ^

Brant's Lighthouse was swallowed by the sea.

8b Varying sentence openings

Most sentences in English begin with the subject, move
to the verb, and continue to an object, with modifiers
tucked in along the way or put at the end. For the most
part, such sentences are fine. Put too many of them in a
row, however, and they become monotonous.

Words, phrases, or clauses modifying the verb can
often be inserted ahead of the subject.

▶ *Eventually a*
~~A~~ few drops of sap ~~eventually~~ began to trickle into
  ^

the pail.

▶ *Just as the sun was coming up, a*
~~A~~ pair of black ducks flew over the pond. ~~just as the~~
  ^   ^

~~sun was coming up.~~

Participial phrases (beginning with verb forms such
as *driving* or *exhausted*) can frequently be moved to the
beginning of a sentence without loss of clarity.

                    D
▶ ~~The committee,~~ ~~d~~iscouraged by the researchers'
                    ^   *the committee*
apparent lack of progress, nearly withdrew funding
                          ^
for the prize-winning experiments.

NOTE: In a sentence that begins with a participial phrase,
the subject of the sentence must name the person or
thing being described. If it doesn't, the phrase dangles.
(See 7c.)

9 Find an appropriate voice.

An appropriate voice is one that suits your subject, engages your audience, and conforms to the conventions of the genre in which you are writing, such as lab reports, informal essays, research papers, business memos, and so on.

In academic and professional writing, certain language is generally considered inappropriate: jargon, clichés, slang, and sexist or biased language.

9a Jargon

Jargon is specialized language used among members of a trade, profession, or group. Use jargon only when readers will be familiar with it; even then, use it only when plain English will not do as well.

JARGON   We outsourced the work to an outfit in Ohio because we didn't have the bandwidth to tackle it in-house.

REVISED   We hired a company in Ohio because we had too few employees to do the work.

Broadly defined, jargon includes puffed-up language designed more to impress readers than to inform them. The following are common examples from business, government, higher education, and the military, with plain English translations in parentheses.

commence (begin)	indicator (sign)
components (parts)	optimal (best)
endeavor (try)	parameters (boundaries, limits)
facilitate (help)	prior to (before)
finalize (finish)	utilize (use)
impact (v.) (affect)	viable (workable)

Sentences filled with jargon are hard to read and often wordy.

▶ The CEO should ~~dialogue~~ *talk* with investors about ~~partnering~~ *working* with clients to buy land in ~~economically~~ *poor* ~~deprived zones.~~ *neighborhoods.*

▶ All ~~employees functioning in the capacity of~~
work-study students ~~are required to give evidence of~~
~~current enrollment.~~

must prove that they are
currently enrolled. ^

9b Clichés

The pioneer who first announced that he had "slept like a log" no doubt amused his companions with a fresh and unlikely comparison. Today, however, that comparison is a cliché, a saying that can no longer add emphasis or surprise. To see just how predictable clichés are, put your hand over the right-hand column below and then finish the phrases given on the left.

cool as a	cucumber
beat around the	bush
busy as a	bee, beaver
crystal	clear
light as a	feather
like a bull	in a china shop
playing with	fire
nutty as a	fruitcake
selling like	hotcakes
water under the	bridge
white as a	sheet, ghost
avoid clichés like the	plague

The solution for clichés is simple: Just delete them. Sometimes you can write around a cliché by adding an element of surprise. One student who had written that she had butterflies in her stomach revised her cliché like this:

> If all of the action in my stomach is caused by butterflies, there must be a horde of them, with horseshoes on.

The image of butterflies wearing horseshoes is fresh and unlikely, not predictable like the original cliché.

9c Slang

Slang is an informal and sometimes private vocabulary that expresses the solidarity of a group such as teenagers, rock musicians, or sports fans. Although it does have a certain vitality, slang is a code that not everyone understands, and it is too informal for most written work.

▶ When the server crashed, three hours of unsaved *we lost*

data, ~~went down the tubes.~~

9d Sexist language

Sexist language excludes, stereotypes, or demeans women or men and should be avoided.

In your writing, avoid referring to any one profession as exclusively male or exclusively female (teachers as women or engineers as men, for example). Also avoid using different conventions when identifying women and men.

▶ All executives' ~~wives~~ *spouses* are invited to the picnic.

▶ Boris Stotsky, attorney, and ~~Mrs.~~ Cynthia Jones, *graphic designer,*
~~mother of three,~~ are running for city council.

Traditionally, *he*, *him*, and *his* were used to refer generically to persons of either sex: *A journalist is motivated by his deadline*. You can avoid such sexist usage in one of three ways: substitute a pair of pronouns (*he or she*, *his or her*); reword in the plural; or revise the sentence to avoid the problem.

▶ A journalist is motivated by his *or her* deadline.

▶ *Journalists are* ~~A journalist is~~ motivated by ~~his deadline.~~ *their deadlines.*

▶ A journalist is motivated by ~~his~~ *a* deadline.

Like *he* and *his*, the nouns *man* and *men* and related words were once used generically to refer to persons of either sex. Use gender-neutral terms instead.

INAPPROPRIATE	APPROPRIATE
chairman	chairperson, chair
congressman	representative, legislator
fireman	firefighter
mailman	mail carrier, postal worker
mankind	people, humans
to man	to operate, to staff
weatherman	meteorologist, forecaster

9e Offensive language

Obviously it is impolite to use offensive terms such as *Polack* or *redneck*, but offensive language can take more subtle forms. When describing groups of people, choose names that the groups currently use to describe themselves.

▶ North Dakota takes its name from the ~~Indian~~ word
     Lakota

  meaning "friend" or "ally."

▶ Many ~~Oriental~~ immigrants have recently settled in
     Asian

  our small town.

Avoid stereotyping a person or a group even if you believe your generalization to be positive.

▶ It was no surprise that Greer, ~~a Chinese American,~~
     an excellent math and science student,

  was selected for the honors chemistry program.

Grammar

10 Make subjects and verbs agree.

In the present tense, verbs agree with their subjects in number (singular or plural) and in person (first, second, or third). The present-tense ending -s is used on a verb if its subject is third-person singular; otherwise the verb takes no ending. Consider, for example, the present-tense forms of the verb *give*:

	SINGULAR	PLURAL
FIRST PERSON	I give	we give
SECOND PERSON	you give	you give
THIRD PERSON	he/she/it gives	they give
	Yolanda gives	parents give

The verb *be* varies from this pattern; it has special forms in *both* the present and the past tense.

PRESENT-TENSE FORMS OF *BE*		**PAST-TENSE FORMS OF** *BE*	
I am	we are	I was	we were
you are	you are	you were	you were
he/she/it is	they are	he/she/it was	they were

This section describes particular situations that can cause problems with subject-verb agreement.

10a Words between subject and verb

Word groups often come between the subject and the verb. Such word groups, usually modifying the subject, may contain a noun that at first appears to be the subject. By mentally stripping away such modifiers, you can isolate the noun that is in fact the subject.

The *samples* on the tray in the lab *need* testing.

▶ High levels of air pollution damages the

respiratory tract.

The subject is *levels*, not *pollution*.

▶ The slaughter of pandas for their pelts ~~have~~ caused
                                            has
the panda population to decline drastically.

The subject is *slaughter*, not *pandas* or *pelts*.

PRACTICE hackerhandbooks.com/pocket
> Grammar > 10–1 to 10–3

NOTE: Phrases beginning with the prepositions *as well as,
in addition to, accompanied by, together with,* and *along with*
do not make a singular subject plural: *The governor as well
as his aide was* [not *were*] *on the plane.*

10b Subjects joined with *and*

Compound subjects joined with *and* are nearly always
plural.

▶ Bleach and ammonia creates a toxic gas when mixed.

EXCEPTION: If the parts of the subject form a single unit,
you may treat the subject as singular: *Bacon and eggs is
always on the menu.*

10c Subjects joined with *or* or *nor*

With compound subjects joined with *or* or *nor*, make the
verb agree with the part of the subject nearer to the verb.

> *is*
▶ If an infant or a child ~~are~~ having difficulty breathing,
    seek medical attention immediately.

> *were*
▶ Neither the lab assistant nor the students ~~was~~ able
    to download the program.

10d Indefinite pronouns such as *someone*

Indefinite pronouns refer to nonspecific persons or things.
The following indefinite pronouns are singular: *anybody,
anyone, anything, each, either, everybody, everyone, everything,
neither, nobody, no one, somebody, someone, something.*

> *was*
▶ Nobody who participated in the taste tests ~~were~~ paid.

> *has*
▶ Each of the essays ~~have~~ been graded.

A few indefinite pronouns (*all, any, none, some*) may
be singular or plural depending on the noun or pronoun
they refer to: *Some of our luggage was lost. Some of the rocks
were slippery. None of his advice makes sense. None of the eggs
were broken.*

10e Collective nouns such as *jury*

Collective nouns such as *jury, committee, audience, crowd, class, family,* and *couple* name a class or a group. In American English, collective nouns are usually treated as singular: They emphasize the group as a unit.

▶ The board of trustees *meets* ~~meet~~ in Denver twice a year.

Occasionally, to draw attention to the individual members of the group, a collective noun may be treated as plural: *The class are debating among themselves.* Many writers prefer to add a clearly plural noun such as *members*: *The class members are debating among themselves.*

NOTE: In general, when fractions or units of measurement are used with a singular noun, treat them as singular; when they are used with a plural noun, treat them as plural: *Three-fourths of the pie has been eaten. One-fourth of the drivers were texting.*

10f Subject after verb

Verbs ordinarily follow subjects. When this normal order is reversed, it is easy to be confused.

▶ Of particular concern *are* ~~is~~ penicillin and tetracycline,

antibiotics used to make animals more resistant

to disease.

The subject, *penicillin and tetracycline,* is plural.

The subject always follows the verb in sentences beginning with *there is* or *there are* (or *there was* or *there were*).

▶ There *were* ~~was~~ a turtle and a snake in the tank.

The subject, *turtle and snake,* is plural, so the verb must be *were*.

10g *Who, which,* and *that*

Like most pronouns, the relative pronouns *who, which,* and *that* have antecedents, nouns or pronouns to which they refer. Relative pronouns used as subjects of subordinate clauses take verbs that agree with their antecedents.

ANT   PN   V

Take a *train that arrives* before 6:00.

Constructions such as *one of the students who* (or *one of the things that*) may cause problems for writers. Do not assume that the antecedent must be *one*. Instead, consider the logic of the sentence.

▶ **Our ability to use language is one of the things**

set

that ~~sets~~ us apart from animals.
        ^

The antecedent of *that* is *things,* not *one.* Several things set us apart from animals.

When the phrase *the only* comes before *one,* you are safe in assuming that *one* is the antecedent of the relative pronoun.

lives

▶ **Carmen is the only one of my friends who ~~live~~**
                                            ^

in my building.

The antecedent of *who* is *one,* not *friends.* Only one friend lives in the building.

10h Plural form, singular meaning

Words such as *athletics, economics, mathematics, physics, politics, statistics, measles,* and *news* are usually singular, despite their plural form.

is

▶ **Politics ~~are~~ among my mother's favorite pastimes.**
        ^

EXCEPTION: Occasionally some of these words, especially *economics, mathematics, politics,* and *statistics,* have plural meanings: *Office politics often affect decisions about hiring and promotion. The economics of the building plan are prohibitive.*

10i Titles, company names, and words mentioned as words

Titles, company names, and words mentioned as words are singular.

▶ *Lost Cities* ~~describe~~ the discoveries of fifty
      describes
      ^

ancient civilizations.

▶ Delmonico Brothers ~~specialize~~ in organic produce
      specializes
      ^

and additive-free meats.

▶ *Controlled substances* ~~are~~ a euphemism for illegal
      is
      ^

drugs.

11 Be alert to other problems with verbs.

Section 10 deals with subject-verb agreement. This section describes a few other potential problems with verbs.

11a Irregular verbs

For all regular verbs, the past-tense and past-participle forms are the same, ending in *-ed* or *-d*, so there is no danger of confusion. This is not true, however, for irregular verbs, such as the following.

BASE FORM	PAST TENSE	PAST PARTICIPLE
begin	began	begun
fly	flew	flown
ride	rode	ridden

The past-tense form, which never has a helping verb, expresses action that occurred entirely in the past. The past participle is used with a helping verb—either with *has, have,* or *had* to form one of the perfect tenses or with *be, am, is, are, was, were, being,* or *been* to form the passive voice.

PAST TENSE	Last July, we *went* to Paris.
PAST PARTICIPLE	We have *gone* to Paris twice.

When you aren't sure which verb form to choose (*went* or *gone, began* or *begun,* and so on), consult the list that begins at the bottom of this page. Choose the past-tense form if your sentence doesn't have a helping verb; choose the past-participle form if it does.

▶ Yesterday we ~~seen~~ a film about rain forests.
     saw
     ^

Because there is no helping verb, the past-tense form *saw* is required.

▶ By the end of the day, the stock market had ~~fell~~
     fallen
     ^

two hundred points.

Because of the helping verb *had*, the past-participle form *fallen* is required.

Distinguishing between *lie* and *lay*   Writers often confuse the forms of *lie* (meaning "to recline or rest on a surface") and *lay* (meaning "to put or place something"). The intransitive verb *lie* does not take a direct object: *The tax forms lie on the table.* The transitive verb *lay* takes a direct object: *Please lay the tax forms on the table.*

In addition to confusing the meanings of *lie* and *lay*, writers are often unfamiliar with the standard English forms of these verbs.

BASE FORM	PAST TENSE	PAST PARTICIPLE	PRESENT PARTICIPLE
lie	lay	lain	lying
lay	laid	laid	laying

Elizabeth was so exhausted that she *lay* down for a nap. [Past tense of *lie*, meaning "to recline"]

The prosecutor *laid* the photograph on a table close to the jurors. [Past tense of *lay*, meaning "to place"]

Letters dating from the Civil War were *lying* in the corner of the chest. [Present participle of *lie*]

The patient had *lain* in an uncomfortable position all night. [Past participle of *lie*]

Common irregular verbs

BASE FORM	PAST TENSE	PAST PARTICIPLE
arise	arose	arisen
awake	awoke, awaked	awaked, awoke
be	was, were	been

BASE FORM	PAST TENSE	PAST PARTICIPLE
beat	beat	beaten, beat
become	became	become
begin	began	begun
bend	bent	bent
bite	bit	bitten, bit
blow	blew	blown
break	broke	broken
bring	brought	brought
build	built	built
burst	burst	burst
buy	bought	bought
catch	caught	caught
choose	chose	chosen
cling	clung	clung
come	came	come
cost	cost	cost
deal	dealt	dealt
dig	dug	dug
dive	dived, dove	dived
do	did	done
draw	drew	drawn
dream	dreamed, dreamt	dreamed, dreamt
drink	drank	drunk
drive	drove	driven
eat	ate	eaten
fall	fell	fallen
fight	fought	fought
find	found	found
fly	flew	flown
forget	forgot	forgotten, forgot
freeze	froze	frozen
get	got	gotten, got
give	gave	given
go	went	gone
grow	grew	grown
hang (suspend)	hung	hung
hang (execute)	hanged	hanged
have	had	had
hear	heard	heard
hide	hid	hidden
hurt	hurt	hurt
keep	kept	kept
know	knew	known
lay (put)	laid	laid
lead	led	led
lend	lent	lent
let (allow)	let	let
lie (recline)	lay	lain

BASE FORM	PAST TENSE	PAST PARTICIPLE
lose	lost	lost
make	made	made
prove	proved	proved, proven
read	read	read
ride	rode	ridden
ring	rang	rung
rise (get up)	rose	risen
run	ran	run
say	said	said
see	saw	seen
send	sent	sent
set (place)	set	set
shake	shook	shaken
shoot	shot	shot
shrink	shrank	shrunk, shrunken
sing	sang	sung
sink	sank	sunk
sit (be seated)	sat	sat
slay	slew	slain
sleep	slept	slept
speak	spoke	spoken
spin	spun	spun
spring	sprang	sprung
stand	stood	stood
steal	stole	stolen
sting	stung	stung
strike	struck	struck, stricken
swear	swore	sworn
swim	swam	swum
swing	swung	swung
take	took	taken
teach	taught	taught
throw	threw	thrown
wake	woke, waked	waked, woken
wear	wore	worn
wring	wrung	wrung
write	wrote	written

11b Tense

Tenses indicate the time of an action in relation to the time of the speaking or writing about that action. The most common problem with tenses—shifting from one tense to another—is discussed in 5b. Other problems with tenses are detailed in this section, after the following survey of tenses.

Survey of tenses Tenses are classified as present, past, and future, with simple, perfect, and progressive forms for each.

The simple tenses indicate relatively simple time relations. The *simple present* tense is used primarily for actions occurring at the time they are being discussed or for actions occurring regularly. The *simple past* tense is used for actions completed in the past. The *simple future* tense is used for actions that will occur in the future. In the following table, the simple tenses are given for the regular verb *walk*, the irregular verb *ride*, and the highly irregular verb *be*.

SIMPLE PRESENT

SINGULAR		PLURAL	
I	walk, ride, am	we	walk, ride, are
you	walk, ride, are	you	walk, ride, are
he/she/it	walks, rides, is	they	walk, ride, are

SIMPLE PAST

SINGULAR		PLURAL	
I	walked, rode, was	we	walked, rode, were
you	walked, rode, were	you	walked, rode, were
he/she/it	walked, rode, was	they	walked, rode, were

SIMPLE FUTURE

I, you, he/she/it, we, they	will walk, ride, be

A verb in one of the perfect tenses (a form of *have* plus the past participle) expresses an action that was or will be completed at the time of another action.

PRESENT PERFECT

I, you, we, they	have walked, ridden, been
he/she/it	has walked, ridden, been

PAST PERFECT

I, you, he/she/it, we, they	had walked, ridden, been

FUTURE PERFECT

I, you, he/she/it, we, they	will have walked, ridden, been

Each of the six tenses has a progressive form used to describe actions in progress. A progressive verb consists of a form of *be* followed by the present participle.

PRESENT PROGRESSIVE

I	am walking, riding, being
he/she/it	is walking, riding, being
you, we, they	are walking, riding, being

PAST PROGRESSIVE

| I, he/she/it | was walking, riding, being |
| you, we, they | were walking, riding, being |

FUTURE PROGRESSIVE

| I, you, he/she/it, we, they | will be walking, riding, being |

PRESENT PERFECT PROGRESSIVE

| I, you, we, they | have been walking, riding, being |
| he/she/it | has been walking, riding, being |

PAST PERFECT PROGRESSIVE

| I, you, he/she/it, we, they | had been walking, riding, being |

FUTURE PERFECT PROGRESSIVE

| I, you, he/she/it, we, they | will have been walking, riding, being |

Special uses of the present tense Use the present tense when writing about literature or when expressing general truths.

▶ The scarlet letter ~~was~~ *is* a punishment placed on

  Hester's breast by the community, and yet it ~~was~~ *is*

  an imaginative product of Hester's own

  needlework.

▶ Galileo taught that the earth ~~revolved~~ *revolves* around

  the sun.

The past perfect tense The past perfect tense is used for an action already completed by the time of another past action. This tense consists of a past participle preceded by *had* (*had worked, had gone*).

▶ We built our cabin forty feet above an abandoned
  had been
  quarry that ~~was~~ flooded in 1920 to create a lake.

▶ By the time dinner was served, the guest of honor
  had
  left.

11c Mood

There are three moods in English: the *indicative*, used for facts, opinions, and questions; the *imperative*, used for orders or advice; and the *subjunctive*, used to express wishes, requests, or conditions contrary to fact. For many writers, the subjunctive is especially challenging.

For wishes and in *if* clauses expressing conditions contrary to fact, the subjunctive is the past-tense form of the verb; in the case of *be*, it is always *were* (not *was*), even if the subject is singular.

> I wish that Jamal *drove* more slowly late at night.

> If I *were* a member of Congress, I would vote for the bill.

TIP: Do not use the subjunctive mood in *if* clauses expressing conditions that exist or may exist: *If Danielle passes* [not *passed*] *the test, she will become a lifeguard.*

Use the subjunctive mood in *that* clauses following verbs such as *ask, insist, recommend,* and *request.* The subjunctive in such cases is the base form of the verb.

> Dr. Chung insists that her students *be* on time.

> We recommend that Dawson *file* form 1050 soon.

12 Use pronouns with care.

Pronouns are words that substitute for nouns: *he, it, them, her, me,* and so on. Pronoun errors are typically related to the four topics discussed in this section:

a. pronoun-antecedent agreement (singular vs. plural)
b. pronoun reference (clarity)
c. pronoun case (personal pronouns such as *I* vs. *me*)
d. pronoun case (*who* vs. *whom*)

12a Pronoun-antecedent agreement

The antecedent of a pronoun is the word the pronoun refers to. A pronoun and its antecedent agree when they are both singular or both plural.

SINGULAR   The *doctor* finished *her* rounds.

PLURAL   The *doctors* finished *their* rounds.

Indefinite pronouns   Indefinite pronouns refer to non-specific persons or things. Even though some of the following indefinite pronouns may seem to have plural meanings, treat them as singular in formal English: *anybody, anyone, anything, each, either, everybody, everyone, everything, neither, nobody, no one, nothing, somebody, someone, something.*

> In this class *everyone* performs at *his or her* [not *their*] own fitness level.

When *they* or *their* refers mistakenly to a singular antecedent such as *everyone*, you will usually have three options for revision:

1. Replace *they* with *he or she* (or *their* with *his or her*).
2. Make the antecedent plural.
3. Rewrite the sentence to avoid the problem.

Because the *he or she* construction is wordy, often the second or third revision strategy is more effective.

▶   If anyone wants to audition, ~~they~~ should sign up.
      he or she

▶   If ~~anyone wants~~ to audition, they should sign up.
      singers want

▶   ~~If anyone~~ wants to audition/~~they~~ should sign up.
      Anyone who

NOTE: The traditional use of *he* (or *his*) to refer to persons of either sex is now widely considered sexist. (See p. 17.)

Generic nouns   A generic noun represents a typical member of a group, such as *a student,* or any member of a group, such as *any lawyer.* Although generic nouns may seem to have plural meanings, they are singular.

> Every *runner* must train rigorously if *he or she wants* [not *they want*] to excel.

When a plural pronoun refers mistakenly to a generic noun, you will usually have the same revision options as for indefinite pronouns.

▶ *he or she wants*
A medical student must study hard if ~~they want~~ to
‸
succeed.

▶ *Medical students*
~~A medical student~~ must study hard if they want to
‸
succeed.

▶ A medical student must study hard ~~if they want~~ to
succeed.

Collective nouns   Collective nouns such as *jury*, *commit-tee*, *audience*, *crowd*, *family*, and *team* name a group. In American English, collective nouns are usually singular because they emphasize the group functioning as a unit.

The planning *committee* granted *its* [not *their*] permission to build.

If the members of the group function individually, however, you may treat the noun as plural: *The family put their signatures on the document.* Or you might add a plural antecedent such as *members* to the sentence: *The family members put their signatures on the document.*

12b Pronoun reference

In the sentence *When Andrew got home, he went straight to bed*, the noun *Andrew* is the antecedent of the pronoun *he*. A pronoun should refer clearly to its antecedent.

Ambiguous reference   Ambiguous reference occurs when the pronoun could refer to two possible antecedents.

▶ *The cake collapsed when Aunt Harriet put it*
~~When Aunt Harriet put the cake~~ on the table/. ~~it~~
‸   ‸
~~collapsed.~~

▶ *"You have*
Tom told James, ~~that he had~~ won the lottery."
‸   ‸

What collapsed—the cake or the table? Who won the lottery—Tom or James? The revisions eliminate the ambiguity.

Implied reference   A pronoun must refer to a specific antecedent, not to a word that is implied but not actually stated.

▶   After braiding Ann's hair, Sue decorated ~~them~~ with
    the braids

    ribbons.

Vague reference of *this, that,* or *which*   The pronouns *this, that,* and *which* should ordinarily refer to specific antecedents rather than to whole ideas or sentences. When a pronoun's reference is too vague, either replace the pronoun with a noun or supply an antecedent to which the pronoun clearly refers.

▶   Television advertising has created new demands for
    prescription drugs. People respond to ~~this~~ by asking
    the ads

    for drugs they may not need.

▶   Romeo and Juliet were both too young to have
    a fact
    acquired much wisdom, ~~and~~ that accounts for

    their rash actions.

Indefinite reference of *they, it,* or *you*   The pronoun *they* should refer to a specific antecedent. Do not use *they* to refer indefinitely to persons who have not been specifically mentioned.

    The board
▶   ~~They~~ announced an increase in sports fees for all

    student athletes.

The word *it* should not be used indefinitely in constructions such as *In the article, it says that. . . .*

    The
▶   ~~In the~~ encyclopedia ~~it~~ states that male moths can

    smell female moths from several miles away.

The pronoun *you* is appropriate only when the writer is addressing the reader directly: *Once you have kneaded the dough, let it rise in a warm place.* Except in informal contexts, however, *you* should not be used to mean "anyone in general." (See the example on p. 34.)

▶ Ms. Pickersgill's *Guide to Etiquette* stipulates that
a guest
~~you~~ should not arrive at a party too early or leave
  ^

too late.

12c Case of personal pronouns (*I* vs. *me* etc.)

The personal pronouns in the following list change what
is known as *case form* according to their grammatical function in a sentence. Pronouns functioning as subjects or
subject complements appear in the *subjective* case; those
functioning as objects appear in the *objective* case; and
those showing ownership appear in the *possessive* case.

SUBJECTIVE CASE	OBJECTIVE CASE	POSSESSIVE CASE
I	me	my
we	us	our
you	you	your
he/she/it	him/her/it	his/her/its
they	them	their

For the most part, you know how to use these forms
correctly. The structures discussed in this section may
tempt you to choose the wrong pronoun.

Compound word groups   You may sometimes be confused when a subject or an object appears as part of a
compound structure. To test for the correct pronoun,
mentally strip away all of the compound structure except
the pronoun in question.

she
▶ While diving for pearls, Ikiko and ~~her~~ found a
                                        ^
sunken boat.

> *Ikiko and she* is the subject of the verb *found*. Strip away the
> words *Ikiko and* to test for the correct pronoun: *she found*
> [not *her found*].

▶ The most traumatic experience for her father and
me
~~I~~ occurred long after her operation.
^

> *Her father and me* is the object of the preposition *for*. Strip
> away the words *her father and* to test for the correct pronoun:
> *for me* [not *for I*].

PRACTICE hackerhandbooks.com/pocket
  > Grammar > 12–7 and 12–8
          > 12–10 and 12–11 (pronoun case review)

When in doubt about the correct pronoun, some writers try to evade the choice by using a reflexive pronoun such as *myself*. Using a reflexive pronoun in such situations is nonstandard.

▶ The Indian cab driver gave my husband and
me
~~myself~~ some good tips on traveling in New Delhi.
  ^

   My husband and me is the indirect object of the verb gave.

Appositives   Appositives are noun phrases that rename nouns or pronouns. A pronoun used as an appositive has the same function (usually subject or object) as the word(s) it renames.

▶ The chief strategists, Dr. Bell and ~~me~~, could not
                                     I,
                                      ^
   agree on a plan.

   The appositive *Dr. Bell and I* renames the subject, *strategists*. Test: *I could not agree on a plan* [not *me could not agree on a plan*].

▶ The reporter interviewed only two witnesses, the
                                     me.
   shopkeeper and ~~I~~.
                   ^

   The appositive *the shopkeeper and me* renames the direct object, *witnesses*. Test: *interviewed me* [not *interviewed I*].

Subject complements   Use subjective-case pronouns for subject complements, which rename or describe the subject and usually follow *be, am, is, are, was, were, being,* or *been.*

▶ During the Lindbergh trial, Bruno Hauptmann
                                         he.
   repeatedly denied that the kidnapper was ~~him~~.
                                             ^

   If *kidnapper was he* seems too stilted, rewrite the sentence: *During the Lindbergh trial, Bruno Hauptmann repeatedly denied that he was the kidnapper.*

We or us before a noun   When deciding whether *we* or *us* should precede a noun, choose the pronoun that would be appropriate if the noun were omitted.

        We
▶ ~~Us~~ tenants would rather fight than move.
   ^

   Test: *We would rather fight* [not *Us would rather fight*].

us

▶ Management is shortchanging ~~we~~ tenants.
    ^

  Test: *Management is shortchanging us* [not *Management is short-changing we*].

Pronoun after *than* or *as*   When a comparison begins with *than* or *as*, your choice of pronoun will depend on your meaning. To test for the correct pronoun, finish the sentence.

I.

▶ My brother is six years older than ~~me.~~
    ^

  Test: *older than I* [*am*].

▶ We respected no other candidate for city council as
      her.
  much as ~~she.~~
       ^

  Test: *as much as* [*we respected*] *her.*

Pronoun before or after an infinitive   An infinitive is the word *to* followed by a verb. Both subjects and objects of infinitives take the objective case.

me

▶ Ms. Wilson asked John and ~~I~~ to drive the senator
    her   ^
  and ~~she~~ to the airport.
     ^

  John and me is the subject and *senator and her* is the object of the infinitive *to drive.*

Pronoun or noun before a gerund   If a pronoun modifies a gerund, use the possessive case: *my, our, your, his, her, its, their.* A gerund is a verb form ending in *-ing* that functions as a noun.

your

▶ The chances of ~~you~~ being hit by lightning are about
       ^
  two million to one.

Nouns as well as pronouns may modify gerunds. To form the possessive case of a noun, use an apostrophe and *-s* (*victim's*) for a singular noun or just an apostrophe (*victims'*) for a plural noun. (See also 19a.)

▶ The old order in France paid a high price for the
  aristocracy's
  ~~aristocracy~~ exploiting the lower classes.
  ^

12d *Who* or *whom*

Who, a subjective-case pronoun, is used for subjects and
subject complements. *Whom*, an objective-case pronoun,
is used for objects. The words *who* and *whom* appear primarily in subordinate clauses or in questions.

In subordinate clauses   When deciding whether to use
who or *whom* in a subordinate clause, check for the word's
function within the clause.

                          whoever
▶ He tells that story to ~~whomever~~ will listen.
                          ^

  Whoever is the subject of *will listen*. The entire subordinate
  clause *whoever will listen* is the object of the preposition *to*.

                                              whom
▶ You will work with our senior engineers, ~~who~~ you
                                              ^
  will meet later.

  Whom is the direct object of the verb *will meet*. This becomes
  clear if you restructure the clause: *you will meet whom later*.

In questions   When deciding whether to use *who* or
whom in a question, check for the word's function within
the question.

  Who
▶ ~~Whom~~ was responsible for creating that computer
  ^
  virus?

  Who is the subject of the verb *was*.

  Whom
▶ ~~Who~~ would you nominate for council president?
  ^

  Whom is the direct object of the verb *would nominate*. This
  becomes clear if you restructure the question: *You would
  nominate whom?*

PRACTICE   hackerhandbooks.com/pocket
   > Grammar > 12–9
             > 12–10 and 12–11 (pronoun case review)

13 Use adjectives and adverbs appropriately.

Adjectives modify nouns or pronouns; adverbs modify verbs, adjectives, or other adverbs.

Many adverbs are formed by adding *-ly* to adjectives (*formal, formally*). But don't assume that all words ending in *-ly* are adverbs or that all adverbs end in *-ly*. Some adjectives end in *-ly* (*lovely, friendly*), and some adverbs don't (*always, here*). When in doubt, consult a dictionary.

13a Adjectives

Adjectives ordinarily precede the nouns they modify. But they can also function as subject complements following linking verbs (usually a form of *be*: *be, am, is, are, was, were, being, been*). When an adjective functions as a subject complement, it describes the subject.

Justice is *blind*.

Verbs such as *smell, taste, look, appear, grow,* and *feel* may also be linking. If the word following one of these verbs describes the subject, use an adjective; if the word modifies the verb, use an adverb.

| ADJECTIVE | The detective looked *cautious*. |
| ADVERB | The detective looked *cautiously* for the fingerprints. |

Linking verbs usually suggest states of being, not actions. For example, to look *cautious* suggests the state of being cautious, whereas to look *cautiously* is to perform an action in a cautious way.

▶ Lori looked ~~well~~ *good* in her new raincoat.

▶ All of us on the debate team felt ~~badly~~ *bad* about our

performance.

The verbs *looked* and *felt* suggest states of being, not actions, so they should be followed by adjectives.

PRACTICE hackerhandbooks.com/pocket
  > Grammar > 13–1 and 13–2

13b Adverbs

Use adverbs to modify verbs, adjectives, and other adverbs.
Adverbs usually answer one of these questions: When?
Where? How? Why? Under what conditions? How often?
To what degree?

Adjectives are often used incorrectly in place of
adverbs in casual or nonstandard speech.

▶ The manager must ensure that the office runs
  smoothly   *efficiently.*
  ~~smooth~~ and ~~efficient.~~
  ^   ^

▶ The chance of recovering any property lost in the
                really
  fire looks ~~real~~ slim.
             ^

The incorrect use of the adjective *good* in place of the
adverb *well* is especially common in casual or nonstandard speech.

                                        well
▶ We were delighted that Nomo had done so ~~good~~
                                          ^

  on the exam.

13c Comparatives and superlatives

Most adjectives and adverbs have three forms: the positive, the comparative, and the superlative.

POSITIVE	COMPARATIVE	SUPERLATIVE
soft	softer	softest
fast	faster	fastest
careful	more careful	most careful
bad	worse	worst
good	better	best

Comparative vs. superlative Use the comparative to
compare two things, the superlative to compare three or
more.

                                              better?
▶ Which of these two brands of toothpaste is ~~best?~~
                                             ^
          most
▶ Hermos is the ~~more~~ qualified of the three applicants.
                ^

Form of comparatives and superlatives   To form comparatives and superlatives of one-syllable adjectives, use the endings *-er* and *-est*: *smooth, smoother, smoothest*. For adjectives with three or more syllables, use *more* and *most* (or *less* and *least*): *exciting, more exciting, most exciting*. Two-syllable adjectives form comparatives and superlatives in both ways: *lovely, lovelier, loveliest; helpful, more helpful, most helpful*.

Some one-syllable adverbs take the endings *-er* and *-est* (*fast, faster, fastest*), but longer adverbs and all of those ending in *-ly* use *more* and *most* (or *less* and *least*).

Double comparatives or superlatives   When you have added *-er* or *-est* to an adjective or an adverb, do not also use *more* or *most* (or *less* or *least*).

▶   All the polls indicated that Gore was more
    likely
    ~~likelier~~ to win than Bush.
    ^

Absolute concepts   Do not use comparatives or superlatives with absolute concepts such as *unique* or *perfect*. Either something is unique or it isn't. It is illogical to suggest that absolute concepts come in degrees.

    unusual
▶   That is the most ~~unique~~ wedding gown I have
    ^

ever seen.

14   Repair sentence fragments.

As a rule, do not treat a piece of a sentence as if it were a sentence. When you do, you create a fragment. To be a sentence, a word group must consist of at least one full independent clause. An independent clause has a subject and a verb, and it either stands alone as a sentence or could stand alone.

You can repair a fragment in one of two ways: Either pull the fragment into a nearby sentence, punctuating the new sentence correctly, or rewrite the fragment as a complete sentence.

adjectives, adverbs • *more* vs. *most* •
-*er* vs. -*est* forms • *unique* etc.

frag
14b

41

14a Fragmented clauses

A subordinate clause is patterned like a sentence, with both a subject and a verb, but it begins with a word that tells readers it cannot stand alone—a word such as *after*, *although*, *because*, *before*, *if*, *so that*, *that*, *though*, *unless*, *until*, *when*, *where*, *who*, or *which*. (For a longer list, see p. 276.)

Most fragmented clauses beg to be pulled into a sentence nearby.

▶ We fear the West Nile virus /, ~~Because~~ *because* it is transmitted

by the common mosquito.

If a fragmented clause cannot be combined gracefully with a nearby sentence, try rewriting it. The simplest way to turn a fragmented clause into a sentence is to delete the opening word or words that mark it as subordinate.

▶ Uncontrolled development is taking a deadly toll on

the environment. ~~So that in~~ *In* many parts of the world,

fragile ecosystems are collapsing.

14b Fragmented phrases

Like subordinate clauses, certain phrases are sometimes mistaken for sentences. They are fragments if they lack a subject, a verb, or both. Frequently a fragmented phrase may simply be pulled into a nearby sentence.

▶ The archaeologists worked slowly /, ~~Examining~~ *examining* and

labeling hundreds of pottery shards.

The word group beginning with *Examining* is a verbal phrase, not a sentence.

▶ Many adults suffer silently from agoraphobia /, ~~A~~ *a*

fear of the outside world.

A fear of the outside world is an appositive phrase, not a sentence.

▶ It has been said that there are only three

    indigenous American art forms /: ~~Jazz,~~ *jazz,* musical

    comedy, and soap operas.

> The list is not a sentence. Notice how easily a colon corrects
> the problem. (See 18b.)

If the fragmented phrase cannot be attached to a nearby sentence, turn the phrase into a sentence. You may need to add a subject, a verb, or both.

▶ Jamie explained how to access the database. *She also taught us* ~~Also~~

    how to submit reports and request vendor payments.

> The revision turns the fragmented phrase into a sentence by
> adding a subject and a verb.

14c Acceptable fragments

Skilled writers occasionally use sentence fragments for emphasis. Although fragments are sometimes appropriate, writers and readers do not always agree on when they are appropriate. Therefore, you will find it safer to write in complete sentences.

15 Revise run-on sentences.

Run-on sentences are independent clauses that have not been joined correctly. An independent clause is a word group that stands alone or could stand alone as a sentence. When two or more independent clauses appear in one sentence, they must be joined in one of these ways:

- with a comma and a coordinating conjunction (*and, but, or, nor, for, so, yet*)
- with a semicolon (or occasionally a colon or a dash)

There are two types of run-on sentences. When a writer puts no mark of punctuation and no coordinating conjunction between independent clauses, the result is a *fused sentence.*

FUSED

Air pollution poses risks to all humans it can be deadly
for people with asthma.

A far more common type of run-on sentence is the
comma splice—two or more independent clauses joined
with a comma and no coordinating conjunction. In some
comma splices, the comma appears alone.

COMMA SPLICE

Air pollution poses risks to all humans, it can be deadly
for people with asthma.

In other comma splices, the comma is accompanied by
a joining word, such as *however*, that is *not* a coordinating
conjunction. (See 15b.)

COMMA SPLICE

Air pollution poses risks to all humans, however, it can
be deadly for people with asthma.

To correct a run-on sentence, you have four choices:

1. Use a comma and a coordinating conjunction.
2. Use a semicolon (or, if appropriate, a colon or a
   dash).
3. Make the clauses into separate sentences.
4. Restructure the sentence, perhaps by subordinating
   one of the clauses.

One of these revision techniques will usually work better
than the others for a particular sentence. The fourth tech-
nique, the one requiring the most extensive revision, is
often the most effective.

CORRECTED WITH COMMA AND COORDINATING CONJUNCTION

Air pollution poses risks to all humans, but it can be
deadly for people with asthma.

CORRECTED WITH SEMICOLON

Air pollution poses risks to all humans; it can be deadly
for people with asthma.

CORRECTED WITH SEPARATE SENTENCES

Air pollution poses risks to all humans. It can be deadly
for people with asthma.

CORRECTED BY RESTRUCTURING

Although air pollution poses risks to all humans, it can
be deadly for people with asthma.

15a Revision with a comma and a coordinating conjunction

When a coordinating conjunction (*and*, *but*, *or*, *nor*, *for*, *so*, *yet*) joins independent clauses, it is usually preceded by a comma.

▶ Most of his friends had made plans for their
             but
  retirement, Tom had not.
         ^

15b Revision with a semicolon (or a colon or a dash)

When the independent clauses are closely related and their relation is clear without a coordinating conjunction, a semicolon is an acceptable method of revision.

▶ Tragedy depicts the individual confronted with the

  fact of death/; comedy depicts the adaptability
         ^

  of human society.

A semicolon is required between independent clauses that have been linked with a conjunctive adverb such as *however* or *therefore* or a transitional phrase such as *in fact* or *of course*. (See p. 62 for longer lists.)

▶ The timber wolf looks like a large German

  shepherd/; however, the wolf has longer legs,
       ^

  larger feet, and a wider head.

If the first independent clause introduces a quoted sentence, use a colon.

▶ Scholar and crime writer Carolyn Heilbrun says this

  about the future/: "Today's shocks are tomorrow's
         ^

  conventions."

Either a colon or a dash may be appropriate when the second clause summarizes or explains the first. (See 18b and 21d.)

15c Revision by separating sentences

If both independent clauses are long—or if one is a question and the other is not—consider making them separate sentences.

▶ Why should we spend money on space exploration/ ?
  We
  ~~we~~ have enough underfunded programs here on
  ^
  Earth.

15d Revision by restructuring the sentence

For sentence variety, consider restructuring the run-on sentence, perhaps by turning one of the independent clauses into a subordinate clause or a phrase.

▶ One of the most famous advertising slogans is
  Wheaties cereal's "Breakfast of Champions," ~~it~~
  which
  was penned in 1933.

▶ Mary McLeod Bethune, ~~was~~ the seventeenth child
  ^
  of former slaves, ~~she~~ founded the National Council
  of Negro Women in 1935.

16 Review grammar concerns for multilingual writers.

16a Verbs

This section offers a brief review of English verb forms and tenses and the passive voice.

Verb forms Every main verb in English has five forms (except *be*, which has eight). These forms are used to create all of the verb tenses in standard English. The following list shows these forms for the regular verb *help* and the irregular verbs *give* and *be*.

PRACTICE hackerhandbooks.com/pocket
  > Grammar > 16–1 to 16–3

	REGULAR (*HELP*)	IRREGULAR (*GIVE*)	IRREGULAR (*BE*)*
BASE FORM	help	give	be
PAST TENSE	helped	gave	was, were
PAST PARTICIPLE	helped	given	been
PRESENT PARTICIPLE	helping	giving	being
-S FORM	helps	gives	is

Be also has the forms *am* and *are*, which are used in the present tense. (See also p. 28.)

Verb tense   Here are descriptions of the tenses and progressive forms in standard English. See also 11b.

The simple tenses show general facts, states of being, and actions that occur regularly.

Simple present tense (base form or *-s* form) expresses general facts, constant states, habitual or repetitive actions, or scheduled future events: *The sun rises in the east. The plane leaves tomorrow at 6:30.*

Simple past tense (base form + *-ed* or *-d* or irregular form) is used for actions that happened at a specific time or during a specific period in the past or for repetitive actions that have ended: *She drove to Montana three years ago. When I was young, I walked to school.*

Simple future tense (*will* + base form) expresses actions that will occur at some time in the future and promises or predictions of future events: *I will call you next week.*

The simple progressive forms show continuing action.

Present progressive (*am, is, are* + present participle) shows actions in progress that are not expected to remain constant or future actions (with verbs such as *go, come, move*): *We are building our house at the shore. They are moving tomorrow.*

Past progressive (*was, were* + present participle) shows actions in progress at a specific past time or a continuing action that was interrupted: *Roy was driving his new car yesterday. When she walked in, we were planning her party.*

Future progressive (*will* + *be* + present participle) expresses actions that will be in progress at a certain time in the future: *Nan will be flying home tomorrow.*

tenses • regular verbs • irregular verbs •
modals (*can, could, may, might,* etc.)

ESL
16a

47

TIP: Certain verbs are not normally used in the progressive: *appear, believe, belong, contain, have, hear, know, like, need, see, seem, taste, think, understand,* and *want.* There are exceptions, however, that you must notice as you encounter them: *We are thinking of buying a summer home.*

The perfect tenses show actions that happened or will happen before another time.

Present perfect tense (*have, has* + past participle) expresses actions that began in the past and continue to the present or actions that happened at an unspecific time in the past: *She has not spoken of her grandfather in a long time. They have traveled to Africa twice.*

Past perfect tense (*had* + past participle) expresses an action that began or occurred before another time in the past: *By the time Hakan was fifteen, he had learned to drive. I had just finished my walk when my brother drove up.* (See also p. 29.)

Future perfect tense (*will* + *have* + past participle) expresses actions that will be completed before or at a specific future time: *By the time I graduate, I will have taken five film study classes.*

The perfect progressive forms show continuous past actions before another time.

Present perfect progressive (*have, has* + *been* + present participle) expresses continuous actions that began in the past and continue to the present: *My sister has been living in Oregon since 2001.*

Past perfect progressive (*had* + *been* + present participle) conveys actions that began and continued in the past until some other past action: *By the time I moved to Georgia, I had been supporting myself for five years.*

Future perfect progressive (*will* + *have* + *been* + present participle) expresses actions that are or will be in progress before another specified time in the future: *By the time we reach the cashier, we will have been waiting in line for an hour.*

Modal verbs The nine modal verbs—*can, could, may, might, must, shall, should, will,* and *would*—are used with the base form of verbs to show certainty, necessity, or possibility. Modals do not change form to indicate tense. (See the examples on p. 48.)

launch
▶ The art museum will ~~launches~~ its fundraising
campaign next month.

speak
▶ We could ~~spoke~~ Portuguese when we were young.

Passive voice When a sentence is written in the passive
voice, the subject receives the action instead of doing it. To
form the passive voice, use a form of *be*—*am, is, are, was,
were, being, be,* or *been*—followed by the past participle of the
main verb. (For appropriate uses of the passive voice, see 2b.)

written
▶ *Dreaming in Cuban* was ~~writing~~ by Cristina García.

be
▶ Senator Dixon will defeated.

NOTE: Verbs that do not take direct objects—such as *occur,
happen, sleep, die,* and *fall*—do not form the passive voice.

16b Articles (*a, an, the*)

Articles and other noun markers Articles (*a, an, the*)
are part of a category of words known as *noun markers* or
determiners. Noun markers identify the nouns that follow them. Besides articles, noun markers include possessive nouns (*Elena's, child's*); possessive pronoun/adjectives
(*my, your, their*); demonstrative pronoun/adjectives (*this,
that*); quantifiers (*all, few, neither, some*); and numbers (*one,
twenty-six*).

ART N
Felix is reading a book about mythology.

ART ADJ N
We took an exciting trip to Alaska last summer.

When to use *a* or *an* Use *a* or *an* with singular count
nouns that refer to one unspecific item (not a whole category). *Count nouns* refer to persons, places, things, or ideas
that can be counted: *one girl, two girls; one city, three cities;
one goose, four geese.*

a
▶ My professor asked me to bring dictionary to class.

> *an*
> We want to rent ⌃apartment close to the lake.

When to use *the* Use *the* with most nouns that the
reader can identify specifically. Usually the identity will
be clear to the reader for one of the following reasons:

1. The noun has been previously mentioned.

> *the*
> A truck cut in front of our van. When truck ⌃
>
> skidded a few seconds later, we almost crashed
>
> into it.

2. A phrase or clause following the noun restricts its
   identity.

> *the*
> Bryce warned me that GPS in his car was not ⌃
>
> working.

3. A superlative adjective such as *best* or *most intelligent*
   makes the noun's identity specific. (See also 13c.)

> *the*
> Brita had best players on her team. ⌃

4. The noun describes a unique person, place, or thing.

> *the*
> During an eclipse, one should not look directly at sun. ⌃

5. The context or situation makes the noun's identity
   clear.

> *the*
> Please don't slam door when you leave. ⌃

6. The noun is singular and refers to a class or category
   of items (most often animals, musical instruments,
   and inventions).

> *The tin*
> ~~Tin~~ whistle is common in traditional Irish music. ⌃

When not to use articles Do not use *a* or *an* with noncount nouns. *Noncount nouns* refer to things or abstract

ideas that cannot be counted or made plural: *salt, silver, air, furniture, patience, knowledge.* (See the chart at the bottom of this page.)

To express an approximate amount of a noncount noun, use a quantifier such as *some* or *more*: *some water, enough coffee, less violence.*

▶ Ava gave us ~~an~~ information about the Peace Corps.

> *some*
▶ Claudia said she had ~~a~~ news that would surprise
  ^

her parents.

Do not use articles with nouns that refer to all of something or something in general.

> *Kindness*
▶ ~~The kindness~~ is a virtue.
  ^

▶ In some parts of the world, ~~the~~ rice is preferred to

all other grains.

Commonly used noncount nouns
Food and drink
beef, bread, butter, candy, cereal, cheese, cream, meat, milk, pasta, rice, salt, sugar, wine
Nonfood substances
air, cement, coal, dirt, gasoline, gold, paper, petroleum, plastic, rain, silver, snow, soap, steel, wood, wool
Abstract nouns
advice, anger, beauty, confidence, courage, employment, fun, happiness, health, honesty, information, intelligence, knowledge, love, poverty, satisfaction, wealth
Other
biology (and other areas of study), clothing, equipment, furniture, homework, jewelry, luggage, machinery, mail, money, news, poetry, pollution, research, scenery, traffic, transportation, violence, weather, work
NOTE: A few noncount nouns can also be used as count nouns: *He had two loves: music and archery.*

When to use articles with proper nouns Do not use articles with most singular proper nouns: *Prime Minister Cameron, Jamaica, Lake Huron, Ivy Street, Mount Everest.* Use *the* with most plural proper nouns: *the McGregors, the Bahamas, the Finger Lakes, the United States.* Also use *the* with large regions, oceans, rivers, and mountain ranges: *the Sahara, the Indian Ocean, the Amazon River, the Rocky Mountains.*

There are, however, many exceptions, especially with geographic names. Note exceptions when you encounter them or consult a native speaker or an ESL dictionary.

16c Sentence structure

This section focuses on the major challenges that multilingual students face when writing sentences in English.

Omitted verbs Some languages do not use linking verbs (*am, is, are, was, were*) between subjects and complements (nouns or adjectives that rename or describe the subject). Every English sentence, however, must include a verb.

▶ Jim ^{*is*} intelligent.

▶ Many streets in San Francisco ^{*are*} very steep.

Omitted subjects Some languages do not require a subject in every sentence. Every English sentence, however, needs a subject.

▶ Your aunt is very energetic. ~~Seems~~ *She seems* young for her age.

EXCEPTION: In commands, the subject *you* is understood but not present in the sentence: *Give me the book.*

The word *it* is used as the subject of a sentence describing the weather or temperature, stating the time, indicating distance, or suggesting an environmental fact. Do not omit *it* in such sentences.

It is raining in the valley and snowing in the mountains.

It is 9:15 a.m.

PRACTICE hackerhandbooks.com/pocket
> Grammar > 16–7 and 16–8

It is three hundred miles to Chicago.

In July, *it* is very hot in Arizona.

In some English sentences, the subject comes after the verb, and a placeholder (called an expletive)—*there* or *it*—comes before the verb.

EXP V ——— S ———   ┌—— S ——┐ V
There are many people here today. (Many people are

here today.)

EXP V   ┌— S —┐   ┌— S —┐   V
It is important to study daily. (To study daily is important.)

                there are
▶ As you know, many religious sects in India.
                ^

Repeated subjects, objects, and adverbs English does not allow a subject to be repeated in its own clause.

▶ The doctor ~~she~~ advised me to cut down on salt.

Do not add a pronoun even when a word group comes between the subject and the verb.

▶ The car that had been stolen ~~it~~ was found.

Do not repeat an object or an adverb in an adjective clause. Adjective clauses begin with relative pronouns (*who, whom, whose, which, that*) or relative adverbs (*when, where*). Relative pronouns usually serve as subjects or objects in the clauses they introduce; another word in the clause cannot serve the same function. Relative adverbs should not be repeated by other adverbs later in the clause.

▶ The cat ran under the car that ~~it~~ was parked on

the street.

The relative pronoun *that* is the subject of the adjective clause, so the pronoun *it* cannot be added as the subject.

If the clause begins with a relative adverb, do not use another adverb with the same meaning later in the clause.

▶ The office where I work ~~there~~ is close to home.

The adverb *there* cannot repeat the relative adverb *where*.

16d Prepositions showing time and place

The chart on this page is limited to three prepositions that show time and place: *at*, *on*, and *in*. Not every possible use is listed in the chart, so don't be surprised when you encounter exceptions and idiomatic uses that you must learn one at a time. For example, in English, we ride *in* a car but *on* a bus, plane, train, or subway.

At, *on*, and *in* to show time and place

Showing time

AT *at* a specific time: *at* 7:20, *at* dawn, *at* dinner

ON *on* a specific day or date: *on* Tuesday, *on* June 4

IN *in* a part of a day: *in* the afternoon, *in* the daytime [but *at* night]

  in a year or month: *in* 1999, *in* July

  in a period of time: finished *in* three hours

Showing place

AT *at* a meeting place or location: *at* home, *at* the club

  at a specific address: living *at* 10 Oak Street

  at the edge of something: sitting *at* the desk

  at the corner of something: turning *at* the intersection

  at a target: throwing the snowball *at* Lucy

ON *on* a surface: placed *on* the table, hanging *on* the wall

  on a street: the house *on* Spring Street

  on an electronic medium: *on* television, *on* the Internet

IN *in* an enclosed space: *in* the garage, *in* an envelope

  in a geographic location: *in* San Diego, *in* Texas

  in a print medium: *in* a book, *in* a magazine

PRACTICE hackerhandbooks.com/pocket
  > Grammar > 16–9

Punctuation

17 The comma

The comma was invented to help readers. Without it, sentence parts can collide into one another unexpectedly, causing misreadings.

CONFUSING   If you cook Elmer will do the dishes.

CONFUSING   While we were eating a rattlesnake approached our campsite.

Add commas in the logical places (after *cook* and *eating*), and suddenly all is clear. No longer is Elmer being cooked, the rattlesnake being eaten.

Various rules have evolved to prevent such misreadings and to guide readers through complex grammatical structures. According to most experts, you should use a comma in the following situations.

17a Before a coordinating conjunction joining independent clauses

When a coordinating conjunction connects two or more independent clauses—word groups that could stand alone as separate sentences—a comma must precede the conjunction. There are seven coordinating conjunctions in English: *and*, *but*, *or*, *nor*, *for*, *so*, and *yet*.

A comma tells readers that one independent clause has come to a close and that another is about to begin.

▶   Jake has no talent for numbers, so he hires someone

to prepare his taxes.

EXCEPTION: If the two independent clauses are short and there is no danger of misreading, the comma may be omitted.

The plane took off and we were on our way.

TIP: Do *not* use a comma to separate compound word groups that are not independent clauses. See 17j.

17b After an introductory word group

Use a comma after an introductory clause or phrase. A comma tells readers that the introductory word group has come to a close and that the main part of the sentence is about to begin. The most common introductory word groups are adverb clauses, prepositional phrases, and participial phrases.

▶ **When Arthur ran his first marathon, he was pleased**
  to finish in under four hours.

▶ **Near a stream at the bottom of the canyon, rangers**
  discovered an abandoned mine.

▶ **Buried under layers of younger rocks, the earth's**
  oldest rocks contain no fossils.

EXCEPTION: The comma may be omitted after a short clause or phrase if there is no danger of misreading.

  In no time we were at 2,800 feet.

17c Between items in a series

Use a comma between all items in a series, including the last two.

▶ **Bubbles of air, leaves, ferns, bits of wood, and**
  insects are often found trapped in amber.

Although some writers view the comma between the last two items as optional, most experts advise using it because its omission can result in ambiguity or misreading.

17d Between coordinate adjectives

Use a comma between coordinate adjectives, those that each modify a noun separately.

▶ **Should patients with severe, irreversible brain**
  damage be put on life support systems?

Adjectives are coordinate if they can be connected with *and*: *severe and irreversible.*

NOTE: Do not use a comma between cumulative adjectives, those that do not each modify the noun separately.

Three large gray shapes moved slowly toward us.

Cumulative adjectives cannot be joined with *and* (not *three and large and gray shapes*).

17e To set off a nonrestrictive element, but not a restrictive element

A *restrictive* element defines or limits the meaning of the word it modifies; it is therefore essential to the meaning of the sentence and is not set off with commas. A *nonrestrictive* element describes a word whose meaning already is clear. Because it is not essential to the meaning of the sentence, it is set off with commas.

RESTRICTIVE (NO COMMAS)

The campers need clothes *that are durable*.

NONRESTRICTIVE (WITH COMMAS)

The campers need sturdy shoes, *which are expensive*.

If you remove a restrictive element from a sentence, the meaning changes significantly, becoming more general than intended. The writer of the first sample sentence does not mean that the campers need clothes in general. The meaning is more restricted: The campers need *durable* clothes.

If you remove a nonrestrictive element from a sentence, the meaning does not change significantly. Some meaning may be lost, but the defining characteristics of the person or thing described remain the same: The campers need *sturdy shoes*, and these happen to be expensive.

Elements that may be restrictive or nonrestrictive include adjective clauses, adjective phrases, and appositives.

Adjective clauses   Adjective clauses, which usually follow the noun or pronoun they describe, begin with a relative pronoun (*who, whom, whose, which, that*) or a relative adverb (*when, where*). When an adjective clause is nonrestrictive, set it off with commas; when it is restrictive, omit the commas.

NONRESTRICTIVE CLAUSE (WITH COMMAS)

▶   The Kyoto Protocol⸴ which was adopted in 1997⸴

   ∧   ∧

   aims to reduce greenhouse gases.

RESTRICTIVE CLAUSE (NO COMMAS)

▶ A corporation/that has government contracts/must

maintain careful personnel records.

NOTE: Use *that* only with restrictive clauses. Many writers use *which* only with nonrestrictive clauses, but usage varies.

Adjective phrases   Prepositional or verbal phrases functioning as adjectives may be restrictive or nonrestrictive. Nonrestrictive phrases are set off with commas; restrictive phrases are not.

NONRESTRICTIVE PHRASE (WITH COMMAS)

▶ The helicopter, with its million-candlepower

spotlight illuminating the area, circled above.

RESTRICTIVE PHRASE (NO COMMAS)

▶ One corner of the attic was filled with newspapers/

dating from the 1920s.

Appositives   An appositive is a noun or pronoun that renames a nearby noun. Nonrestrictive appositives are set off with commas; restrictive appositives are not.

NONRESTRICTIVE APPOSITIVE (WITH COMMAS)

▶ Darwin's most important book, *On the Origin of*

Species, was the result of many years of research.

RESTRICTIVE APPOSITIVE (NO COMMAS)

▶ The song/"Firework/" was blasted out of amplifiers.

17f To set off transitional and parenthetical expressions, absolute phrases, and contrasted elements

Transitional expressions   Transitional expressions serve as bridges between sentences or parts of sentences. They include conjunctive adverbs such as *however, therefore,* and *moreover* and transitional phrases such as *for example* and *as a matter of fact.* For a longer list, see page 62.

When a transitional expression appears between independent clauses in a compound sentence, it is preceded by a semicolon and usually followed by a comma.

▶ **Minh did not understand our language; moreover,**

he was unfamiliar with our customs.

When a transitional expression appears at the beginning of a sentence or in the middle of an independent clause, it is usually set off with commas.

▶ **In fact, stock values rose after the company's press**

release.

▶ **Natural foods are not always salt-free; celery, for**

example, is high in sodium.

Parenthetical expressions Expressions that are distinctly parenthetical, interrupting the flow of a sentence, should be set off with commas.

▶ **Evolution, so far as we know, doesn't work this way.**

Absolute phrases An absolute phrase consists of a noun followed by a participle or participial phrase. It modifies the whole sentence and should be set off with commas.

```
┌────── ABSOLUTE PHRASE ──────┐
  N   ┌──── PARTICIPLE ────┐
```
Our grant having been approved, we were at last

able to begin the archaeological dig.

Contrasted elements Sharp contrasts beginning with words such as *not* and *unlike* are set off with commas.

▶ **The Epicurean philosophers sought mental, not**

bodily, pleasures.

17g To set off nouns of direct address, the words *yes* and *no*, interrogative tags, and mild interjections

▶ **Forgive me, Angela, for forgetting our date.**

▶ **Yes, the loan will probably be approved.**

▶ The film was faithful to the book, wasn't it?

▶ Well, cases like this are difficult to decide.

17h To set off direct quotations introduced with expressions such as *he said*

▶ "Happiness in marriage is entirely a matter of chance,"

says Charlotte Lucas in *Pride and Prejudice* (69; ch. 6).

17i With dates, addresses, and titles

Dates   In dates, the year is set off from the rest of the sentence with commas.

▶ On December 12, 1890, orders were sent out for

the arrest of Sitting Bull.

EXCEPTIONS: Commas are not needed if the date is inverted or if only the month and year are given: *The 15 April 2011 deadline is approaching. May 2006 was a surprisingly cold month.*

Addresses   The elements of an address or a place name are separated by commas. A zip code, however, is not preceded by a comma.

▶ Greg lived at 708 Spring Street, Washington,

Illinois 61571.

Titles   If a title follows a name, set off the title with a pair of commas.

▶ Sandra Barnes, MD, was appointed to the board.

17j Misuses of the comma

Do not use commas unless you have good reasons for using them. In particular, avoid using commas in the following situations.

BETWEEN COMPOUND ELEMENTS THAT ARE NOT INDEPENDENT CLAUSES

▶ Marie Curie discovered radium/and later applied

her work on radioactivity to medicine.

TO SEPARATE A VERB FROM ITS SUBJECT

▶ Zoos large enough to give the animals freedom to
roam/are becoming more popular.

BETWEEN CUMULATIVE ADJECTIVES (See p. 56.)

▶ We found an old/maroon hatbox.

TO SET OFF RESTRICTIVE ELEMENTS (See pp. 57–58.)

▶ Drivers/who think they own the road/make
cycling a dangerous sport.

▶ Margaret Mead's book/*Coming of Age in Samoa*/
caused controversy when it was published.

AFTER A COORDINATING CONJUNCTION

▶ Occasionally TV talk shows are performed live,
but/more often they are taped.

AFTER *SUCH AS* OR *LIKE*

▶ Plants such as/begonias and impatiens add color
to a shady garden.

BEFORE *THAN*

▶ Touring Crete was more thrilling for us/than
visiting the Greek islands frequented by the rich.

BEFORE A PARENTHESIS

▶ At InterComm, Sylvia began at the bottom/(with
only a cubicle and a swivel chair), but within three
years she had been promoted to supervisor.

TO SET OFF AN INDIRECT (REPORTED) QUOTATION

▶ Samuel Goldwyn once said/that a verbal contract
isn't worth the paper it's written on.

WITH A QUESTION MARK OR AN EXCLAMATION POINT

▶ "Why don't you try it?/" she coaxed.

18 The semicolon and the colon

18a The semicolon

The semicolon is used between independent clauses not joined with a coordinating conjunction. It can also be used between items in a series containing internal punctuation.

The semicolon is never used between elements of unequal grammatical rank.

Between independent clauses When two independent clauses appear in one sentence, they are usually linked with a comma and a coordinating conjunction (*and, but, or, nor, for, so, yet*). The coordinating conjunction signals the relation between the clauses. If the relation is clear without a conjunction, a writer may choose to connect the clauses with a semicolon instead.

> In film, a low-angle shot makes the subject look powerful; a high-angle shot does just the opposite.

A writer may also connect the clauses with a semicolon and a conjunctive adverb such as *however* or a transitional phrase such as *for example*.

> Many corals grow very gradually; in fact, the creation of a coral reef can take centuries.

CONJUNCTIVE ADVERBS

accordingly, also, anyway, besides, certainly, consequently, conversely, finally, furthermore, hence, however, incidentally, indeed, instead, likewise, meanwhile, moreover, nevertheless, next, nonetheless, now, otherwise, similarly, specifically, still, subsequently, then, therefore, thus

TRANSITIONAL PHRASES

after all, as a matter of fact, as a result, at any rate, at the same time, even so, for example, for instance, in addition, in conclusion, in fact, in other words, in the first place, on the contrary

NOTE: A semicolon must be used whenever a coordinating conjunction does not appear between independent clauses. To use merely a comma—or to use a comma and a conjunctive adverb or transitional expression—creates an error known as a *comma splice*. (See 15.)

Between items in a series containing internal punctuation Items in a series are usually separated by commas. If one or more of the items contain internal punctuation, however, a writer may use semicolons for clarity.

> Classic science fiction sagas include *Star Trek*, with Captain Kirk, Dr. McCoy, and Mr. Spock; *Battlestar Galactica*, with its Cylons; and *Star Wars*, with Han Solo, Luke Skywalker, and Darth Vader.

Misuses of the semicolon Do not use a semicolon in the following situations.

BETWEEN AN INDEPENDENT CLAUSE AND A SUBORDINATE CLAUSE

▶ The media like to portray my generation as lazy;,

although polls show that we work as hard as the

twentysomethings before us.

BETWEEN AN APPOSITIVE AND THE WORD IT REFERS TO

▶ We were fascinated by the species *Argyroneta*

aquatica;, a spider that lives underwater.

TO INTRODUCE A LIST

▶ Some birds are flightless;: emus, penguins, and

ostriches.

BETWEEN INDEPENDENT CLAUSES JOINED BY *AND*, *BUT*, *OR*, *NOR*, *FOR*, *SO*, OR *YET*

▶ Five of the applicants had worked with spread-

sheets;, but only one was familiar with database

management.

18b The colon

Main uses of the colon A colon can be used after an independent clause to direct readers' attention to a list, an appositive, or a quotation.

A LIST

The routine includes the following: twenty knee bends, fifty leg lifts, and five minutes of running in place.

AN APPOSITIVE

My roommate is guilty of two of the seven deadly sins: gluttony and sloth.

A QUOTATION

Consider the words of Benjamin Franklin: "There never was a good war or a bad peace."

For other ways of introducing quotations, see pages 69–70.

A colon may also be used between independent clauses if the second summarizes or explains the first.

Faith is like love: It cannot be forced.

The second clause may begin with a capital or a lowercase letter: *Minds are like parachutes: They* [or *they*] *function only when open.* (See 22e.)

Conventional uses   Use a colon after the salutation in a formal letter, to indicate hours and minutes, to show proportions, between a title and a subtitle, and to separate city and publisher in bibliographic entries.

Dear Sir or Madam:

5:30 p.m.

The ratio of women to men was 2:1.

Alvin Ailey: A Life in Dance

Boston: Bedford, 2012

NOTE: In biblical references, a colon is ordinarily used between chapter and verse (Luke 2:14). MLA recommends a period (Luke 2.14).

Misuses of the colon   A colon must be preceded by an independent clause. Therefore, avoid using it in the following situations.

BETWEEN A VERB AND ITS OBJECT OR COMPLEMENT

▶   Some important vitamins found in vegetables are̸

vitamin A, thiamine, niacin, and vitamin C.

BETWEEN A PREPOSITION AND ITS OBJECT

▶ The heart's two pumps each consist of̷ an upper

chamber, or atrium, and a lower chamber, or

ventricle.

AFTER *SUCH AS, INCLUDING,* OR *FOR EXAMPLE*

▶ The NCAA regulates college athletic teams,

including̷ basketball, baseball, softball,

and football.

19 The apostrophe

The apostrophe indicates possession and marks contractions. In addition, it has a few conventional uses.

19a To indicate possession

The apostrophe is used to indicate that a noun or an indefinite pronoun is possessive. Possessives usually indicate ownership, as in *Tim's hat, the editor's desk,* or *someone's gloves.* Frequently, however, ownership is only loosely implied: *the tree's roots, a day's work.* If you are not sure whether a word is possessive, try turning it into an *of* phrase: *the roots of the tree, the work of a day.*

When to add -'s   Add -'s if the noun does not end in -s or if the noun is singular and ends in -s or an s sound.

Luck often propels a rock musician's career.

Thank you for refunding the children's money.

Lois's sister spent last year in India.

Her article presents an overview of Marx's teachings.

EXCEPTION: If pronunciation would be awkward with an apostrophe and an -s, some writers use only the apostrophe: *Sophocles'.*

PRACTICE   hackerhandbooks.com/pocket
  > Punctuation > 19–1 and 19–2

When to add only an apostrophe   If the noun is plural and ends in -*s*, add only an apostrophe.

Both diplomats' briefcases were searched by guards.

Joint possession   To show joint possession, use -'*s* (or -*s*') with the last noun only; to show individual possession, make all nouns possessive.

Have you seen Joyce and Greg's new camper?

Hernando's and Maria's expectations were quite different.

Compound nouns   If a noun is compound, use -'*s* (or -*s*') with the last element.

Her father-in-law's sculpture won first place.

Indefinite pronouns such as *someone*   Use -'*s* to indicate that an indefinite pronoun is possessive. Indefinite pronouns refer to no specific person or thing: *anyone, everyone, someone, no one*, and so on.

This diet will improve almost anyone's health.

NOTE: Possessive pronouns (*its, his*, and so on) do not use an apostrophe. (See 19d.)

19b To mark contractions

In a contraction, an apostrophe takes the place of missing letters.

It's a shame that Frank can't go on the tour.

It's stands for *it is, can't* for *cannot*.
The apostrophe is also used to mark the omission of the first two digits of a year (*the class of '13*) or years (*the '60s generation*).

19c Conventional uses

An apostrophe typically is not used to pluralize numbers, abbreviations, letters, or words mentioned as words. Note the few exceptions and be consistent in your writing.

Plural numbers and abbreviations   Do not use an apostrophe in the plural of any numbers (including decades) or of any abbreviations.

Peggy skated nearly perfect figure 8s.

We've paid only four IOUs out of six.

Plural letters Italicize the letter and use roman (regular) font style for the -*s* ending. Use of an apostrophe is usually optional; MLA recommends the apostrophe.

Two large *J*s [or *J*'s] were painted on the door.

Plural of words mentioned as words Italicize the word and use roman (regular) font style for the -*s* ending.

We've heard enough *maybe*s.

Words mentioned as words may also appear in quotation marks. When you choose this option, use the apostrophe: *We've heard enough "maybe's."*

19d Misuses of the apostrophe

Do not use an apostrophe in the following situations.

WITH NOUNS THAT ARE PLURAL BUT NOT POSSESSIVE

outpatients
▶ Some ~~outpatient's~~ have special parking permits.
　　　　^

IN THE POSSESSIVE PRONOUNS *ITS, WHOSE, HIS, HERS, OURS, YOURS,* **AND** *THEIRS*

its
▶ Each area has ~~it's~~ own conference room.
　　　　　　　　　^

It's means "it is." The possessive pronoun *its* contains no apostrophe despite the fact that it is possessive.

20 Quotation marks

Quotation marks are used to enclose direct quotations. They are also used around some titles and to set off words used as words.

20a To enclose direct quotations

Direct quotations of a person's words, whether spoken or written, must be in quotation marks (see p. 68).

"The contract negotiations are stalled," the executive told reporters, "but I'll bring both sides together."

EXCEPTION: When a long quotation has been set off from the text by indenting, quotation marks are not needed. (See pp. 112–13, 170–71, and 214.)

Use single quotation marks to enclose a quotation within a quotation.

> According to Paul Eliott, Eskimo hunters "chant an ancient magic song to the seal they are after: 'Beast of the sea! Come and place yourself before me in the early morning!' "

NOTE: Do not use quotation marks around indirect quotations, which report what a person said without using the person's exact words: *The executive pledged to find a compromise even though negotiations had broken down.*

20b Around titles of short works

Use quotation marks around titles of newspaper and magazine articles, poems, short stories, songs, episodes of television and radio programs, and chapters or subdivisions of books.

> The poem "Mother to Son" is by Langston Hughes.

NOTE: Titles of books, plays, Web sites, television and radio programs, films, magazines, and newspapers are put in italics. (See pp. 81–82.)

20c To set off words used as words

Although words used as words are ordinarily italicized (see p. 82), quotation marks are also acceptable.

> The words "affect" and "effect" are frequently confused.

20d Other punctuation with quotation marks

This section describes the conventions to observe in placing various marks of punctuation inside or outside quotation marks. It also explains how to punctuate when introducing quoted material.

Periods and commas   Place periods and commas inside quotation marks.

> "I'm here for my service-learning project," I told the teacher. "I'd like to become a reading specialist."

This rule applies to single and double quotation marks, and it applies to all uses of quotation marks.

EXCEPTION: In MLA and APA parenthetical in-text citations, the period follows the citation in parentheses. MLA: *According to Cole, "The instruments of science have vastly extended our senses" (53).* APA: *According to Cole (1999), "The instruments of science have vastly extended our senses" (p. 53).*

Colons and semicolons   Put colons and semicolons outside quotation marks.

> Harold wrote, "I regret that I cannot attend the fundraiser for AIDS research"; his letter, however, contained a contribution.

Question marks and exclamation points   Put question marks and exclamation points inside quotation marks unless they apply to the whole sentence.

> Contrary to tradition, bedtime at my house is marked by "Mommy, can I tell you a story now?"

> Have you heard the old proverb "Do not climb the hill until you reach it"?

In the first sentence, the question mark applies only to the quoted question. In the second sentence, the question mark applies to the whole sentence.

Introducing quoted material   After a word group introducing a quotation, use a colon, a comma, or no punctuation at all, whichever is appropriate in context.

If a quotation has been formally introduced, a colon is appropriate. A formal introduction is a full independent clause, not just an expression such as *he said* or *she writes*.

> Lance Morrow views personal ads as an art form: "The personal ad is like a haiku of self-celebration, a brief solo played on one's own horn."

If a quotation is introduced or followed by an expression such as *he said* or *she writes*, use a comma.

Stephen Leacock once said, "I am a great believer in luck, and I find the harder I work the more I have of it."

"You can be a little ungrammatical if you come from the right part of the country," writes Robert Frost.

When you blend a quotation into your own sentence, use either a comma or no punctuation, depending on the way the quotation fits into your sentence structure.

The champion could, as he put it, "float like a butterfly and sting like a bee."

Virginia Woolf wrote in 1928 that "a woman must have money and a room of her own if she is to write fiction" (4).

If a quotation appears at the beginning of a sentence, use a comma after it unless the quotation ends with a question mark or an exclamation point.

"I've always thought of myself as a reporter," claimed American poet Gwendolyn Brooks (162).

"What is it?" I asked, bracing myself.

If a quoted sentence is interrupted by explanatory words, use commas to set off the explanatory words.

"With regard to air travel," Stephen Ambrose notes, "Jefferson was a full century ahead of the curve" (53).

If two successive quoted sentences from the same source are interrupted by explanatory words, use a comma before the explanatory words and a period after them.

"It's considered unseemly to discuss one's personal finances in public," Lionel Shriver writes. "But I'm not very polite" (28).

20e Misuses of quotation marks

Avoid using quotation marks in the following situations.

FAMILIAR SLANG, TRITE EXPRESSIONS, OR HUMOR

▶ The economist emphasized that 5 percent was a

/"ballpark figure./"

INDIRECT QUOTATIONS

▶ After finishing the exam, Chuck said that /he was

due for a coffee break. /

NOTE: Do not use quotation marks around the title of your
own essay.

21 Other marks

21a The period

Use a period to end all sentences except direct questions
or genuine exclamations.

Celia asked whether the picnic would be canceled.

A period is conventionally used with personal titles,
Latin abbreviations, and designations for time.

Mr.	i.e.	a.m. (or AM)
Ms.	e.g.	p.m. (or PM)
Dr.	etc.	

NOTE: If a sentence ends with a period marking an abbreviation, do not add a second period.

A period is not used for the following: US Postal
Service abbreviations for states, abbreviations for organization and country names, academic degrees, and designations for eras.

CA	UNESCO	FCC	NATO	BS	BC
NY	AFL-CIO	IRS	USA	PhD	BCE

21b The question mark

Use a question mark after a direct question.

What is the horsepower of a 747 engine?

NOTE: Use a period, not a question mark, after an indirect
question, one that is reported rather than asked directly.

He asked me who was teaching the mythology course.

PRACTICE hackerhandbooks.com/pocket
   > Punctuation > 21–1

21c The exclamation point

Use an exclamation point after a sentence that expresses exceptional feeling or deserves special emphasis.

> We yelled to the police officer, "He's not drunk! He's in diabetic shock!"

Do not overuse the exclamation point.

▶ **In the fisherman's memory, the fish lives on,**

increasing in length and weight each year, until it is

big enough to shade a fishing boat⸌.

This sentence doesn't need to be pumped up with an exclamation point. It is emphatic enough without it.

21d The dash

The dash may be used to set off parenthetical material that deserves special emphasis. When typing, use two hyphens to form a dash (- -), with no spaces before or after the dash. (If your word processing program has what is known as an "em-dash" (—), you may use it instead, with no space before or after it.)

Use a dash to introduce a list, a restatement, an amplification, or a striking shift in tone or thought.

> Along the wall are the bulk liquids—sesame seed oil, honey, safflower oil, and half-liquid peanut butter.

> Peter decided to focus on his priorities—applying to graduate school, getting financial aid, and finding a roommate.

> Kiere took a few steps back, came running full speed, kicked a mighty kick—and missed the ball.

In the first two examples, the writer could also use a colon. (See 18b.) The colon is more formal than the dash and not quite as dramatic.

Use a pair of dashes to set off parenthetical material that deserves special emphasis or to set off an appositive that contains commas.

> Everything that went wrong—from the peeping Tom at her window to my head-on collision—was blamed on our move.

In my hometown, people's basic needs—food, clothing, and shelter—are less costly than in Denver.

TIP: Unless you have a specific reason for using the dash, avoid it. Unnecessary dashes create a choppy effect.

21e Parentheses

Use parentheses to enclose supplemental material, minor digressions, and afterthoughts.

Nurses record patients' vital signs (temperature, pulse, and blood pressure) several times a day.

Use parentheses to enclose letters or numbers labeling items in a series.

There are three points of etiquette in poker: (1) allow someone to cut the cards, (2) don't forget to ante up, and (3) never stack your chips.

TIP: Do not overuse parentheses. Often a sentence reads more gracefully without them.

▶ Research shows that seventeen million ~~(estimates~~

from

^

~~run as high as~~ twenty-three million~~)~~ Americans

to

^

have diabetes.

21f Brackets

Use brackets to enclose any words or phrases you have inserted into an otherwise word-for-word quotation.

Audubon reports that "if there are not enough young to balance deaths, the end of the species [California condor] is inevitable" (4).

The *Audubon* article did not contain the words *California condor* in the sentence quoted.

The Latin word "sic" in brackets indicates that an error in a quoted sentence appears in the original source.

According to the review, Nelly Furtado's performance was brilliant, "exceding [sic] the expectations of even her most loyal fans."

21g The ellipsis mark

Use an ellipsis mark, three spaced periods, to indicate that you have deleted material from an otherwise word-for-word quotation.

> Harmon (2011) noted, "During hibernation, heart rate would drop to nine beats per minute between breaths . . . and then speed up with each inhale."

If you delete a full sentence or more in the middle of a quoted passage, use a period before the three ellipsis dots.

NOTE: Do not use the ellipsis mark at the beginning or end of a quotation unless it is important, for clarity, to indicate that the passage quoted is from the middle of a sentence.

21h The slash

Use the slash to separate two or three lines of poetry that have been run into your text. Add a space both before and after the slash.

> In the opening lines of "Jordan," George Herbert pokes fun at popular poems of his time: "Who says that fictions only and false hair / Become a verse? Is there in truth no beauty?"

Use the slash sparingly, if at all, to separate options: *pass/fail*, *producer/director*. Put no space around the slash. Avoid using expressions such as *he/she* and *his/her* and the awkward construction *and/or*.

Mechanics

22 Capitalization

In addition to the following guidelines, a good dictionary can tell you when to use capital letters.

22a Proper vs. common nouns

Proper nouns and words derived from them are capitalized; common nouns are not. Proper nouns name specific persons, places, and things. All other nouns are common nouns.

The following types of words are usually capitalized: names of deities, religions, religious followers, and sacred books; words of family relationships used as names; particular places; nationalities and their languages, races, and tribes; educational institutions, departments, degrees, particular courses; government departments, organizations, political parties; historical movements, periods, events, documents; specific electronic sources; and trade names.

PROPER NOUNS	COMMON NOUNS
God (used as a name)	a god
Book of Common Prayer	a sacred book
Uncle Pedro	my uncle
Father (used as a name)	my father
Lake Superior	a picturesque lake
the Capital Center	a center for the arts
the South	a southern state
Wrigley Field	a baseball stadium
University of Wisconsin	a good university
Geology 101	a geology course
Veterans Administration	a federal agency
Phi Kappa Psi	a fraternity
the Democratic Party	a political party
the Enlightenment	the eighteenth century
the Great Depression	a recession
the Treaty of Versailles	a treaty
the World Wide Web, the Web	a home page
the Internet, the Net	a computer network
Advil	a painkiller

Months, holidays, and days of the week are capitalized: *May*, *Labor Day*, *Monday*. The seasons and numbers of the days of the month are not: *summer*, *the fifth of June*.

Names of school subjects are capitalized only if they are names of languages: *geology*, *history*, *English*, *French*.

Names of particular courses are capitalized: *Geology 101, Principles of Economics.*

NOTE: Do not capitalize common nouns to make them seem important: *Our company is currently hiring technical support staff* [not *Company, Technical Support Staff*].

22b Titles with proper names

Capitalize a title when used as part of a proper name but usually not when used alone.

> Prof. Margaret Burnes; Dr. Sinyee Sein; John Scott Williams Jr.; Anne Tilton, LLD

> District Attorney Mill was ruled out of order.

> The district attorney was elected for a two-year term.

Usage varies when the title of an important public figure is used alone: *The president* [or *President*] *vetoed the bill.*

22c Titles of works

Major words should be capitalized in both titles and subtitles of works such as books, articles, and songs. Minor words—articles, prepositions, and coordinating conjunctions—are not capitalized unless they are the first or last word of a title or subtitle.

> *The Impossible Theater: A Manifesto*

> "Man in the Middle"

> "I Want to Hold Your Hand"

22d First word of a sentence or quoted sentence

The first word of a sentence should be capitalized. Capitalize the first word of a quoted sentence but not a quoted phrase.

> In *Time* magazine, Robert Hughes writes, "There are only about sixty Watteau paintings on whose authenticity all experts agree" (102).

> Russell Baker has written that sports are "the opiate of the masses" (46).

If a quoted sentence is interrupted by explanatory words, do not capitalize the first word after the interruption.

"When we all think alike," he said, "no one is thinking."

22e First word following a colon

Capitalize the first word after a colon if it begins an independent clause.

I came to a startling conclusion: The house must be haunted.

NOTE: MLA and *Chicago* styles use a lowercase letter to begin an independent clause following a colon. APA style uses a capital letter. CSE style uses a lowercase letter except for a direct quotation that is a complete sentence.

22f Abbreviations

Capitalize abbreviations for departments and agencies of government, other organizations, and corporations; capitalize trade names and the call letters of radio and television stations.

EPA, FBI, DKNY, IBM, Xerox, WCRB, KNBC-TV

23 Abbreviations, numbers, and italics

23a Abbreviations

Use abbreviations only when they are clearly appropriate.

Appropriate abbreviations   Use standard abbreviations for titles immediately before and after proper names.

TITLES BEFORE PROPER NAMES	TITLES AFTER PROPER NAMES
Ms. Nancy Linehan	Thomas Hines Jr.
Dr. Margaret Simmons	Anita Lor, PhD
Rev. John Stone	Robert Simkowski, MD
St. Joan of Arc	William Lyons, MA
Prof. James Russo	Polly Stern, DDS

Do not abbreviate a title if it is not used with a proper name:
My history professor [not *prof.*] *was an expert on naval warfare.*

Familiar abbreviations for the names of organizations,
corporations, and countries are also acceptable: *CIA*, *FBI*,
NAACP, *EPA*, *YMCA*, *NBC*, *USA*.

> The CIA was established in 1947 by the National
> Security Act.

When using an unfamiliar abbreviation (such as NAB
for National Association of Broadcasters) throughout a
paper, write the full name followed by the abbreviation in
parentheses at the first mention of the name. You may use
the abbreviation in the rest of the paper.

Other commonly accepted abbreviations include *BC*,
AD, *a.m.*, *p.m.*, *No.*, and *$*. The abbreviation *BC* ("before
Christ") follows a date, and *AD* ("*anno Domini*") precedes
a date. Acceptable alternatives are *BCE* ("before the common era") and *CE* ("common era").

40 BC (or 40 BCE)	4:00 a.m. (or AM)	No. 12 (or no. 12)
AD 44 (or 44 CE)	6:00 p.m. (or PM)	$150

Avoid using *a.m.*, *p.m.*, *No.*, or *$* when not accompanied
by a specific figure: *We set off for the lake early in the morning* [not *a.m.*].

Inappropriate abbreviations In formal writing, abbreviations for the following are not commonly accepted.

PERSONAL NAME   Charles (*not* Chas.)

UNITS OF MEASUREMENT   pound (*not* lb.)

DAYS OF THE WEEK   Monday (*not* Mon.)

HOLIDAYS   Christmas (*not* Xmas)

MONTHS   January, February (*not* Jan., Feb.)

COURSES OF STUDY   political science (*not* poli. sci.)

DIVISIONS OF WRITTEN WORKS   chapter, page (*not* ch., p.)

STATES AND COUNTRIES   Florida (*not* FL or Fla.)

PARTS OF A BUSINESS NAME   Adams Lighting Company
(*not* Adams Lighting Co.); Kim and Brothers, Inc.
(*not* Kim and Bros., Inc.)

Although Latin abbreviations are appropriate in footnotes and bibliographies and in informal writing, use the
appropriate English phrases in formal writing.

cf. (Latin *confer*, "compare")

e.g. (Latin *exempli gratia*, "for example")

et al. (Latin *et alii*, "and others")

etc. (Latin *et cetera*, "and so forth")

i.e. (Latin *id est*, "that is")

N.B. (Latin *nota bene*, "note well")

23b Numbers

Spell out numbers of one or two words. Use figures for numbers that require more than two words to spell out.

▶ The 1980 eruption of Mount St. Helens blasted
   sixteen   *230*
ash ~~16~~ miles into the sky and devastated ~~two~~
  ^

~~hundred thirty~~ square miles of land.

If a sentence begins with a number, spell out the number or rewrite the sentence.

   One hundred fifty
▶ ~~150~~ children in our program need expensive
  ^

dental treatment.

Generally, figures are acceptable for the following.

DATES   July 4, 1776; 56 BC; AD 30

ADDRESSES   77 Latches Lane, 519 West 42nd Street

PERCENTAGES   55 percent (or 55%)

FRACTIONS, DECIMALS $1/2$, 0.047

SCORES   7 to 3, 21–18

STATISTICS   average age 37

SURVEYS   4 out of 5

EXACT AMOUNTS OF MONEY $105.37, $0.05

DIVISIONS OF BOOKS   volume 3, chapter 4, page 189

DIVISIONS OF PLAYS   act 3, scene 3 (or act III, scene iii)

IDENTIFICATION NUMBERS   serial no. 1098

TIME OF DAY   4:00 p.m., 1:30 a.m.

spelling out numbers • using numerals •
italics • titles of books, films, etc.

ital
23c
81

NOTE: Academic styles vary for handling numbers in the text of a paper. In the humanities, MLA and *Chicago* spell out numbers below 101 and round numbers (*forty million*); they use numerals for specific numbers above one hundred (*234*). In the social sciences and the sciences, APA and CSE spell out the numbers one through nine and use numerals for all other numbers.

23c Italics

This section describes conventional uses for italics: for titles of works; names of ships, aircraft, and spacecraft; foreign words; and words as words.

NOTE: If your instructor prefers underlining, simply substitute underlining for italics in the examples in this section.

Titles of works   Titles of the following types of works are italicized.

TITLES OF BOOKS   *The Known World, Middlesex, Encarta*

MAGAZINES   *Time, Scientific American, Salon.com*

NEWSPAPERS   the *Baltimore Sun,* the *Orlando Sentinel*

PAMPHLETS   *Common Sense, Facts about Marijuana*

LONG POEMS   *The Waste Land, Paradise Lost*

PLAYS   *King Lear, Wicked*

FILMS   *Casablanca, The Hurt Locker*

TELEVISION PROGRAMS   *American Idol, Frontline*

RADIO PROGRAMS   *All Things Considered*

MUSICAL COMPOSITIONS   *Porgy and Bess*

CHOREOGRAPHIC WORKS   *Brief Fling*

WORKS OF VISUAL ART   *American Gothic*

COMIC STRIPS   *Dilbert*

ELECTRONIC DATABASES   *ProQuest*

WEB SITES   *ZDNet, Google*

ELECTRONIC GAMES   *Dragon Age, Call of Duty*

The titles of other works, such as short stories, essays, songs, and short poems, are enclosed in quotation marks. (See 20b.)

NOTE: Do not use italics when referring to the Bible; titles of books in the Bible (Genesis, not *Genesis*); the titles of legal documents (the Constitution, not the *Constitution*); or the titles of your own papers.

Names of ships, aircraft, spacecraft Italicize names of specific ships, aircraft, and spacecraft.

> *Queen Mary 2, Spirit of St. Louis, Challenger*

Foreign words Italicize foreign words used in an English sentence.

> Caroline's *joie de vivre* should be a model for all of us.

EXCEPTION: Do not italicize foreign words that have become part of the English language—"laissez-faire," "fait accompli," "modus operandi," and "per diem," for example.

Words as words, etc. Italicize words used as words, letters mentioned as letters, and numbers mentioned as numbers.

> Tomás assured us that the chemicals could probably be safely mixed, but his *probably* stuck in our minds.

> Some toddlers have trouble pronouncing the letters *f* and *s*.

> A big *3* was painted on the stage door.

NOTE: Quotation marks may be used instead of italics to set off words mentioned as words. (See 20c.)

Inappropriate italics Italicizing to emphasize words or ideas is distracting and should be used sparingly.

24 Spelling and the hyphen

24a Spelling

A word processing program equipped with a spell checker is a useful tool, but be aware of its limitations. A spell checker will not tell you how to spell words not listed in its dictionary; nor will it help you catch words commonly confused, such as *accept* and *except*, or common typographical errors, such as *own* for *won*. You will still need to proofread, and for some words you may need to turn to the dictionary.

NOTE: To check for correct use of commonly confused words (*accept* and *except*, *its* and *it's*, and so on), consult section 46, the glossary of usage.

Major spelling rules If you need to improve your spelling, review the following rules and exceptions.

1. In general, use *i* before *e* except after *c* and except when sounded like "ay," as in *neighbor* and *weigh*.

I BEFORE *E*	relieve, believe, sieve, niece, fierce, frieze
E BEFORE *I*	receive, deceive, sleigh, freight, eight
EXCEPTIONS	seize, either, weird, height, foreign, leisure

2. Generally, drop a final silent *-e* when adding a suffix that begins with a vowel. Keep the final *-e* if the suffix begins with a consonant.

desire, desiring   achieve, achievement
remove, removable   care, careful

Words such as *changeable*, *judgment*, *argument*, and *truly* are exceptions.

3. When adding *-s* or *-ed* to words ending in *-y*, ordinarily change *-y* to *-i* when the *-y* is preceded by a consonant but not when it is preceded by a vowel.

comedy, comedies   monkey, monkeys
dry, dried   play, played

With proper names ending in *-y*, however, do not change the *-y* to *-i* even if it is preceded by a consonant: *the Dougherty family*, *the Doughertys*.

4. If a final consonant is preceded by a single vowel *and* the consonant ends a one-syllable word or a stressed syllable, double the consonant when adding a suffix beginning with a vowel.

bet, betting   occur, occurrence
commit, committed

5. Add *-s* to form the plural of most nouns; add *-es* to singular nouns ending in *-s*, *-sh*, *-ch*, and *-x*.

table, tables	church, churches
paper, papers	dish, dishes
agenda, agendas	fox, foxes

Ordinarily add *-s* to nouns ending in *-o* when the *-o* is preceded by a vowel. Add *-es* when the *-o* is preceded by a consonant.

radio, radios	hero, heroes
video, videos	tomato, tomatoes

To form the plural of a hyphenated compound word, add the *-s* to the chief word even if it does not appear at the end.

mother-in-law, mothers-in-law

NOTE: English words derived from other languages such as Latin, Greek, or French sometimes form the plural as they would in their original language.

medium, media	chateau, chateaux
criterion, criteria	

Spelling variations   Following is a list of some common words spelled differently in American and British English. Consult a dictionary for others.

AMERICAN	BRITISH
canceled, traveled	cancelled, travelled
color, humor	colour, humour
judgment	judgement
check	cheque
realize, apologize	realise, apologise
defense	defence
program	programme
anemia, anesthetic	anaemia, anaesthetic
theater, center	theatre, centre
fetus	foetus
mold, smolder	mould, smoulder
civilization	civilisation
connection, inflection	connexion, inflexion
licorice	liquorice

24b The hyphen

In addition to the following guidelines, a dictionary will
help you make decisions about hyphenation.

Compound words   The dictionary will tell you whether
to treat a compound word as a hyphenated compound
(*water-repellent*), as one word (*waterproof*), or as two words
(*water table*). If the compound word is not in the dictionary, treat it as two words.

▶   The prosecutor did not cross‑examine any witnesses.

▶   Imogen kept her sketches in a small note book.

▶   Alice walked through the looking glass into a

backward world.

Words functioning together as an adjective   When
two or more words function together as an adjective
before a noun, connect them with a hyphen. Generally,
do not use a hyphen when such compounds follow the
noun.

▶   Pat Hobbs is not yet a well‑known candidate.

▶   After our television campaign, Pat Hobbs will be

well known.

Do not use a hyphen to connect *-ly* adverbs to the words
they modify.

▶   A slowly moving truck tied up traffic.

NOTE: In a series, hyphens are suspended: *Do you prefer
first-, second-, or third-class tickets?*

Conventional uses   Hyphenate the written form of
fractions and of compound numbers from twenty-one
to ninety-nine. Also use the hyphen with the prefixes *all-*,
ex-, and *self-* and with the suffix *-elect.*

▶   One‑fourth of my income goes for rent.

▶   The charity is funding more self‑help projects.

Hyphenation at ends of lines Set your word processing program to not hyphenate words at the end of a
line of text. This setting ensures that only words that
already contain a hyphen may be broken at the end of
a line.

E-mail addresses, URLs, and other electronic addresses
need special attention when they occur at the end of a
line of text. Do not insert a hyphen to divide electronic
addresses. Instead, break an e-mail address after the @
symbol or before a period. Break a URL after a slash or
a double slash or before any other mark of punctuation.
(For specific documentation styles, see 34a, 39a, 44a, and
45b.)

Research

College research assignments ask you to pose a question worth exploring, to read widely in search of possible answers, to interpret what you read, to draw reasoned conclusions, and to support those conclusions with valid and well-documented evidence.

This section and the color-coded sections that follow—MLA (red), APA (green), *Chicago* (blue), and CSE (orange)—will help you write your paper and properly document your sources in the style your instructor requires.

25 Posing a research question

Working within the guidelines of your assignment, pose a few questions that seem worth researching—questions that you want to explore, that you feel would interest your audience, and about which there is a substantial debate. As you formulate possible questions, make sure that they are appropriate lines of inquiry for a research paper. Choose questions that are narrow (not too broad), challenging (not too bland), and grounded (not too speculative).

25a Choosing a narrow question

If your initial question is too broad, given the length of the paper you plan to write, look for ways to restrict your focus. Here, for example, is how two students narrowed their initial questions.

TOO BROAD	NARROWER
What are the hazards of fad diets?	What are the hazards of low-carbohydrate diets?
What are the benefits of stricter auto emissions standards?	How will stricter auto emissions standards create new, more competitive auto industry jobs?

25b Choosing a challenging question

Your research paper will be more interesting to both you and your audience if you base it on an intellectually challenging line of inquiry. Try to draft questions that provoke thought or engage readers in a debate.

TOO BLAND	CHALLENGING
What is obsessive-compulsive disorder?	Why is obsessive-compulsive disorder so difficult to treat?
How does DNA testing work?	How reliable is DNA testing?

You may need to address a bland question in the course of answering a more challenging one, but it would be a mistake to use the bland question as the focus for the whole paper.

25c Choosing a grounded question

Finally, you will want to make sure that your research question is grounded, not too speculative. Although speculative questions—such as those that address morality or beliefs—are worth asking and may receive some attention in a research paper, they are inappropriate central questions. The central argument of a research paper should be grounded in facts.

TOO SPECULATIVE	GROUNDED
Is it wrong to share pornographic personal photos by cell phone?	What role should the US government play in regulating mobile content?
Do scientists have the right to conduct medical experiments on animals?	How have breakthroughs in technology made medical experiments on animals increasingly unnecessary?

26 Finding appropriate sources

Depending on your research question, some sources will prove more useful than others. For example, if your research question addresses a historical issue, you might look at reference works, books, scholarly articles, and primary sources such as speeches. If your research question addresses a current political issue, however, you might turn to magazine and newspaper articles, Web sites, and government documents.

26a Locating reference works

For some topics, you may want to begin your search by consulting general or specialized reference works. General reference works include encyclopedias, almanacs, atlases, and biographical references. Many specialized reference works are available: *Encyclopedia of Bioethics*, *Almanac of American Politics*, *The Historical and Cultural Atlas of African Americans*, and *The New Grove Dictionary of Music and Musicians*, to name a few. Reference works can help you learn about a topic, but you will need to consult more in-depth sources as you write.

26b Locating articles

Libraries subscribe to a variety of databases (sometimes called *periodical* or *article databases*) that give students access to articles and other materials without charge. Older works that have not been digitized will not be available in databases; you may need to consult a print index as well.

What databases offer   Your library's databases can lead you to articles in newspapers, magazines, and scholarly or technical journals. General databases cover several subject areas; subject-specific databases cover one subject area in depth. Your library might subscribe to some of the following databases.

GENERAL DATABASES

> *Academic Search Premier.* A database that indexes popular and scholarly journals.
>
> *Expanded Academic ASAP.* A database that indexes the contents of magazines, newspapers, and scholarly journals.
>
> *JSTOR.* A full-text archive of scholarly journals from many disciplines.
>
> *LexisNexis.* A set of databases particularly strong in news, business, legal, and political topics.
>
> *ProQuest.* A database of periodical articles.

SUBJECT-SPECIFIC DATABASES

> *ERIC.* An education database.
>
> *MLA Bibliography.* A database of literary criticism.
>
> *PsycINFO.* A database of psychology research.
>
> *PubMed.* A database with abstracts of medical studies.

Many databases include the full text of at least some articles; others list only citations or citations with short summaries called *abstracts*. When the full text is not available, a citation will give you enough information to track down an article.

Refining keyword searches in databases and search engines

Although command terms and characters vary among databases and Web search engines, some of the most common functions are listed here.

- Use quotation marks around words that are part of a phrase: "gateway drug".

- Use AND to connect words that must appear in a document: hyperactivity AND children. Some search engines require a plus sign instead: hyperactivity+children.

- Use NOT in front of words that must not appear in a document: Persian Gulf NOT war. Some search engines require a minus sign (hyphen) instead: Persian Gulf -war.

- Use OR if only one of the terms must appear in a document: "mountain lion" OR cougar.

- Use an asterisk as a substitute for letters that might vary: "marine biolog*" (to find *marine biology* or *marine biologist*).

- Use parentheses to group a search expression and combine it with another: (standard OR student OR test*) AND reform.

NOTE: Many search engines and databases offer an advanced search option for refining your search with filters for phrases that should or should not appear, date restrictions, and so on.

How to search a database To find articles on your topic in a database, start by searching with keywords, terms related to the information you need. If the first keyword you try results in no matches, experiment with synonyms. If your keyword search results in too many matches, narrow it by using one of the strategies in the chart above.

26c Locating books

The books your library owns are listed along with other resources in its catalog. You can search the catalog by author, title, or subject.

If your search calls up too few results, try different keywords or search for books on broader topics. If your search gives you too many results, try the strategies in the chart at the top of this page.

Use a book's call number to find the book on the shelf. When you're retrieving the book, take time to scan other books in the area since they are likely to cover the same topic.

26d Locating other sources online

You can find a variety of reliable resources using online tools beyond those offered by your library. For example, government agencies post information on their Web sites, and the sites of many organizations are filled with information about current issues. Museums and libraries often post digital versions of primary sources, such as photographs, political speeches, and classic literary texts.

Although the Internet can be a rich source of information, it lacks quality control. Anyone can publish to the Web, so you'll need to evaluate online sources with special care (see 27c).

This section describes the following Internet resources: search engines, directories, digital archives, government and news sites, blogs, and wikis.

Search engines When using a search engine, such as *Google* or *Yahoo!*, focus your search as narrowly as possible. You can sharpen your search by using the tips listed in the chart on page 91 or by using a search engine's advanced search form.

Directories Unlike search engines, which hunt for Web pages automatically, directories are put together by information specialists who arrange reputable sites by topic: education, health, politics, and so on.

Try the following directories for scholarly research:

Internet Scout Project: http://scout.wisc.edu/Archives

Librarian's Internet Index: http://lii.org

Open Directory Project: http://dmoz.org

WWW Virtual Library: http://vlib.org

Digital archives Archives like the following can help you find primary resources: the texts of poems, books, speeches, and historically significant documents; photographs; and political cartoons.

American Memory: http://memory.loc.gov

Avalon Project: http://yale.edu/lawweb/avalon/ avalon.htm

Eurodocs: http://eudocs.lib.byu.edu

Google Books: http://books.google.com

Google Scholar: http://scholar.google.com

Making of America: http://moa.umdl.umich.edu

Online Books Page: http://onlinebooks.library.upenn
.edu

Government and news sites For current topics, both government and news sites can prove useful. Many government agencies at every level provide online information. Government-maintained sites include resources such as facts and statistics, legal texts, government reports, and searchable reference databases. Here are just a few government sites:

Census Bureau: http://www.census.gov

Fedstats: http://www.fedstats.gov

GPO Access: http://www.gpoaccess.gov

United Nations: http://www.un.org

University of Michigan Documents Center: http://
www.lib.umich.edu/m/moagrp

Many news organizations offer up-to-date information online. Some require registration and may charge fees for some articles. (Find out if your library subscribes to news sites that you can access at no charge.) The following news sites offer many free resources:

BBC: http://www.bbc.co.uk

Google News: http://news.google.com

Kidon Media-Link: http://www.kidon.com/media-link

New York Times: http://nytimes.com

Reuters: http://www.reuters.com

Blogs A blog (short for *Weblog*) is a site that contains text or multimedia entries usually written and maintained by one person, with comments contributed by readers. Though some blogs are personal or devoted to partisan politics, many journalists and academics maintain blogs that cover topics of interest to researchers. The following Web sites can lead you to a wide range of blogs:

Academic Blog Portal: http://academicblogs.org

Google Blog Search: http://www.google.com/blogsearch

Science Blogs: http://scienceblogs.com

Technorati: http://technorati.com

Wikis A wiki is a collaborative Web site with many contributors and with content that may change frequently. *Wikipedia*, the collaborative online encyclopedia, is one of the most frequently consulted wikis.

In general, *Wikipedia* may be helpful if you're checking for something that is common knowledge or looking for current information about a topic in contemporary culture. (For a discussion of common knowledge in various disciplines, see pp. 108, 166–67, and 210.) However, many scholars do not consider *Wikipedia* and wikis in general to be appropriate sources for college research. Authorship is not limited to experts; articles may be written or changed by anyone. When possible, locate and cite another, more reliable source for any useful information you find in a wiki.

27 Evaluating sources

You can often locate dozens or even hundreds of potential sources for your topic—far more than you will have time to read. Your challenge will be to determine what kinds of sources you need and to find a reasonable number of quality sources.

Later, once you have decided on sources worth consulting, your challenge will be to read them with an open mind and a critical eye.

27a Selecting sources

Determining how sources contribute to your writing
How you plan to use sources affects how you evaluate them. Sources can have various functions in a paper. You can use them to

- provide background information or context for your topic
- explain terms or concepts that your readers might not understand
- provide evidence for your argument
- lend authority to your argument
- offer counterevidence and alternative interpretations

Determining if a source is scholarly

Many college assignments require you to use scholarly
sources. Written by experts for a knowledgeable audience,
these sources often go into more depth than books and
articles written for a general audience. To determine if a
source is scholarly, look for the following:

- Formal language and presentation
- Authors with academic or scientific credentials
- Footnotes or a bibliography documenting the works
  cited by the author in the source
- Original research and interpretation (rather than a
  summary of other people's work)
- Quotations from and analysis of primary sources
- A description of research methods or a review of related
  research

See pages 96–97 for a sample scholarly source and popular
source.

For examples of how student writers use sources for a variety of purposes, see 31, 37, and 42.

Scanning search results   The chart on page 91 shows
how to refine your searches. This section explains how to
scan through the results for the most useful and reliable
sources.

Databases   Most article databases (see p. 90) provide at
least the following information to help you decide if a
source is relevant, current, scholarly enough, and a suitable length.

Title and brief description (How relevant?)

Date (How current?)

Name of periodical (How scholarly?)

Length (How extensive in coverage?)

Book catalogs   A book's title and date of publication are
often your first clues as to whether the book is worth consulting. If a title looks interesting, you can click on it for
further information.

Search engines   Because anyone can publish a Web site,
legitimate sources and unreliable sources live side-by-side
online. Look for the following clues about the probable

Common features of a scholarly source

1 Formal presentation with abstract and research methods
2 Includes review of previous research studies
3 Reports original research
4 Includes references
5 Multiple authors with academic credentials

FIRST PAGE OF ARTICLE

Cyberbullying: Using Virtual Scenarios to Educate and Raise Awareness

Vivian H. Wright, Joy J. Burnham, Christopher T. Inman, and
Heather N. Ogorchock

Abstract

This study examined cyberbullying in three distinct phases to facilitate a multifaceted understanding of cyberbullying. The phases included (a) a quantitative survey, (b) a qualitative focus group, and (c) development of educational scenarios/simulations (within the Second Life virtual environment). Phase III was based on adolescent feedback about cyberbullying from Phases I and II of this study. In all three phases, adolescent reactions to cyberbullying were examined and reported to raise awareness and have the potential to be powerful tools in helping schools address problems such as cyberbullying education and prevention. (Keywords: cyberbullying, virtual worlds, Second Life, teacher education, counselor education)

Introduction

Cyberbullying has gained attention and recognition in recent years (Beale & Hall, 2007; Carney, 2008; Casey-Canon, Hayward, & Gowen, 2001; Kowalski & Limber, 2007; Li, 2007; Shariff, 2005). The increased interest and awareness of cyberbullying relates to such factors as the national media attention after several publicized cyberbullying tragedies (Maag, 2007; Stelter, 2008; Zifcak, 2006), the attenuation of communication between... and computer network connection... technology use among youth. Non... youth, presently there remains a cr... cyberbullying and its possible effect... lescents. Because cyberbullying has... systems (i.e., home, school, and the co... "school professionals" (Li, 2007, p. 1778), and mental health providers must not only be made aware of cyberbullying and its consequences, but must also have access to ways to deal with this growing concern.

Two years ago, cyberbullying was considered to be a "new territory" for exploration (Li, 2007, p. 1778) because there was limited information about bullying through "electronic means" (Li, p. 1780). In contrast, today studies on cyberbullying, including some descriptions of the worst cyberbullying incidences (Maag, 2007; Stelter, 2008; Zifcak, 2006), are becoming more prevalent (Beale & Hall, 2007; Carney, 2008; Kowalski & Limber, 2007; Li, 2007). At this time, there is a need to raise awareness about the effects of cyberbullying and to create educational opportunities to serve multiple audiences (i.e. teachers, teacher educators, school administrators, school counselors, mental health professionals, students, parents) in the quest to identify and hopefully prevent cyberbullying in the future. Consequently, to facilitate a multifaceted understanding of

cyberbullying, this study sought to examine cyberbullying through three phases: (a) a quantitative survey, (b) a qualitative focus group, and (c) development of the educational scenarios/simulations (i.e., using virtual world avatars similar to those used in Linden Lab's (1993) Second Life (SL; http://secondlife.com) based on adolescent feedback from Phases I and II of this study). Adolescent reactions to cyberbullying in all three phases of this study were examined and reported with two aims in mind: (a) to raise awareness of cyberbullying, and (b) to educate others about cyberbullying.

Defining Cyberbullying

Cyberbullying has been described as a traumatic experience that can lead to physical, cognitive, emotional, and social consequences (Carney, 2008; Casey-Canon et al., 2001; Patchin & Hinduja, 2006). Cyberbullying has been defined as "bullying through the e-mail, instant messaging, in a chat room, on a website, or though digital messages or images sent to a cell phone" (Kowalski & Limber, 2007, p. 822). There are numerous methods to engage in cyberbullying, including e-mail, instant messaging, online gaming, chat rooms, and text messaging (Beale & Hall, 2007; Li, 2007). In addition, cyberbullying appears in different forms than traditional bullying. For example, Beale and Hall (2007), Mason (2007), and Willard (2008) found that at least seven different types of cyberbullying exist, including:

Research suggests that cyberbullying has distinct gender and age differences. According to the literature, girls are more likely to be online and to cyberbully (Beale & Hall, 2007; Kowalski & Limber, 2007; Li, 2006, 2007). This finding is "opposite of what happens off-line," where boys are

- ... ...ating similarly, including a person not sharing certain information
- Exclusion: excluding someone purposefully

Research suggests that cyberbullying has distinct gender and age differences. According to the literature, girls are more likely to be online and to cyberbully (Beale & Hall, 2007; Kowalski & Limber, 2007; Li, 2006, 2007). This finding is "opposite of what happens off-line," where boys are more likely to bully than girls (Beale & Hall, p. 8). Age also appears to be a factor in cyberbullying. Cyberbullying increases in the elementary years, peaks during the middle school years, and declines in the high school years (Beale & Hall). Based on the literature, cyberbullying is a growing concern among middle school-aged children (Beale & Hall; Hinduja & Patchin, 2008; Kowalski & Limber, 2007; Li, 2007; Pellegrini & Bartini, 2000; Smith, Mahdavi, Carvalho, & Tippett, 2006; Williams & Guerra, 2007). Of the middle school grades, 6th grade students are usually the

Volume 26/ Number 1 Fall 2009 Journal of Computing in Teacher Education 35

EXCERPTS FROM OTHER PAGES

3 Table 2: Percentage of Students Who Experienced Cyberbullying through Various Methods

	E-mail	Facebook	MySpace	Cell Phone	Online Video	Chat Rooms
Victim	35.3%	11.8%	52.9%	50%	14.7%	11.8%
Bully	17.6%	0%	70.6%	47.1%	11.8%	5.9%

4 References

Bainbridge, W. S. (2007, July). The scientific research potential of virtual worlds. *Science, 317,* 472–476.

Beale, A., & Hall, K. (2007, September/October). Cyberbullying:
What... 81, 8...

5 *Vivian H. Wright is an associate professor of instructional technology at the Uni... of Alabama. In addition to teaching in the graduate program, Dr. Wright works with teacher educators on innovative ways to infuse technology in the curriculum...*

Wright, Vivian H., et al. "Cyberbullying: Using Virtual Scenarios to Educate and Raise Awareness." *Journal of Computing in Teacher Education* 26.1 (2009): 35–42.

Common features of a popular source

1 Provocative title
2 Written by a staff reporter, not an expert
3 Presents anecdotes about the topic
4 Presents a summary of research but no original research
5 No consistent citation of sources

FIRST PAGE OF ARTICLE

Technology

The cyber-bullies are always with you...

The anonymity of the internet makes it easy for bu...
to ruin the lives of their teenage victims

PHIL MCKENNA

RYAN HALLIGAN was taunted for months. Classmates spread rumours via instant messaging that the 13-year-old boy was gay. A popular female classmate pretended to like him and chatted with him over the internet only to copy their personal exchanges and share them with her friends. Unable to cope, Halligan, of Essex Junction, Vermont, killed himself.

Gail Jones, a 15-year-old from Tranmere near Liverpool in the UK took her life after receiving, at one point, 20 silent calls on her cellphone every 30 minutes. Her father, Glyn, suspects a final call in the middle of the night pushed her over the edge.

These are extreme but far from unique examples of the devastation wrought by cyber-bullying. Since Halligan died in 2003 and Jones in 2000, many more children are logging on to the internet, so it's likely that online bullying, including sending threatening messages, displaying private messages and photos online, is also increasing.

A study last month by the Pew Internet & American Life Project based in Washington DC found that one-third of US teenage internet users have been targets of cyber-bullying (*New Scientist*, 7 July, p 23). Meanwhile, as online communication evolves from instant messaging and chatrooms

The anonymity of the internet makes it easy to ruin the lives of their teenage victims

PHIL MCKENNA

RYAN HALLIGAN was taunted for months. Classmates spread rumours via instant messaging that the 13-year-old boy was gay. A popular female classmate pretended to like him and chatted with him online only to copy their personal exchanges and share them with her friends. Unable to cope, Halligan, of Essex Junction, Vermont, killed himself.

These are extreme... unique examples of devastation wrought bullying. Since Hallig 2003 and Jones in 20 more children are lo the internet, so it's li online bullying, inclu sending threatening posting embarrassin photos online, is also A study last mont

I was a kid, playground bullying stopped when the bell rang and you went back inside or when you went home at the end of the day.

physical bullying.

One reason for this is the sheer number of people who can view something that is posted online. "It would be bad enough if a teen was cyber-bullied by one person, but nobody else... The humiliation of a video seen by hundreds or thousands of your peers is devastating," says Robin Kowalski, a psychologist at Clemson University in South Carolina and co-author of the book...

A study last month by the Pew Internet & American Life Project based in Washington DC found that one-third of US teenage internet users have been targets

is how they communicate." A 2007 Pew study found that 93 per cent of US teens use the internet and 61 per cent go online daily.

The internet doesn't just amplify the effect of bullying, however. The many options to remain anonymous when online, by using pseudonyms for instant messaging, say, means people can write things they would not dare to if their identity was known.

Anonymity was at the heart of a 2001 incident when a student at an elite high school in New York City set up a web page that let students vote anonymously on who they felt was their most

ONLINE BULLIES ATTACK ADULTS TOO

Known best as a problem facing teens, cyber-bullying affects adults too. Inhabitants of virtual worlds, from film stars to teachers have all been victims.

Second Life is designed for adults and to access most locations you are supposed to be at least 18 years old. Yet nearly 2000 abuse reports are filed each day, says Linden Labs of San Francisco, who created Second Life. "It's adults hassling other adults," says Thomas Chesney of the University of Nottingham, UK, who has encountered pushing, swearing and shooting there.

Chesney and colleagues recently set

up an office in Second Life where they interviewed more than 100 inhabitants about bullying. Chesney says that because many people come to Second Life with a background in gaming, they bring preconceived notions of violence and aggression with them. "They're playing games like World of Warcraft — where the aim is to kill everybody — and they take that attitude into Second Life," he says. "It's a bit depressing that we haven't progressed beyond hassling one other, but not surprising given all we know about workplace bullying."

Teachers have also been victims.

Tired of insults from students on websites such as RateMyteachers.co.uk, the UK Association of Teachers and lecturers said earlier this year that it is ready to go to court in support of teachers who have been libelled online. The union would target publishers of websites directly, not the children who post disparaging comments.

Meanwhile in South Korea, celebrities have been the high-profile victims of anonymous cyber-bullying attacks, reportedly including TV star Jeong Da-bin and pop singer Yuni, who both later committed suicide.

www.newscientist.com

26 | NewScientist | 21 July 2007

EXCERPT FROM ANOTHER PAGE

"The lack of face-to-face contact might tempt bullies to new levels of cruelty"

communication. "There is a distancing of the self and immediacy in response that we don't have in any other form of communication," she says. "On the computer, it's like it's not really you."

So what can be done? Led by Ruth Aylett of Heriot-Watt University in Edinburgh, UK,

Meanwhile, some governments have taken legislative action. In January 2006, the US Congress passed a law making it a federal crime to "annoy, abuse, threaten or harass" another person over the internet. Approximately 36 states have enacted similar legislation. And in South Korea, the "internet real-

McKenna, Phil. "The Cyber-Bullies Are Always with You. . . ."
New Scientist July 2007: 26-27.

relevance, currency, and reliability of a site—but be aware that the clues are by no means foolproof.

Title, keywords, and lead-in text (How relevant?)

A date (How current?)

An indication of the site's sponsor or purpose (How reliable?)

The URL, especially the domain name extension: for example, .com, .edu, .gov, or .org (How relevant? How reliable?)

27b Reading with an open mind and a critical eye

As you begin reading the sources you have chosen, keep an open mind. Do not let your personal beliefs prevent you from listening to new ideas and opposing viewpoints. Your research question—not a snap judgment about the question—should guide your reading.

When you read critically, you are not necessarily judging an author's work harshly; you are simply examining its

Evaluating all sources

Checking for signs of bias

- Does the author or publisher endorse political or religious views that could affect objectivity?

- Is the author or publisher associated with a special-interest group, such as Greenpeace or the National Rifle Association, that might present a narrow view of an issue?

- How fairly does the author treat opposing views?

- Does the author's language show signs of bias?

Assessing an argument

- What is the author's central claim or thesis?

- How does the author support this claim—with relevant and sufficient evidence or with anecdotes or emotional examples?

- Are statistics accurate and used fairly? Does the author explain where the statistics come from?

- Are any of the author's assumptions questionable?

- Does the author consider opposing arguments and refute them persuasively?

assumptions, assessing its evidence, and weighing its conclusions. For a checklist on evaluating sources, see page 98.

27c Assessing Web sources with special care

Web sources can provide valuable information, but verify-
ing their credibility may take time. Even sites that appear
to be professional and fair-minded may contain questionable information. Before using a Web source in your paper,
make sure you know who created the material and for
what purpose. The following chart provides a checklist for
evaluating Web sources.

Evaluating Web sources

Authorship

■ Is there an author? You may need to do some clicking
  and scrolling to find the author's name. Check the home
  page or an "about this site" link.

■ Can you tell whether an author is knowledgeable and
  credible? If the author's qualifications aren't listed on the
  site, look for links to the author's home page, which may
  provide evidence of his or her expertise.

Sponsorship

■ Who, if anyone, sponsors the site? The sponsor of a site
  is often named and described on the home page.

■ What does the URL tell you? The domain name
  extension often indicates the type of group hosting the
  site: commercial (.com), educational (.edu), nonprofit
  (.org), governmental (.gov), military (.mil), or network
  (.net). URLs may also indicate a country of origin: .uk
  (United Kingdom) or .jp (Japan), for instance.

Purpose and audience

■ Why was the site created: To argue a position? To sell a
  product? To inform readers?

■ Who is the site's intended audience?

Currency

■ How current is the site? Check for the date of
  publication or the latest update.

■ How current are the site's links? If many of the links
  no longer work, the site may be outdated for your
  purposes.

28 Managing information; avoiding plagiarism

Whether you decide to keep records on paper or on your computer—or both—you will need methods for managing information: maintaining a working bibliography, keeping track of source materials, and taking notes without plagiarizing your sources. (For more on avoiding plagiarism, see 30 for MLA style, 36 for APA style, and 41 for *Chicago* style.)

28a Maintaining a working bibliography

Keep a record of any sources you decide to consult. This record, called a *working bibliography*, will help you compile the list of sources that will appear at the end of your paper. The format of this list depends on the documentation style you are using. (For MLA style, see 33b; for APA style, see 38b; for *Chicago* style, see 43c; for CSE style, see 45b.)

Once you have created a working bibliography, you can annotate it. Writing several brief sentences summarizing key points of a source in your own words will help you identify how the source relates to your argument and to your other sources. Clarifying the source's ideas at this stage will help you separate them from your own ideas and avoid plagiarizing them later.

SAMPLE ANNOTATED BIBLIOGRAPHY ENTRY (MLA STYLE)

Gonsalves, Chris. "Wasting Away on the Web." *eWeek.com*. Ziff Davis Enterprise Holdings, 8 Aug. 2005. Web. 16 Feb. 2009.

> In this editorial, Gonsalves considers the implications **1** of several surveys, including one in which 61% of respondents said that their companies have the right to spy on them. The **2** author agrees with this majority, claiming that it's fine if his company chooses to monitor him as long as the company discloses its monitoring practices. He argues that "the days of **3** Internet freedom at work are justifiably finished," adding that he would prefer not to know the extent of the surveillance. Gonsalves writes for *eWeek.com*, a publication focused on technology products. He presents himself as an employee who **4** is comfortable with being monitored, but his job may be a

MODELS hackerhandbooks.com/pocket

> Model papers > MLA annotated bibliography: Orlov
> APA annotated bibliography: Haddad

source of bias. This editorial contradicts some of my other   **5**
sources, which claim that employees want to know and
should know all the details of their company's monitoring
procedures.

1 Summarize the source.

2 Annotations should be three to seven sentences long.

3 Use quotations sparingly. Put quotation marks around any
words from the source.

4 Evaluate the source for bias and relevance.

5 Interpret the relationship between this source and others in the
bibliography.

28b Keeping track of source materials

Save a copy of each source. Many databases will allow you
to e-mail, save, or print citations or full texts of articles,
and you can easily download, copy, or take screen shots of
information from the Web.

Working with saved files or printouts—as opposed to
relying on memory or hastily written notes—lets you high-
light key passages and make notes in the margins of the
source as you read. You also reduce the chances of uninten-
tional plagiarism, since you will be able to compare your use
of a source in your paper with the actual source, not just
with your notes.

NOTE: It's especially important to keep print or electronic
copies of Web sources, which may change or even become
inaccessible over time. Make sure that your copy includes
the site's URL and your date of access.

28c Avoiding unintentional plagiarism
as you take notes

When you take notes, be very careful to identify borrowed
words and phrases as quotations. Even if you half-copy
the author's sentences—either by mixing the author's
phrases with your own without using quotation marks
or by plugging your synonyms into the author's sentence
structure—you are committing plagiarism, a serious academic offense.

Summarizing and paraphrasing ideas and quoting
exact language are three ways of taking notes. Be sure to

include exact page references for all three types of notes, since you will need the page numbers later if you use the information in your paper. (See the following chart for advice about avoiding plagiarism.)

Integrating and citing sources to avoid plagiarism

Source text

> Our language is constantly changing. Like the Mississippi, it keeps forging new channels and abandoning old ones, picking up debris, depositing unwanted silt, and frequently bursting its banks. In every generation there are people who deplore changes in the language and many who wish to stop its flow. But if our language stopped changing it would mean that American society had ceased to be dynamic, innovative, pulsing with life — that the great river had frozen up.
>
> — Robert MacNeil and William Cran,
> *Do You Speak American?*, p. 1

NOTE: The examples in this chart follow MLA style (see 33). For information on APA, *Chicago*, and CSE styles, see 38, 43, and 45, respectively.

If you are using an exact sentence from a source, with no changes . . . → . . . put quotation marks around the sentence. Use a signal phrase and include a page number in parentheses.

MacNeil and Cran write, "Our language is constantly changing" (1).

If you are using a few exact words from the source but not an entire sentence . . . → . . . put quotation marks around the exact words that you have used from the source. Use a signal phrase and include a page number in parentheses.

Some people, according to MacNeil and Cran, "deplore changes in the language" (1).

If you are using near-exact words from the source but changing some word forms (*I* to *she*, *walk* to *walked*) or adding words to clarify and make the quotation flow with your own text . . .	→	. . . put quotation marks around the quoted words and put brackets around the changes you have introduced. Include a signal phrase and follow the quotation with the page number in parentheses.

MacNeil and Cran compare the English language to the Mississippi River, which "forg[es] new channels and abandon[s] old ones" (1).

MacNeil and Cran write, "In every generation there are people who deplore changes in the [English] language and many who wish to stop its flow" (1).

If you are paraphrasing or summarizing the source, using the author's ideas but not any of the author's exact words . . .	→	. . . introduce the ideas with a signal phrase and put the page number at the end of your sentence. Do not use quotation marks. (See 30, 36, and 41.)

MacNeil and Cran argue that changes in the English language are natural and that they represent cultural progress (1).

If you have used the source's sentence structure but substituted a few synonyms for the author's words . . .	→	STOP! This is a form of plagiarism even if you use a signal phrase and a page number. Change your sentence by using one of the techniques given in this chart or in 31, 37, or 42.

PLAGIARIZED

MacNeil and Cran claim that, like a river, English creates new waterways and discards old ones.

INTEGRATED AND CITED CORRECTLY

MacNeil and Cran claim, "Like the Mississippi, [English] keeps forging new channels and abandoning old ones" (1).

MLA Papers

Most English and some humanities instructors will ask you to document your sources with the Modern Language Association (MLA) system of citations described in 33. When writing an MLA paper based on sources, you face three main challenges: (1) supporting a thesis, (2) citing your sources and avoiding plagiarism, and (3) integrating quotations and other source material.

29   Supporting a thesis

Most research assignments ask you to form a thesis, or main idea, and to support that thesis with well-organized evidence.

29a   Forming a thesis

Once you have read a variety of sources and considered your issue from different perspectives, you are ready to form a working thesis—a one-sentence (or occasionally a two-sentence) statement of your central idea. The thesis expresses not just your opinion but also your informed, reasoned judgment. Usually your thesis will appear at the end of the first paragraph (see p. 159).

Your ideas may change as you learn more about your subject through reading and writing. You can revise your working thesis as you draft.

In a research paper, your thesis will answer the central question that you pose, as in the following examples.

PUBLIC POLICY QUESTION

Should employers monitor their employees' online activities in the workplace?

POSSIBLE THESIS

Employers should not monitor their employees' online activities because electronic surveillance can compromise workers' privacy.

LITERATURE QUESTION

What does Stephen Crane's short story "The Open Boat" reveal about the relationship between humans and nature?

POSSIBLE THESIS

In Stephen Crane's gripping tale "The Open Boat," four men lost at sea discover not only that nature is indifferent to their fate but also that their own particular talents make little difference as they struggle for survival.

MEDIA STUDIES QUESTION

What statement does the television show *House* make about the patient's right to choose or decline medical treatment?

POSSIBLE THESIS

On the television show *House*, Dr. House frequently accuses his patients of ignorance or deceit and sometimes manipulates them into undergoing treatment they do not want. Despite these negative qualities, Dr. House usually emerges as the hero, demonstrating that medical expertise is more valuable than a patient's right to make decisions about treatment.

Notice that each of these thesis statements takes a stand on a debatable issue—an issue about which intelligent, well-meaning people might disagree. Each writer's job will be to convince such people that his or her view is worth taking seriously.

29b Organizing your ideas

The body of your paper will consist of evidence in support of your thesis. To get started, list your key points, as student writer Anna Orlov did in this rough outline.

- Employers monitor workers more efficiently with electronic surveillance.

- Companies may have financial and legal reasons to monitor employees' Internet usage.

- But monitoring employees' Internet usage may create distrust and lower worker productivity.

- Current laws do little to protect employees' privacy rights, so employees and employers must negotiate the risks and benefits of electronic surveillance.

After you have written a rough draft, a more formal outline can help you shape the complexities of your argument.

29c Using sources to inform and support your argument

Sources can play several different roles as you develop your points.

Providing background information or context You can use facts and statistics to support generalizations or to establish the importance of your topic.

Explaining terms or concepts Explain words, phrases, or ideas that might be unfamiliar to your readers. Quoting or paraphrasing a source can help you define terms and concepts in accessible language.

Supporting your claims Back up your assertions with facts, examples, and other evidence from your research.

Lending authority to your argument Expert opinion can give weight to your argument. But don't rely on experts to make your argument for you. Construct your argument in your own words and cite authorities in the field to support your position.

Anticipating and countering objections Do not ignore sources that seem to contradict your position or that offer arguments different from your own. Instead, use them to give voice to opposing ideas and interpretations before you counter them.

30 Avoiding plagiarism

Your research paper is a collaboration between you and your sources. To be fair and ethical, you must acknowledge your debt to the writers of those sources. When you acknowledge your sources, you avoid plagiarism, a serious academic offense.

Three different acts are considered plagiarism: (1) failing to cite quotations and borrowed ideas, (2) failing to enclose borrowed language in quotation marks, and (3) failing to put summaries and paraphrases in your own words.

PRACTICE hackerhandbooks.com/pocket
> MLA > 30–1 to 30–6

30a Citing quotations and borrowed ideas

When you cite sources, you give credit to writers from whom you've borrowed words and ideas. You also let your readers know where your information comes from so that they can evaluate the original source.

You must cite anything you borrow from a source, including direct quotations; statistics and other specific facts; visuals such as cartoons, graphs, and diagrams; and any ideas you present in a summary or a paraphrase.

The only exception is common knowledge—information your readers could easily find in general sources. For example, most encyclopedias will tell readers that Alfred Hitchcock directed *Notorious* in 1946 and that Emily Dickinson published only a handful of her many poems during her lifetime.

When you have seen information repeatedly in your reading, you don't need to cite it. However, when information has appeared in only one or two sources, when it is highly specific (as with statistics), or when it is controversial, you should cite the source.

MLA recommends a system of in-text citations. Here, briefly, is how the MLA citation system usually works:

1. The source is introduced by a signal phrase that names its author.
2. The material being cited is followed by a page number in parentheses.
3. At the end of the paper, a list of works cited, arranged alphabetically by authors' last names (or by titles for works with no authors), gives complete publication information about the source.

IN-TEXT CITATION

Legal scholar Jay Kesan points out that the law holds employers liable for employees' actions such as violations of copyright laws, the distribution of offensive or graphic sexual material, and illegal disclosure of confidential information (312).

ENTRY IN THE LIST OF WORKS CITED

Kesan, Jay P. "Cyber-Working or Cyber-Shirking? A First Principles Examination of Electronic Privacy in the Workplace." *Florida Law Review* 54.2 (2002): 289-332. Print.

This basic MLA format varies for different types of sources. For a detailed discussion of other models, see 33.

30b Enclosing borrowed language in quotation marks

To show that you are using a source's exact phrases or sentences, enclose them in quotation marks unless they have been set off from the text by indenting (see pp. 112–13). To omit the quotation marks is to claim—falsely—that the language is your own. Such an omission is plagiarism even if you have cited the source.

ORIGINAL SOURCE

> Without adequate discipline, the World Wide Web can be a tremendous time sink; no other medium comes close to matching the Internet's depth of materials, interactivity, and sheer distractive potential.
> —Frederick Lane, *The Naked Employee*, p. 142

PLAGIARISM

Frederick Lane points out that if people do not have adequate discipline, the World Wide Web can be a tremendous time sink; no other medium comes close to matching the Internet's depth of materials, interactivity, and sheer distractive potential (142).

BORROWED LANGUAGE IN QUOTATION MARKS

Frederick Lane points out that for those not exercising self-control, "the World Wide Web can be a tremendous time sink; no other medium comes close to matching the Internet's depth of materials, interactivity, and sheer distractive potential" (142).

30c Putting summaries and paraphrases in your own words

A summary condenses information from a source; a paraphrase conveys the information using about the same number of words as in the original source. When you summarize or paraphrase, you must name the source and restate the source's meaning in your own words. You commit plagiarism if you half-copy the author's sentences—either by mixing the author's phrases with your own without using quotation marks or by plugging your synonyms into the author's sentence structure.

The first paraphrase of the source on page 110 is plagiarized—even though the source is cited—because too much of its language is borrowed from the original. The underlined words have been copied exactly (without quotation marks). Also, the writer has echoed the sentence structure of the source, merely substituting some synonyms (*restricted* for *limited*, *modern era* for *computer age*, *monitoring* for *surveillance*, and *inexpensive* for *cheap*).

ORIGINAL SOURCE

> In earlier times, surveillance was limited to the information that a supervisor could observe and record firsthand and to primitive counting devices. In the computer age surveillance can be instantaneous, unblinking, cheap, and, maybe most importantly, easy.
>> — Carl Botan and Mihaela Vorvoreanu,
>> "What Do Employees Think about
>> Electronic Surveillance at Work?," p. 126

PLAGIARISM: UNACCEPTABLE BORROWING

Scholars Carl Botan and Mihaela Vorvoreanu argue that in earlier times monitoring of employees was restricted to the information that a supervisor could observe and record firsthand. In the modern era, monitoring can be instantaneous, inexpensive, and, most importantly, easy (126).

To avoid plagiarizing an author's language, don't look at the source while you are summarizing or paraphrasing. After you've restated the author's idea in your own words, return to the source and check that you haven't used the author's language or sentence structure or misrepresented the author's ideas.

ACCEPTABLE PARAPHRASE

Scholars Carl Botan and Mihaela Vorvoreanu claim that the nature of workplace surveillance has changed over time. Before the arrival of computers, managers could collect only small amounts of information about their employees based on what they saw or heard. However, because computers are now standard workplace technology, employers can monitor employees efficiently (126).

31 Integrating nonfiction sources

Quotations, summaries, paraphrases, and facts will help you develop your argument, but they cannot speak for you. You can use several strategies to integrate information from research sources into your paper while maintaining your own voice.

31a Using quotations appropriately

Limiting your use of quotations In your writing, keep the emphasis on your own ideas. Do not quote excessively. Except for the following legitimate uses of quotations, use your own words to summarize and paraphrase your sources and to explain your points.

WHEN TO USE QUOTATIONS

- When language is especially vivid or expressive
- When exact wording is needed for technical accuracy
- When it is important to let the debaters of an issue explain their positions in their own words
- When the words of an authority lend weight to an argument
- When the language of a source is the topic of your discussion (as in an analysis or interpretation)

It is not always necessary to quote full sentences from a source. Often you can integrate words or phrases from a source into your own sentence structure.

Kizza and Ssanyu observe that technology in the workplace has been accompanied by "an array of problems that needed quick answers," such as electronic monitoring to prevent security breaches (4).

Using the ellipsis mark To condense a quoted passage, you can use the ellipsis mark (three periods, with spaces between) to indicate that you have omitted words. What remains must be grammatically complete.

Lane acknowledges the legitimate reasons that many companies have for monitoring their employees' online activities, particularly management's concern about preventing "the theft of information that can be downloaded to a . . . disk, e-mailed to oneself . . . , or even posted to a Web page for the entire world to see" (12).

The writer has omitted from the source the words *floppy or Zip* before *disk* and *or a confederate* after *oneself.*

If you want to omit a full sentence or more, use a period before the three ellipsis dots.

Charles Lewis, director of the Center for Public Integrity,
points out that "by 1987, employers were administering nearly
2,000,000 polygraph tests a year to job applicants and
employees. . . . Millions of workers were required to produce
urine samples under observation for drug testing . . ." (22).

Ordinarily, do not use an ellipsis mark at the beginning
or at the end of a quotation. Your readers will understand
that the quoted material is taken from a longer passage.
The only exception occurs when you have dropped words
at the end of the final quoted sentence. In such cases, put
three ellipsis dots before the closing quotation mark and
the parentheses, as in the previous example.

Using brackets Brackets allow you to insert your own
words into quoted material—to clarify a confusing reference or to make the quoted words fit grammatically into
the context of your writing.

Legal scholar Jay Kesan notes that "a decade ago, losses [from
employees' computer crimes] were already mounting to five
billion dollars annually" (311).

To indicate an error such as a misspelling, insert [sic],
including the brackets, right after the error.

Setting off long quotations When you quote more
than four typed lines of prose or more than three lines of
poetry, set off the quotation by indenting it one inch
from the left margin.

Long quotations should be introduced by an informative sentence, usually followed by a colon. Quotation
marks are unnecessary because the indented format tells
readers that the passage is taken word-for-word from the
source.

Botan and Vorvoreanu examine the role of gender in
company practices of electronic surveillance:

> By the middle 1990s, estimates of the proportion of
> surveilled employees that were women ranged from
> 75% to 85%. . . . Ironically, this gender imbalance
> in workplace surveillance may be evening out today
> because advances in surveillance technology are
> making surveillance of traditionally male dominated

> fields, such as long-distance truck driving, cheap,
>
> easy, and frequently unobtrusive. (127)

At the end of an indented quotation, the parenthetical
citation goes outside the final punctuation mark.

31b Using signal phrases to integrate sources

When you include a paraphrase, summary, or direct quotation in your paper, introduce it with a *signal phrase* that
names the author of the source and provides some context for the source material. (See the chart on page 114 for
a list of verbs commonly used in signal phrases.)

Marking boundaries   Readers need to move smoothly
from your words to the words of a source. Avoid dropping quotations into the text without warning. Provide
clear signal phrases, including at least the author's name,
to indicate the boundary between your words and the
source's words.

DROPPED QUOTATION

Some experts have argued that a range of legitimate concerns
justifies employer monitoring of employee Internet usage.
"Employees could accidentally (or deliberately) spill confidential
corporate information . . . or allow worms to spread throughout
a corporate network" (Tynan).

QUOTATION WITH SIGNAL PHRASE

Some experts have argued that a range of legitimate concerns
justifies employer monitoring of employee Internet usage. As *PC
World* columnist Daniel Tynan points out, companies that don't
monitor network traffic can be penalized for their ignorance:
"Employees could accidentally (or deliberately) spill confidential
corporate information . . . or allow worms to spread throughout
a corporate network."

Establishing authority   The first time you mention a
source, include in the signal phrase the author's title, credentials, or experience to help your readers recognize the
source's authority and your own credibility as a responsible
researcher who has located reliable sources.

SOURCE WITH NO CREDENTIALS

Jay Kesan points out that the law holds employers liable for employees' actions such as violations of copyright laws, the distribution of offensive or graphic sexual material, and illegal disclosure of confidential information (312).

SOURCE WITH CREDENTIALS

Legal scholar Jay Kesan points out that the law holds employers liable for employees' actions such as violations of copyright laws, the distribution of offensive or graphic sexual material, and illegal disclosure of confidential information (312).

Introducing summaries and paraphrases Introduce most summaries and paraphrases with a signal phrase that names the author and places the material in the context of your argument. Readers will then understand that everything between the signal phrase and the parenthetical citation summarizes or paraphrases the cited source.

Without the signal phrase (highlighted) in the following example, readers might think that only the quotation at the end is being cited, when in fact the whole paragraph is based on the source.

Frederick Lane believes that the personal computer has posed new challenges for employers worried about workplace productivity. Whereas early desktop computers were primitive enough to prevent employees from using them to waste time, the machines have become so sophisticated that they now make non-work-related computer activities easy and inviting. Perhaps most problematic from the employer's point of view, Lane asserts, is giving employees access to the Internet, "roughly the equivalent of installing a gazillion-channel television set for each employee" (15-16).

Sometimes a summary or a paraphrase does not require a signal phrase. When the context makes clear where the cited material begins, you may omit the signal phrase and include the author's last name in parentheses.

Integrating statistics and other facts When you are citing a statistic or another specific fact, a signal phrase is often not necessary. In most cases, readers will understand that the citation refers to the statistic or fact (not to the whole paragraph).

Using signal phrases in MLA papers

To avoid monotony, try to vary both the language and the placement of your signal phrases.

Model signal phrases

In the words of researchers Greenfield and Davis, ". . ."

As legal scholar Jay Kesan has noted, ". . ."

The ePolicy Institute, an organization that advises companies about reducing risks from technology, reports that ". . ."

". . . ," writes Daniel Tynan, ". . ."

". . . ," attorney Schmitt claims.

Kizza and Ssanyu offer a persuasive counterargument: ". . ."

Verbs in signal phrases

Are you providing background, explaining a concept, supporting a claim, lending authority, or refuting a belief? Choose a verb that is appropriate for the way you are using the source.

acknowledges	contends	insists
adds	declares	notes
admits	denies	observes
agrees	describes	points out
argues	disputes	refutes
asserts	emphasizes	rejects
believes	endorses	reports
claims	grants	responds
compares	illustrates	suggests
confirms	implies	writes

NOTE: In MLA style, use the present or present perfect tense (*argues* or *has argued*) to introduce source material unless you include a date that specifies the time of the original author's writing.

Roughly 60% of responding companies reported disciplining employees who had used the Internet in ways the companies deemed inappropriate; 30% had fired their employees for those transgressions (Greenfield and Davis 347).

There is nothing wrong, however, with using a signal phrase to introduce statistics and other facts.

Putting source material in context A signal phrase can help you connect your own ideas with those of another writer by clarifying how the source will contribute to your paper.

If you use another writer's words, you must explain how those words relate to your point; you must put the source in context. It's a good idea to embed a quotation between sentences of your own that interpret the source and link the quotation to your paper's argument. (See also 31c.)

QUOTATION WITH EFFECTIVE CONTEXT

The difference, Lane argues, between these old methods of data gathering and electronic surveillance involves quantity:

> Technology makes it possible for employers to gather enormous amounts of data about employees, often far beyond what is necessary to satisfy safety or productivity concerns. And the trends that drive technology—faster, smaller, cheaper—make it possible for larger and larger numbers of employers to gather ever-greater amounts of personal data. (3-4)

In an age when employers can collect data whenever employees use their computers—when they send e-mail, surf the Web, or even arrive at or depart from their workstations—the challenge for both employers and employees is to determine how much is too much.

31c Synthesizing sources

When you synthesize multiple sources in a research paper, you create a conversation about your research topic. You show readers how the ideas of one source relate to those of another by connecting and analyzing the ideas in the context of your argument. Keep the emphasis on your own writing. The thread of your argument should be easy to identify and to understand, with or without your sources.

In the following sample synthesis, Anna Orlov uses her own analyses to shape the conversation among her sources. She does not simply string quotations together or allow sources to overwhelm her writing. In her final sentence, she explains to readers how the various sources support her argument.

SAMPLE SYNTHESIS (DRAFT)

1   Productivity is not easily measured in the wired workplace. As a result, employers find it difficult to determine how much freedom to allow their employees. On the one hand, computers and Internet access give employees powerful tools to carry out their jobs; on the other hand, the same technology offers constant temptations to avoid work. As a 2005 study by *Salary.com* and *America Online* indicates, the Internet ranked as the top choice among employees for ways of wasting time on the job (Frauenheim).

> Student writer

> Source 1

2 Chris Gonsalves, an editor for *eWeek.com,* argues that technology has changed the terms between employers and employees: "While bosses can easily detect and interrupt water-cooler chatter," he writes, "the employee who is shopping at Lands' End or IMing with fellow fantasy baseball managers may actually appear to be working." The gap between observable behaviors and actual online activities has motivated some employers to invest in surveillance programs.

> Source 2

> Student writer

3   Many experts, however, disagree with employers' assumption that online monitoring can increase productivity. Employment law attorney Joseph Schmitt argues that, particularly for salaried employees, "a company shouldn't care whether employees spend one or 10 hours on the Internet as long as they are getting their jobs done—and provided that they are not accessing inappropriate sites" (qtd. in Verespej). Other experts even argue that time spent on personal

> Source 3

> Student writer

4 Internet browsing can actually be productive for companies. According to Bill Coleman, an executive at Salary.com, "Personal Internet use and casual office conversations often turn into new business ideas or suggestions for gaining operating efficiencies" (qtd. in Frauenheim). Employers, in other words, may benefit from showing more faith in their employees' ability to exercise their autonomy.

> Source 4

> Student writer

1 Student writer Anna Orlov begins with a claim that needs support.

2 Signal phrases indicate how sources contribute to Orlov's paper and show that the ideas that follow are not her own.
3 Orlov presents a counterposition to extend her argument.
4 Orlov builds her case — each quoted passage offers a more detailed claim or example in support of her larger claim.

32 Integrating literary quotations

Smoothly integrating quotations from a literary work into your own text can present challenges. Do not be surprised to find yourself puzzling over the most graceful way to tuck in a short phrase or the clearest way to introduce a more extended passage from the work.

NOTE: The parenthetical citations at the ends of examples in this section tell readers where the quoted words can be found. They indicate the lines of a poem; the act, scene, and lines of a play; or the page number of a quotation from a short story or a novel. (For guidelines on citing literary works, see pp. 128–29.)

32a Introducing literary quotations

When writing about nonfiction articles and books, you will introduce every quotation with a signal phrase naming the author (see p. 115). When writing about a single work of fiction, however, you do not need to include the author's name each time you quote from the work. Mention the author's name in the introduction to your paper; in your discussion of the work, refer, as appropriate, to the narrator of a story, the speaker of a poem, or the characters in a play. Make sure, however, that you do not confuse the author of the work with the narrator, speaker, or characters.

INAPPROPRIATE

Poet Andrew Marvell describes his fear of death like this: "But at my back I always hear / Time's wingèd chariot hurrying near" (21-22).

APPROPRIATE

Addressing his beloved in an attempt to win her sexual favors, the speaker of the poem argues that death gives them no time to waste: "But at my back I always hear / Time's wingèd chariot hurrying near" (21-22).

When you quote the words of a narrator, speaker,
or character in a literary work, you should name who is
speaking and provide a context for the quoted words. In
the following example, the quoted dialogue is from Tennessee Williams's play *The Glass Menagerie*.

Laura is so completely under Amanda's spell that when urged
to make a wish on the moon, she asks, "What shall I wish for,
Mother?" (1.5.140).

For examples of quoted dialogue from a short story,
see page 161.

32b Avoiding shifts in tense

Because it is conventional to write about literature in
the present tense (see p. 29) and because literary works
often use other tenses, you will need to exercise some care
when weaving quotations into your own text. A first-draft
attempt may result in an awkward shift, as it did for one
student who was writing about Nadine Gordimer's short
story "Friday's Footprint."

TENSE SHIFT

When Rita sees Johnny's relaxed attitude, "she blushed, like a
wave of illness" (159).

To avoid the distracting shift from present tense (*sees*) to
past tense (*blushed*), the writer decided to paraphrase the
reference to Rita's blushing and reduce the length of the
quotation.

REVISED

When Rita sees Johnny's relaxed attitude, she is overcome with
embarrassment, "like a wave of illness" (159).

The writer could have changed the quotation to present
tense, using brackets to indicate the change: *When Rita
sees Johnny's relaxed attitude, "she blushe[s], like a wave of
illness"* (159). (See also p. 112 for the use of brackets.)

32c Formatting and citing literary passages

MLA guidelines for formatting and citing quotations
differ somewhat for short stories or novels, poems, and
plays.

Short stories or novels If a quotation from a short story or a novel takes up four or fewer typed lines in your paper, put it in quotation marks and run it into the text of your essay. Include a page number in parentheses after the quotation.

The narrator of Eudora Welty's "Why I Live at the P.O.," known to us only as "Sister," makes many catty remarks about her enemies. For example, she calls Mr. Whitaker "this photographer with the pop-eyes" (46).

If a quotation from a short story or a novel is five typed lines or longer in your paper, set the quotation off from the text by indenting it one inch from the left margin; do not use quotation marks. (See also pp. 112–13.) Put the page number in parentheses after the final mark of punctuation.

Sister's tale begins with "I," and she makes every event revolve around herself, even her sister's marriage:

> I was getting along fine with Mama, Papa-Daddy, and Uncle Rondo until my sister Stella-Rondo just separated from her husband and came back home again. Mr. Whitaker! Of course I went with Mr. Whitaker first, when he first appeared here in China Grove, taking "Pose Yourself" photos, and Stella-Rondo broke us up. (46)

Poems Enclose quotations of three or fewer lines of poetry in quotation marks within your text, and indicate line breaks with a slash with a space on each side. Include line numbers in parentheses at the end of the quotation. For the first reference, use the word "lines." Thereafter, use just numbers.

The opening of Frost's "Fire and Ice" strikes a conversational tone: "Some say the world will end in fire, / Some say in ice" (lines 1-2).

When you quote four or more lines of poetry, set the quotation off from the text by indenting one inch and omit the quotation marks. Put the line numbers in parentheses after the final mark of punctuation.

The opening stanza of Louise Bogan's "Women" startles readers by presenting a negative stereotype of women:

> Women have no wilderness in them,
> They are provident instead,
> Content in the tight hot cell of their hearts
> To eat dusty bread. (lines 1-4)

Plays If a quotation from a play takes up four or fewer typed lines in your paper and is spoken by only one character, put quotation marks around it and run it into the text of your essay. Whenever possible, include the act number, scene number, and line numbers in parentheses at the end of the quotation. Separate the numbers with periods and use arabic numerals unless your instructor prefers roman numerals.

Two attendants silently watch as the sleepwalking Lady Macbeth subconsciously struggles with her guilt: "Here's the smell of blood still. All the perfumes of Arabia will not sweeten this little hand" (5.1.50-51).

33 MLA documentation style

In English and other humanities classes, you may be asked to use the MLA (Modern Language Association) system for documenting sources, which is set forth in the *MLA Handbook for Writers of Research Papers*, 7th ed. (New York: MLA, 2009).

To document sources, MLA recommends in-text citations that refer readers to a list of works cited at the end of the paper. The works cited list gives all the sources cited in the paper, arranged alphabetically by authors' last names (or by titles for works that have no authors). The author's name (or the work's title) is used in a signal phrase or in parentheses to cite the source in the text of the paper.

33a MLA in-text citations

MLA in-text citations are made with a combination of signal phrases and parenthetical references. A signal phrase introduces information taken from a source (a quotation, summary, paraphrase, or fact); usually the signal phrase includes the author's name. The parenthetical reference comes after the cited material, often at the end of the sentence. It includes at least a page number (except for unpaginated sources, such as those found online). In the models in this section, the elements of the in-text citation are highlighted.

PRACTICE hackerhandbooks.com/pocket
 > MLA > 33–1 to 33–3

IN-TEXT CITATION

Kwon points out that the Fourth Amendment does not give employees any protections from employers' "unreasonable searches and seizures" (6).

Readers can look up the author's last name in the alphabetized list of works cited, where they will learn the work's title and other publication information. If readers decide to consult the source, the page number will direct them to the passage that has been cited.

Basic rules for print and electronic sources   The MLA system of in-text citations, which depends heavily on authors' names and page numbers, was created with print sources in mind. Although many online sources have unclear authorship and lack page numbers, the basic rules are the same for print and electronic sources.

The models in this section (items 1–5) show how the MLA system usually works and explain what to do if your source has no author or page numbers.

■ **1. Author named in a signal phrase**   Ordinarily, introduce the material being cited with a signal phrase that includes the author's name. (See also 31b.)

Frederick Lane reports that employers can monitor their employees with "a hidden video camera pointed at an employee's monitor" and can even position a camera "so that a number of monitors [can] be viewed at the same time" (147).

The signal phrase—*Frederick Lane reports*—names the author; the parenthetical citation gives the page number of the book in which the quoted words may be found.

Notice that the period follows the parenthetical citation. When a quotation ends with a question mark or an exclamation point, leave the end punctuation inside the quotation mark and add a period at the end of your sentence.

O'Connor asks a critical question: "When does Internet surveillance cross the line between corporate responsibility and invasion of privacy?" (16).

■ **2. Author named in parentheses**   If a signal phrase does not name the author, put the author's last name in parentheses along with the page number. Use no punctuation between the name and the page number.

Companies can monitor employees' keystrokes without legal penalty, but they may have to combat low morale as a result (Lane 129).

■ **3. Author unknown** Either use the complete title in a signal phrase or use a short form of the title in parentheses. Titles of books are italicized; titles of articles are put in quotation marks.

A popular keystroke logging program operates invisibly on workers' computers and provides supervisors with details of the workers' online activities ("Automatically").

If the author is an organization or a government agency, see item 8 on pages 125–26.

NOTE: See item 5 on page 134 for works cited entries for sources with unknown authors.

■ **4. Page number unknown** Do not include the page number if a work lacks page numbers, as is the case with many Web sources. Even if a printout from a Web site shows page numbers, treat the source as unpaginated because not all printouts give the same page numbers. (When the pages of a Web source are stable, as in PDF files, supply a page number in your in-text citation.)

As a 2005 study by *Salary.com* and *America Online* indicates, the Internet ranked as the top choice among employees for ways of wasting time on the job; it beat talking with co-workers—the second most popular method—by a margin of nearly two to one (Frauenheim).

If a source has numbered paragraphs or sections, use "par." (or "pars.") or "sec." (or "secs.") in the parentheses: (Smith, par. 4). Notice that a comma follows the author's name.

■ **5. One-page source** If the source is one page long, MLA allows (but does not require) you to omit the page number. Even so, it's a good idea to supply the page number because without it readers may not know where your citation ends or, worse, may not realize that you have provided a citation at all.

Anush Yegyazarian reports that in 2000 the National Labor
Relations Board's Office of the General Counsel helped win
restitution for two workers who had been dismissed because their
employers were displeased by the employees' e-mails about work-
related issues (62). The case points to the ongoing struggle to
define what constitutes protected speech in the workplace.

Variations on the basic rules This section describes
the MLA guidelines for handling a variety of situations not covered by the basic rules in items 1–5. These
rules for in-text citations are the same for both print and
online sources.

■ **6. Two or three authors** Name the authors in a signal phrase, as in the following example, or include their
last names in the parenthetical reference: (Kizza and
Ssanyu 2).

Kizza and Ssanyu note that "employee monitoring is a dependable,
capable, and very affordable process of electronically or otherwise
recording all employee activities at work" and elsewhere (2).

When three authors are named in the parentheses, separate the names with commas: (Alton, Davies, and Rice 56).

■ **7. Four or more authors** Name all of the authors or
include only the first author's name followed by "et al."
(Latin for "and others"). The format you use should
match the format in your works cited entry (see item 3
on p. 133).

The study was extended for two years, and only after results were
reviewed by an independent panel did the researchers publish their
findings (Blaine et al. 35).

■ **8. Organization as author** When the author is a corporation or an organization, name that author either in
the signal phrase or in the parentheses. (For a government
agency as author, see item 16 on p. 127.)

According to a 2001 survey of human resources managers by the
American Management Association, more than three-quarters of the
responding companies reported disciplining employees for "misuse
or personal use of office telecommunications equipment" (2).

In the list of works cited, the American Management Association is treated as the author and alphabetized under *A*. When you give the organization name in parentheses, abbreviate common words in the name: "Assn.," "Dept.," "Natl.," "Soc.," and so on.

In a 2001 survey of human resources managers, more than three-quarters of the responding companies reported disciplining employees for "misuse or personal use of office telecommunications equipment" (Amer. Management Assn. 2).

■ **9. Authors with the same last name** If your list of works cited includes works by two or more authors with the same last name, include the author's first name in the signal phrase or first initial in the parentheses.

Estimates of the frequency with which employers monitor employees' use of the Internet each day vary widely (A. Jones 15).

■ **10. Two or more works by the same author** Mention the title of the work in the signal phrase or include a short version of the title in the parentheses.

The American Management Association and ePolicy Institute have tracked employers' practices in monitoring employees' e-mail use. The groups' 2003 survey found that one-third of companies had a policy of keeping and reviewing employees' e-mail messages ("2003 E-mail" 2); in 2005, more than 55% of companies engaged in e-mail monitoring ("2005 Electronic" 1).

Titles of articles and other short works are placed in quotation marks; titles of books are italicized.

■ **11. Two or more works in one citation** To cite more than one source in the parentheses, give the citations in alphabetical order and separate them with a semicolon.

Several researchers have analyzed the reasons that companies monitor employees' use of the Internet at work (Botan and Vorvoreanu 128-29; Kesan 317-19; Kizza and Ssanyu 3-7).

■ **12. Encyclopedia or dictionary entry** Unless an entry in an encyclopedia or a dictionary has an author, the source will be alphabetized in the list of works cited under the word or entry that you consulted (see item 24 on p. 140).

Either in your text or in the parenthetical citation, mention the word or entry. No page number is required, since readers can easily look up the word or entry.

The word *crocodile* has a surprisingly complex etymology ("Crocodile").

■ **13. Multivolume work** If your paper cites more than one volume of a multivolume work, indicate in the parentheses the volume you are referring to, followed by a colon and the page number.

In his studies of gifted children, Terman describes a pattern of accelerated language acquisition (2: 279).

■ **14. Entire work** Use the author's name in a signal phrase or in parentheses. There is no need to use a page number.

Lane explores the evolution of surveillance in the workplace.

■ **15. Selection in an anthology** Put the name of the author of the selection (not the editor of the anthology) in the signal phrase or the parentheses.

In "Love Is a Fallacy," the narrator's logical teachings disintegrate when Polly declares that she should date Petey because "[h]e's got a raccoon coat" (Shulman 379).

In the list of works cited, the work is alphabetized by the author's last name (Shulman), not by the name of the editor of the anthology. (See item 21 on pp. 139 and 140.)

■ **16. Government document** When a government agency is the author, you will alphabetize it in the list of works cited under the name of the government, such as United States or Great Britain (see item 66 on p. 153). For this reason, you must name the government as well as the agency in your in-text citation.

Online monitoring by the United States Department of the Interior over a one-week period found that employees' use of "sexually explicit and gambling websites . . . accounted for over 24 hours of Internet use" (3).

■ **17. Historical document** For a historical document, such as the United States Constitution, provide the document title, neither italicized nor in quotation marks, along with article and section numbers. In parenthetical citations, use common abbreviations such as "art." and "sec." and abbreviations of well-known titles (US Const., art. 1, sec. 2).

While the United States Constitution provides for the formation of new states (art. 4, sec. 3), it does not explicitly allow or prohibit the secession of states.

For other historical documents, cite as you would any other work, by the first element in the works cited entry (see item 67 on p. 153).

■ **18. Legal source** For legislative acts (laws) and court cases, name the act or case either in a signal phrase or in parentheses. Italicize the names of cases but not the names of acts.

The Jones Act of 1917 granted US citizenship to Puerto Ricans.

In 1857, Chief Justice Roger B. Taney declared in *Dred Scott v. Sandford* that blacks, whether enslaved or free, could not be citizens of the United States.

■ **19. Indirect source (source quoted in another source)** When a writer's or a speaker's quoted words appear in a source written by someone else, begin the parenthetical citation with the abbreviation "qtd. in."

According to Bill Coleman, an executive at *Salary.com,* "Personal Internet use and casual office conversations often turn into new business ideas or suggestions for gaining operating efficiencies" (qtd. in Frauenheim).

Literary works and sacred texts Literary works and sacred texts are usually available in a variety of editions. Your list of works cited will specify which edition you are using. When possible, give enough information—book parts, play divisions, line numbers—so that readers can locate the cited passage in any edition of the work.

■ **20. Literary work without parts or line numbers** When a work such as a short story, a novel, or a play has no parts or line numbers, cite the page number.

At the end of Kate Chopin's "The Story of an Hour," Mrs. Mallard drops dead upon learning that her husband is alive. In the final irony of the story, doctors report that she has died of a "joy that kills" (25).

■ **21. Verse play or poem**   If possible, give act, scene, and line numbers for a verse play. Use arabic numerals and separate the numbers with periods.

In Shakespeare's *King Lear*, Gloucester, blinded for suspected treason, learns a profound lesson from his tragic experience: "A man may see how this world goes / with no eyes" (4.2.148-49).

For a poem, cite the part, stanza, and line numbers, if it has them, separated with periods.

The Green Knight claims to approach King Arthur's court "because the praise of you, prince, is puffed so high, / And your manor and your men are considered so magnificent" (1.12.258-59).

For a poem that is not divided into numbered parts or stanzas, use line numbers. For a first reference, use the word "lines": (lines 5-8). Thereafter use just the numbers: (12-13).

■ **22. Novel with numbered divisions**   Give the page number followed by a semicolon, and then indicate the book, part, or chapter in which the passage may be found. Use abbreviations such as "bk.," "pt.," and "ch."

One of Kingsolver's narrators, teenager Rachel, pushes her vocabulary beyond its limits. For example, Rachel complains that being forced to live in the Congo with her missionary family is "a sheer tapestry of justice" because her chances of finding a boyfriend are "dull and void" (117; bk. 2, ch. 10).

■ **23. Sacred text**   When citing a sacred text such as the Bible or the Qur'an, name the edition in your works cited entry (see item 25 on p. 140). In your parenthetical citation, give the book, chapter, and verse (or their equivalent), separated with periods. Common abbreviations for books of the Bible are acceptable.

Consider the words of Solomon: "If your enemy is hungry, give him bread to eat; and if he is thirsty, give him water to drink" (*Oxford Annotated Bible*, Prov. 25.21).

The title of a sacred work is italicized when it refers to a specific edition of the work, as in the preceding example. If you refer to the book in a general sense in your text, neither italicize it nor put it in quotation marks. (See also 23c.)

The Bible and the Qur'an provide allegories that help readers understand how to lead a moral life.

33b MLA list of works cited

An alphabetized list of works cited, which appears at the end of your research paper, gives publication information for each of the sources you have cited in the paper. Include only sources that you have quoted, summarized, or paraphrased. (For information about preparing the list, see pp. 157–58; for sample lists of works cited, see pp. 160 and 162.)

When a publisher is required in a works cited entry, give the city of publication without a state name. Shorten publishers' names, usually to the first principal word; abbreviate "University" and "Press" in the names of university publishers: UP of Florida. For the date of publication, use the date on the title page or the most recent date on the copyright page.

Include the medium in which a work was published, produced, or delivered. Usually put the medium at the end of the entry, capitalized but neither italicized nor in quotation marks. Typical designations for the medium are "Print," "Web," "Television," "CD," "Film," "DVD," "Photograph," "Performance," "Lecture," and "MP3 file."

Listing authors (print and online) Alphabetize entries in the list of works cited by authors' last names (or by title if a work has no author).

NAME CITED IN TEXT
According to Nancy Flynn, . . .

BEGINNING OF WORKS CITED ENTRY
Flynn, Nancy.

Directory to MLA works cited models

■ 1. Single author

author: last
name first   title (book)   city of
publication   publisher   date   medium

Wood, James. *How Fiction Works.* New York: Farrar, 2008. Print.

■ 2. Two or three authors

first author:
last name first   second author:
in normal order   title (book)

Gourevitch, Philip, and Errol Morris. *Standard Operating Procedure.*

city of
publication   publisher   date   medium

New York: Penguin, 2008. Print.

first author:
last name first   other authors:
in normal order   title (newspaper article)

Farmer, John, John Azzarello, and Miles Kara. "Real Heroes, Fake

date of
newspaper title   publication   page(s)   medium

Stories." *New York Times* 14 Sept. 2008: WK10. Print.

■ 3. Four or more authors

first author:
last name first   other authors:
in normal order

Harris, Shon, Allen Harper, Chris Eagle, and Jonathan Ness.

title (book)   edition
number   city of
publication   publisher   date   medium

Gray Hat Hacking. 2nd ed. New York: McGraw, 2007. Print.

Name all the authors or name the first author followed by
"et al." (Latin for "and others"). In an in-text citation, use
the same form for the authors' names as you use in the
works cited entry. See item 7 on page 125.

■ 4. Organization as author

author: organization name,
not abbreviated   title (book)

National Wildlife Federation. *Rain Check: Conservation Groups*

city of
publication

Monitor Mercury Levels in Milwaukee's Rain. Ann Arbor:

publisher,
with common abbreviations   date   medium

Natl. Wildlife Federation, 2001. Print.

Your in-text citation should also treat the organization as
the author (see item 8 on pp. 125–26).

■ **5. Unknown author**

Article or other short work

title (newspaper article)   label   newspaper title
"Poverty, by Outdated Numbers." Editorial. *Boston Globe*

date of publication page(s) medium
20 Sept. 2008: A16. Print.

title (TV episode) title (TV program) producer network station city of broadcast
"Heat." *Frontline*. Prod. Martin Smith. PBS. KTWU, Topeka,

date of broadcast medium
21 Oct. 2008. Television.

For other examples of an article with no author and of a television program, see items 12 and 58, respectively.

Book, entire Web site, or other long work

title (book) city of publication publisher date medium
New Concise World Atlas. New York: Oxford UP, 2007. Print.

title (Web site)
Women of Protest: Photographs from the Records of the National

sponsor of site no date medium date of access
Woman's Party. Lib. of Cong., n.d. Web. 29 Sept. 2008.

Before concluding that the author of an online source is unknown, check carefully. The name of the author may appear at the end of the source, in tiny print, or on another page of the site, such as the home page. Also remember that an organization or a government agency may be the author (see items 4 and 66).

■ **6. Two or more works by the same author**   First alphabetize the works by title (ignoring the article *A*, *An*, or *The* at the beginning of a title). Use the author's name for the first entry only; for subsequent entries, use three hyphens followed by a period. The hyphens must stand for exactly the same name or names as in the first entry.

Knopp, Lisa. *Field of Vision*. Iowa City: U of Iowa P, 1996.
    Print.
---. *The Nature of Home: A Lexicon and Essays*. Lincoln: U of
    Nebraska P, 2002. Print.

Articles in periodicals (print) This section shows how
to prepare works cited entries for articles in print journals,
magazines, and newspapers. See "Listing authors" on
page 130 and items 1–6 for how to handle basic parts of the
entries. See also "Online sources" (pp. 141–50).

For articles appearing on consecutive pages, provide the
range of pages (see items 7 and 8). When an article does not
appear on consecutive pages, give the first page number
followed by a plus sign: 32+. For dates requiring a month,
abbreviate all but May, June, and July. For an illustrated citation of an article in a print periodical, see page 136.

■ 7. Article in a journal (paginated by volume or by issue)

author: last
name first · · · · · · · · · · · article title

Blackburn, Robin. "Economic Democracy: Meaningful, Desirable,

journal · volume,
title · issue · year · page(s) · medium

Feasible?" *Daedalus* 136.3 (2007): 36-45. Print.

■ 8. Article in a monthly magazine

Lanting, Frans. "Life: A Journey through Time." *Audubon*
Nov.-Dec. 2006: 48-52. Print.

■ 9. Article in a weekly magazine

von Drehle, David. "The Ghosts of Memphis." *Time* 7 Apr. 2008:
34-37. Print.

■ 10. Article in a daily newspaper

Page number with section letter

McKenna, Phil. "It Takes Just One Village." *New York Times*
23 Sept. 2008, New England ed.: D1. Print.

Page number with section number

Knox, David Blake. "Lord Archer, Storyteller." *Sunday Independent*
[Dublin] 14 Sept. 2008, sec. 2: 9. Print.

■ 11. Article with a title in its title
Use single quotation
marks around a title of a short work or a quoted term that
appears in an article title. Italicize a title or term normally
italicized.

Shen, Min. "'Quite a Moon!' The Archetypal Feminine in *Our Town*."
American Drama 16.2 (2007): 1-14. Print.

Citation at a glance
Article in a periodical (MLA)

To cite an article in a print periodical in MLA style, include the following elements:

1 Author of article
2 Title and subtitle of article
3 Title of periodical
4 Volume and issue numbers (for journal)
5 Date or year of publication
6 Page number(s) of article
7 Medium

TITLE PAGE

FIRST PAGE OF ARTICLE

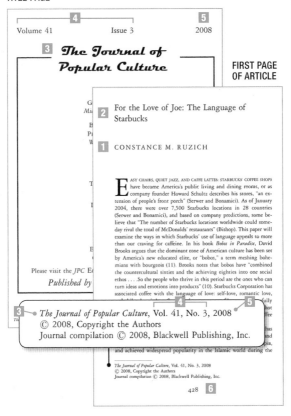

WORKS CITED ENTRY FOR AN ARTICLE IN A PRINT PERIODICAL

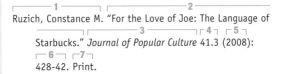

Ruzich, Constance M. "For the Love of Joe: The Language of Starbucks." *Journal of Popular Culture* 41.3 (2008): 428-42. Print.

For more on citing print periodical articles in MLA style, see pages 135 and 137.

■ **12. Editorial or other unsigned article**

"Getting the Message: Communicating Electronically with Doctors
Can Spur Honesty from Young Patients." Editorial. *Columbus*
[OH] *Dispatch* 19 June 2008: 10A. Print.

■ **13. Letter to the editor**

Morris, David. "Fiercely Proud." Letter. *Progressive* Feb. 2008:
6. Print.

■ **14. Review** Begin with the name of the reviewer and
the title of the review, if it has one. Add the words "Rev. of"
and the title of the work reviewed, followed by the author,
director, or other significant contributor. If the review has
no author and no title, begin with "Rev. of" and alphabetize
the entry by the first principal word in the title of the work
reviewed.

Lane, Anthony. "Dream On." Rev. of *The Science of Sleep* and
Renaissance, dir. Michel Gondry. *New Yorker* 25 Sept. 2006:
155-57. Print.

Dodge, Chris. Rev. of *The Radical Jack London: Writings on War and
Revolution,* ed. Jonah Raskni. *Utne Reader* Sept.-Oct. 2008:
35. Print.

Books (print) Items 15–30 apply to print books. For
electronic and online books, see items 37–39. For an illustrated citation of a print book, see page 138.

■ **15. Basic format for a book**

author: last
name first · · · · · book title · · · · · city of
publication

Sacks, Oliver. *Musicophilia: Tales of Music and the Brain.* New York:

publisher date medium
Knopf, 2007. Print.

■ **16. Book with an author and an editor** The abbreviation "Ed." means "Edited by," so it is the same for one or
multiple editors.

Plath, Sylvia. *The Unabridged Journals of Sylvia Plath.* Ed. Karen V.
Kukil. New York: Anchor-Doubleday, 2000. Print.

Citation at a glance
Book (MLA)

To cite a print book in MLA style, include the following elements:

1 Author
2 Title and subtitle
3 City of publication
4 Publisher
5 Date of publication
6 Medium

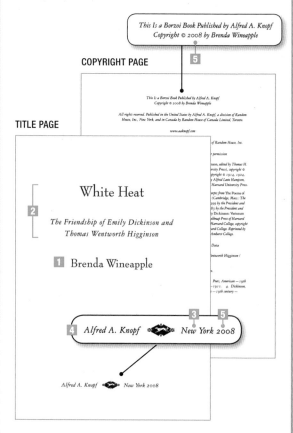

This Is a Borzoi Book Published by Alfred A. Knopf
Copyright © 2008 by Brenda Wineapple

5

COPYRIGHT PAGE

This Is a Borzoi Book Published by Alfred A. Knopf
Copyright © 2008 by Brenda Wineapple

All rights reserved. Published in the United States by Alfred A. Knopf, a division of Random House, Inc., New York, and in Canada by Random House of Canada Limited, Toronto.

www.aaknopf.com

TITLE PAGE

White Heat

2

The Friendship of Emily Dickinson and
Thomas Wentworth Higginson

1 Brenda Wineapple

3   **5**

4 Alfred A. Knopf ◆ New York 2008

Alfred A. Knopf ◆ New York 2008

WORKS CITED ENTRY FOR A PRINT BOOK

```
┌─────1─────┐ ┌──────────2──────────
Wineapple, Brenda. White Heat: The Friendship of Emily

                                    ┐ ┌─3─┐
     Dickinson and Thomas Wentworth Higginson. New York:
     ┌─4─┐ ┌─5─┐ ┌─6─┐
     Knopf, 2008. Print.
```

For more on citing print books in MLA style, see pages 137–41.

■ **17. Book with an author and a translator** "Trans." means "Translated by," so it is the same for one or multiple translators.

Scirocco, Alfonso. *Garibaldi: Citizen of the World*. Trans. Allan
  Cameron. Princeton: Princeton UP, 2007. Print.

■ **18. Book with an editor** Begin with the editor's name. For one editor, use "ed." after the name; for multiple editors, use "eds."

Lago, Mary, Linda K. Hughes, and Elizabeth MacLeod Walls, eds. *The
  BBC Talks of E. M. Forster, 1929-1960*. Columbia: U of Missouri
  P, 2008. Print.

■ **19. Graphic narrative or illustrated book** For a book that combines text and illustrations, begin your citation with the person you wish to emphasize (writer, illustrator, artist) and list any other contributors after the title of the book.

Weaver, Dustin, illus. *The Tenth Circle*. By Jodi Picoult. New York:
  Washington Square, 2006. Print.

Moore, Alan. *V for Vendetta*. Illus. David Lloyd. New York:
  Vertigo-DC Comics, 2008. Print.

■ **20. Entire anthology**

Dumanis, Michael, and Cate Marvin, eds. *Legitimate Dangers:
  American Poets of the New Century*. Louisville: Sarabande,
  2006. Print.

■ **21. One or more selections from an anthology**

One selection from anthology

author of selection: title of
last name first   selection   title of anthology

Brouwer, Joel. "The Spots." *Legitimate Dangers: American Poets*

                                editor(s) of anthology:
                                in normal order

of the New Century. Ed. Michael Dumanis and Cate Marvin.

  city of   page(s) of
 publication   publisher   date selection medium

Louisville: Sarabande, 2006. 51-52. Print.

For two or more selections from an anthology, see page 140. For an illustrated citation of a selection from a print anthology, see pages 142–43.

Two or more selections, with separate anthology entry

Provide an entry for the entire anthology (see item 20) and give a shortened entry for each selection. Use the medium only in the entry for the complete anthology.

author of selection | title of selection | editor(s) of anthology: last name(s) only | pages(s) of selection

Brouwer, Joel. "The Spots." Dumanis and Marvin 51-52.

editor(s) of anthology | title of anthology

Dumanis, Michael, and Cate Marvin, eds. *Legitimate Dangers:*

city of publication | publisher

American Poets of the New Century. Louisville: Sarabande,

date | medium

2006. Print.

author of selection | title of selection | editor(s) of anthology: last name(s) only | page(s) of selection

Keith, Sally. "Orphean Song." Dumanis and Marvin 195-96.

■ **22. Edition other than the first**   If the book has a translator or an editor in addition to the author, give the name of the translator or editor before the edition number, using the abbreviation "Trans." for "Translated by" (see item 17) or "Ed." for "Edited by" (see item 16).

Auletta, Ken. *The Underclass*. 2nd ed. Woodstock: Overlook, 2000.
Print.

■ **23. Multivolume work**   See item 13 on page 127 for an in-text citation of a multivolume work.

Stark, Freya. *Letters*. Ed. Lucy Moorehead. 8 vols. Salisbury:
Compton, 1974-82. Print.

■ **24. Encyclopedia or dictionary entry**

Posner, Rebecca. "Romance Languages." *The Encyclopaedia
Britannica: Macropaedia*. 15th ed. 1987. Print.

"Sonata." *The American Heritage Dictionary of the English Language*.
4th ed. 2000. Print.

■ **25. Sacred text**

The Oxford Annotated Bible with the Apocrypha. Ed. Herbert G. May
and Bruce M. Metzger. New York: Oxford UP, 1965. Print. Rev.
Standard Vers.

The Qur'an: Translation. Trans. Abdullah Yusuf Ali. Elmhurst:
Tahrike, 2000. Print.

■ 26. Foreword, introduction, preface, or afterword

Bennett, Hal Zina. Foreword. *Shimmering Images: A Handy Little
Guide to Writing Memoir*. By Lisa Dale Norton. New York:
Griffin-St. Martin's, 2008. xiii-xvi. Print.

Ozick, Cynthia. "Portrait of the Essay as a Warm Body."
Introduction. *The Best American Essays 1998*. Ed. Ozick.
Boston: Houghton, 1998. xv-xxi. Print.

■ 27. Book with a title in its title

Woodson, Jon. *A Study of Joseph Heller's* Catch-22: *Going Around
Twice*. New York: Lang, 2001. Print.

■ 28. Book in a series
After the medium of publication, give the series name as it appears on the title page, followed by the series number, if any.

Douglas, Dan. *Assessing Languages for Specific Purposes*.
Cambridge: Cambridge UP, 2000. Print. Cambridge Applied
Linguistics Ser.

■ 29. Republished book

Trilling, Lionel. *The Liberal Imagination*. 1950. Introd. Louis
Menand. New York: New York Review of Books, 2008. Print.

■ 30. Publisher's imprint
Give the name of the imprint (a division of a publishing company), a hyphen, and the name of the publisher.

Ackroyd, Peter. *The Fall of Troy*. New York: Talese-Doubleday, 2007. Print.

Online sources MLA guidelines assume that readers can locate most online sources by entering the author, title, or other identifying information in a search engine or a database. Consequently, the *MLA Handbook* does not require a Web address (URL) in citations for online sources. If your instructor requires one, see the note at the end of item 31 on page 144.

MLA style calls for a sponsor or a publisher in works cited entries for most online sources. If a source has no sponsor or publisher, use the abbreviation "N.p." (for "No publisher") in the sponsor position. If there is no

Citation at a glance
Selection from an anthology (MLA)

To cite a selection from a print anthology in MLA style, include the following elements:

1 Author of selection
2 Title of selection
3 Title and subtitle of anthology
4 Editor(s) of anthology
5 City of publication
6 Publisher
7 Date of publication
8 Page number(s) of selection
9 Medium

TITLE PAGE

3 ASIAN-AMERICAN LITERATURE

An Anthology

4 Shirley Geok-lin Lim
University of California, Santa Barbara

6 NTC Publishing Group
a division of NTC/Contemporary Publishing Company
Lincolnwood, Illinois USA

5 Lincolnwood, Illinois USA

FROM COPYRIGHT PAGE

Published by NTC/Contemporary Publishing Group, Inc.
4255 West Touhy Avenue, Lincolnwood (Chicago), Illinois 60646-1975 U.S.A.
©2000 NTC/Contemporary Publishing Group, Inc.

7

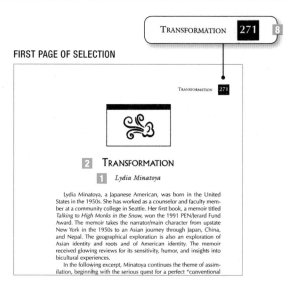

FIRST PAGE OF SELECTION

2 TRANSFORMATION

1 *Lydia Minatoya*

Lydia Minatoya, a Japanese American, was born in the United States in the 1950s. She has worked as a counselor and faculty member at a community college in Seattle. Her first book, a memoir titled *Talking to High Monks in the Snow*, won the 1991 PEN/Jerard Fund Award. The memoir takes the narrator/main character from upstate New York in the 1950s to an Asian journey through Japan, China, and Nepal. The geographical exploration is also an exploration of Asian identity and roots and of American identity. The memoir received glowing reviews for its sensitivity, humor, and insights into bicultural experiences.

In the following excerpt, Minatoya continues the theme of assimilation, beginning with the serious quest for a perfect "conventional

WORKS CITED ENTRY FOR A SELECTION FROM A PRINT ANTHOLOGY

—— 1 ——   ——— 2 ———   —— 3 ——

Minatoya, Lydia. "Transformation." *Asian-American*

———— 4 ————

Literature: An Anthology. Ed. Shirley Geok-lin Lim.

—— 5 ——   —6— —7— —8— —9—

Lincolnwood: NTC, 2000. 271-75. Print.

For more on citing selections from print anthologies in MLA style, see pages 139 and 140.

date of publication or update, use "n.d." (for "no date") after the sponsor. For an article in an online journal or an article from a database, give page numbers if they are available; if they are not, use the abbreviation "n. pag." (See item 33 on p. 146.)

■ 31. Entire Web site

Web site with author

author: last name first   title of Web site   sponsor of site (personal page)

Peterson, Susan Lynn. *The Life of Martin Luther*. Susan Lynn Peterson,

update   medium   date of access: day + month + year

2005.   Web.   24 Jan. 2009.

Web site with organization (group) as author

organization name: sponsor:
not abbreviated   title of Web site   abbreviated

American Library Association. *American Library Association*. ALA,

                date of access:
update medium   day + month + year

     2008. Web. 14 Jan. 2009.

Web site with no author

title of Web site   sponsor of site   update

Margaret Sanger Papers Project. History Dept., New York U, 18 Oct. 2000.

            date of access:
medium   day + month + year

    Web. 6 Jan. 2009.

Web site with no title

Use the label "Home page" or another appropriate description in place of a title.

Yoon, Mina. Home page. Oak Ridge Natl. Laboratory, 28 Dec. 2006. Web.

     12 Jan. 2009.

NOTE: If your instructor requires a URL for Web sources, include the URL, enclosed in angle brackets, at the end of the entry. When a URL in a works cited entry must be divided at the end of a line, break it after a double slash or a slash. Do not insert a hyphen.

Peterson, Susan Lynn. *The Life of Martin Luther*. Susan Lynn Peterson,

     2005. Web. 24 Jan. 2009. <http://www.susanlynnpeterson.com/

     index_files/luther.htm>.

■ **32. Short work from a Web site** Short works include articles, poems, and other documents that are not book length or that appear as internal pages on a Web site. For an illustrated citation of a short work from a Web site, see page 145.

Short work with author

author: last   title of
name first   title of short work   Web site

Shiva, Vandana. "Bioethics: A Third World Issue." *NativeWeb*.

         no update   date of access:
sponsor   date medium   day + month + year

    NativeWeb, n.d. Web. 22 Jan. 2010.

For a short work with no author, see page 146.

Citation at a glance
Short work from a Web site (MLA)

To cite a short work from a Web site in MLA style, include the following elements:

1. Author of short work (if any)
2. Title of short work
3. Title of Web site
4. Sponsor of Web site ("N.p." if none)
5. Update date ("n.d." if none)
6. Medium
7. Date you accessed the source

INTERNAL PAGE OF WEB SITE

FOOTER ON HOME PAGE

the local area. It houses the most extensive collection of art, artifacts, and manuscri
pertaining to American whaling in the age of sail - late eighteenth century to the ear
twentieth, when sailing ships dominated merchant trade and whaling.

18 Johnny Cake Hill | New Bedford, MA | 02740-6398 | Tel. (508) 997-0046
Fax: (508) 997-0018 | Library Fax: (508) 207-1064

©Copyright 2009 Old Dartmouth Historical Society / New Bedford Whaling Museum

WORKS CITED ENTRY FOR A SHORT WORK FROM A WEB SITE

"Overview of American Whaling." *New Bedford Whaling Museum.*
Old Dartmouth Hist. Soc./New Bedford Whaling Museum,
2009. Web. 27 Oct. 2009.

For more on citing sources from Web sites in MLA style, see pages 141–46.

Short work with no author

| title of short work | title of Web site | sponsor of site | update |

"Sister Aimee." *American Experience*. PBS Online, 2 Apr. 2007.

| medium | date of access: day + month + year |

Web. 30 Oct. 2010.

■ **33. Article in an online journal**   Use the abbreviation "n. pag." for an online journal that is not paginated.

Mason, John Edwin. "'Mannenberg': Notes on the Making of an Icon
and Anthem." *African Studies Quarterly* 9.4 (2007): n. pag.
Web. 23 Feb. 2010.

■ **34. Article in an online magazine**

Burton, Robert. "The Certainty Epidemic." *Salon.com*. Salon Media
Group, 29 Feb. 2008. Web. 18 Jan. 2010.

■ **35. Article in an online newspaper**

Smith, Andrew D. "Poll: More than 70% of US Workers Use Internet
on the Job." *Dallasnews.com*. Dallas Morning News, 25 Sept.
2008. Web. 29 Sept. 2010.

■ **36. Article from a database**   For an illustrated citation
of an article from a database, see page 147.

| author of source: last name first | title of article | journal title | volume, issue | year | page(s) |

Heyen, William. "Sunlight." *American Poetry Review* 36.2 (2007): 55-56.

| database name | medium | date of access: day + month + year |

Expanded Academic ASAP. Web. 24 Mar. 2010.

Barrera, Rebeca María. "A Case for Bilingual Education." *Scholastic
Parent and Child* Nov.-Dec. 2004: 72-73. *Academic Search Premier*.
Web. 1 Feb. 2009.

Williams, Jeffrey J. "Why Today's Publishing World Is Reprising the
Past." *Chronicle of Higher Education* 13 June 2008: n. pag.
LexisNexis Academic. Web. 29 Sept. 2009.

■ **37. E-book (electronic book)**

Tolstoy, Leo. *War and Peace*. Trans. Richard Pevear and Larissa
Volokhonsky. New York: Knopf, 2010. Nook file.

Citation at a glance
Article from a database (MLA)

To cite an article from a database in MLA style, include the following elements:

1 Author of article
2 Title of article
3 Title of periodical
4 Volume and issue numbers (for journal)
5 Date or year of publication
6 Page number(s) of article ("n. pag." if none)
7 Name of database
8 Medium
9 Date you accessed the source

ON-SCREEN VIEW OF DATABASE RECORD

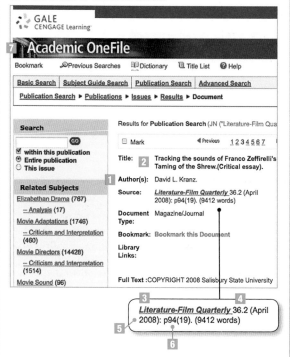

GALE
CENGAGE Learning

7 Academic OneFile

Bookmark   Previous Searches   Dictionary   Title List   Help

Basic Search   Subject Guide Search   Publication Search   Advanced Search

Publication Search ▶ Publications ▶ Issues ▶ Results ▶ Document

Search

[GO]
☑ within this publication
◉ Entire publication
○ This issue

Related Subjects
Elizabethan Drama (767)
-- Analysis (17)
Movie Adaptations (1746)
-- Criticism and Interpretation (460)
Movie Directors (14428)
-- Criticism and Interpretation (1514)
Movie Sound (96)

Results for **Publication Search** (JN ("Literature-Film Qua

☐ Mark   ◀ Previous   1 2 3 4 5 6 7

Title: **2** Tracking the sounds of Franco Zeffirelli's Taming of the Shrew.(Critical essay).

Author(s): **1** David L. Kranz.

Source: **3** *Literature-Film Quarterly* 36.2 (April 2008): p94(19). (9412 words)

Document Type: Magazine/Journal

Bookmark: Bookmark this Document

Library Links:

Full Text :COPYRIGHT 2008 Salisbury State University

3 *Literature-Film Quarterly* **4** 36.2 (April 2008): **5** p94(19). (9412 words) **6**

WORKS CITED ENTRY FOR AN ARTICLE FROM A DATABASE

┌── 1 ──┐ ┌────── 2 ──────
Kranz, David L. "Tracking the Sounds of Franco Zeffirelli's
   ┌──────── 3 ────────┐ ┌ 4 ┐
   The Taming of the Shrew." *Literature-Film Quarterly* 36.2
   ┌ 5 ┐ ┌ 6 ┐ ┌──── 7 ────┐ ┌ 8 ┐┌── 9 ──┐
   (2008): 94-112. *Academic OneFile*. Web. 28 Oct. 2009.

For more on citing articles from a database in MLA style, see item 36.

147

■ **38. Online book-length work** Cite as you would a short work from a Web site (see item 32), but italicize the title of the work.

author: last
name first   title of long poem   title of Web site   sponsor of site

Milton, John. *Paradise Lost: Book I. Poetryfoundation.org.* Poetry

update medium date of access: day + month + year

Foundation, 2008. Web. 14 Dec. 2009.

Give the print publication information for the work, if available (see items 15–30), followed by the title of the Web site, the medium, and your date of access.

author: last
name first   book title

Jacobs, Harriet A. *Incidents in the Life of a Slave Girl: Written by Herself.* Ed.

editor of   city of
original book   publication year   title of Web site

L. Maria Child. Boston, 1861. *Documenting the American South.*

medium date of access: day + month + year

Web. 3 Feb. 2010.

■ **39. Part of an online book**

Adams, Henry. "Diplomacy." *The Education of Henry Adams.* Boston:

Houghton, 1918. N. pag. *Bartleby.com: Great Books Online.* Web.

8 Jan. 2010.

■ **40. Digital archives** Digital archives are online collections of documents or records—books, letters, photographs, data—that have been converted to digital form. Cite publication information for the original document, if available. Then give the location of the document, if any, neither italicized nor in quotation marks; the name of the archive, italicized; the medium ("Web"); and your date of access.

Fiore, Mark. *Shockwaves.* 18 Oct. 2001. *September 11 Digital*

Archive. Web. 3 Apr. 2009.

Oblinger, Maggie. Letter to Charlie Thomas. 31 Mar. 1895. Nebraska

State Hist. Soc. *Prairie Settlement: Nebraska Photographs and*

Family Letters, 1862-1912. Web. 3 Nov. 2009.

■ **41. Online poem** Cite as you would a short work from a Web site (item 32) or part of an online book (item 39).

Bell, Acton [Anne Brontë]. "Mementos." *Poems by Currer, Ellis, and Acton Bell*. London, 1846. N. pag. *A Celebration of Women Writers*. Web. 18 Sept. 2009.

■ **42. Entire blog (Weblog)**   Cite as you would an entire Web site (see item 31).

Gristmill. Grist Magazine, 2008. Web. 19 Jan. 2009.

■ **43. Entry or comment in a blog (Weblog)**   Cite as you would a short work from a Web site (see item 32).

"Social Media: Facebook and MySpace as University Curricula." *Open Education*. Open Education.net, n.d. Web. 19 Sept. 2008.

Cynthia. Weblog comment. *Open Education*. Open Education.net, 8 Jan. 2010. Web. 14 Feb. 2010.

■ **44. Online video clip**   Cite as you would a short work from a Web site (see item 32).

Murphy, Beth. "Tips for a Good Profile Piece." *YouTube*. YouTube, 7 Sept. 2008. Web. 19 Apr. 2010.

■ **45. Online review**
Greer, W. R. "Who's the Fairest One of All?" Rev. of *Mirror, Mirror*, by Gregory Maguire. *Reviewsofbooks.com*. Reviewsofbooks.com, 2003. Web. 26 Oct. 2009.

■ **46. E-mail message**
Lowe, Walter. "Review Questions." Message to the author. 15 Mar. 2010. E-mail.

■ **47. Posting to an online discussion list**
Fainton, Peter. "Re: Backlash against New Labour." *Media Lens Message Board*. Media Lens, 7 May 2008. Web. 2 June 2008.

■ **48. Entry in a wiki**   A wiki is an online reference that is openly edited by its users. Treat an entry in a wiki as you would a short work from a Web site (see item 32). Because wiki content is collectively edited and can be updated frequently, do not include an author.

"Hip Hop Music." *Wikipedia*. Wikimedia Foundation, 2 Mar. 2010. Web. 18 Mar. 2010.

"Negation in Languages." *UniLang Wiki*. UniLang, 12 Jan. 2009.

> Web. 9 Mar. 2010.

Audio and visual sources (including online versions)

■ **49. Digital file** A digital file is any document or image that exists in digital form, independent of a Web site. To cite a digital file, begin with information required for the source (such as a photograph, a report, a sound recording, or a radio program), following the guidelines throughout 33b. Then for the medium, indicate the type of file: "JPEG file," "PDF file," "MP3 file," and so on.

```
              photographer        photograph title    date of
                                                    composition   location of photograph
```
Hine, Lewis W. *Girl in Cherryville Mill*. 1908. Prints and Photographs

```
                              medium:
                              file type
```
> Div., Lib. of Cong. JPEG file.

"Scenes from a Recession." *This American Life*. Narr. Ira Glass. NPR,

> 30 Mar. 2009. MP3 file.

National Institute of Mental Health. *What Rescue Workers Can Do*.

> Washington: US Dept. of Health and Human Services, 2006.
>
> PDF file.

■ **50. Podcast** If you view or listen to a podcast online, cite it as you would a short work from a Web site (see item 32). If you download the podcast and view or listen to it on a computer or portable player, cite it as a digital file (see item 49).

Podcast online

"Calculating the Demand for Charter Schools." Narr. David

> Guenthner. *Texas PolicyCast*. Texas Public Policy Foundation,
>
> 28 Aug. 2008. Web. 10 Jan. 2009.

Podcast downloaded as digital file

"Calculating the Demand for Charter Schools." Narr. David

> Guenthner. *Texas PolicyCast*. Texas Public Policy Foundation,
>
> 28 Aug. 2008. MP3 file.

■ **51. Musical score**

Handel, G. F. *Messiah: An Oratorio*. N.d. *CCARH Publications: Scores

> and Parts*. Center for Computer Assisted Research in the
>
> Humanities, 2003. Web. 5 Jan. 2009.

■ 52. Sound recording

Bizet, Georges. *Carmen*. Perf. Jennifer Laramore, Thomas
Moser, Angela Gheorghiu, and Samuel Ramey. Bavarian
State Orch. and Chorus. Cond. Giuseppe Sinopoli. Warner,
1996. CD.

Blige, Mary J. "Be without You." *The Breakthrough*. Geffen,
2005. CD.

■ 53. Film

Frozen River. Dir. Courtney Hunt. Perf. Melissa Leo, Charlie McDermott,
and Misty Upham. Sony, 2008. Film.

■ 54. DVD or Blu-ray Disc (BD)

Forster, Marc, dir. *Finding Neverland*. Perf. Johnny Depp, Kate
Winslet, Julie Christie, Radha Mitchell, and Dustin Hoffman.
Miramax, 2004. DVD.

■ 55. Special feature on a DVD or Blu-ray Disc (BD)

"Sweeney's London." Prod. Eric Young. *Sweeney Todd: The Demon
Barber of Fleet Street*. Dir. Tim Burton. DreamWorks, 2007. DVD.
Disc 2.

■ 56. CD-ROM

"Pimpernel." *The American Heritage Dictionary of the English
Language*. 4th ed. Boston: Houghton, 2006. CD-ROM.

■ 57. Computer software or video game

Firaxis Games. *Sid Meier's Civilization Revolution*. Take-Two
Interactive, 2008. Xbox 360.

■ 58. Radio or television program

"Machines of the Gods." *Ancient Discoveries*. History Channel.
14 Oct. 2008. Television.

"Elif Shafak: Writing under a Watchful Eye." *Fresh Air*. Narr. Terry
Gross. Natl. Public Radio, 6 Feb. 2007. *NPR.org*. Web. 22 Feb.
2009.

■ 59. Radio or television interview

De Niro, Robert, Barry Levinson, and Art Linson. Interview by
Charlie Rose. *Charlie Rose*. PBS. WGBH, Boston, 13 Oct. 2008.
Television.

■ **60. Live performance**

The Brothers Size. By Tarell Alvin McCraney. Dir. Bijan Sheibani.
  Young Vic Theatre, London. 15 Oct. 2008. Performance.

Symphony no. 4 in G. By Gustav Mahler. Cond. Mark Wigglesworth.
  Perf. Juliane Banse and Boston Symphony Orch. Symphony
  Hall, Boston. 17 Apr. 2009. Performance.

■ **61. Lecture or public address**

Wellbery, David E. "On a Sentence of Franz Kafka." Franke Inst.
  for the Humanities. Gleacher Center, Chicago. 1 Feb. 2006.
  Lecture.

■ **62. Work of art**   For artworks found online, omit the
medium of composition and include the title of the Web site,
the medium ("Web"), and your date of access.

Constable, John. *Dedham Vale*. 1802. Oil on canvas. Victoria and
  Albert Museum, London.

Hessing, Valjean. *Caddo Myth*. 1976. Joslyn Art Museum, Omaha.
  Joslyn Art Museum. Web. 19 Apr. 2009.

■ **63. Cartoon**

Keefe, Mike. "Veterans Affairs Overruns." Cartoon. *Denverpost.com*.
  Denver Post, 11 Oct. 2009. Web. 12 Dec. 2009.

■ **64. Advertisement**

Truth by Calvin Klein. Advertisement. *Vogue* Dec. 2000: 95-98.
  Print.

Arbella Insurance. Advertisement. *Boston.com*. NY Times, n.d. Web.
  3 Sept. 2009.

■ **65. Map or chart**

Joseph, Lori, and Bob Laird. "Driving While Phoning Is Dangerous."
  Chart. *USA Today* 16 Feb. 2001: 1A. Print.

"Serbia." Map. *Syrena Maps*. Syrena, 2 Feb. 2001. Web. 17 Mar. 2009.

Other sources (including online versions)   This section includes a variety of sources not covered elsewhere.
For online sources, consult the appropriate model in this
section and also see items 31–48.

■ 66. Government document

government   department   agency

United States. Dept. of the Interior. Office of Inspector General.

document title

"Excessive Indulgences: Personal Use of the Internet at the

Web site title

Department of the Interior." *Office of Inspector General*.

publication   date of access:
publisher/sponsor   date medium day + month + year

Dept. of the Interior, Sept. 1999. Web. 20 May 2010.

Canada. Minister of Indian Affairs and Northern Dev. *Gathering
    Strength: Canada's Aboriginal Action Plan*. Ottawa: Minister of
    Public Works and Govt. Services Can., 2000. Print.

■ 67. Historical document

Jefferson, Thomas. First Inaugural Address. 1801. *The American
    Reader*. Ed. Diane Ravitch. New York: Harper, 1990. 42-44. Print.

The Virginia Declaration of Rights. 1776. *A Chronology of US
    Historical Documents*. U of Oklahoma Coll. of Law, 2008. Web.
    23 Feb. 2009.

■ 68. Legal source

Legislative act (law)

Begin with the name of the act, neither italicized nor in
quotation marks. Then provide the act's Public Law number; its Statutes at Large volume and page numbers; its
date of enactment; and the medium of publication.

Electronic Freedom of Information Act Amendments of 1996.
    Pub. L. 104-231. 110 Stat. 3048. 2 Oct. 1996. Print.

Court case

Name the first plaintiff and the first defendant. Then give
the volume, name, and page numbers of the law report;
the court name; the year of the decision; and publication
information. Do not italicize the name of the case. (In the
text of the paper, the name of the case is italicized; see
item 18 on p. 128.)

Utah v. Evans. 536 US 452. Supreme Court of the US. 2002.
    Supreme Court Collection. Legal Information Inst., Cornell U
    Law School, n.d. Web. 30 Apr. 2008.

■ 69. Pamphlet or brochure

Commonwealth of Massachusetts. Dept. of Jury Commissioner.
  A Few Facts about Jury Duty. Boston: Commonwealth of
  Massachusetts, 2004. Print.

■ 70. Unpublished dissertation

Jackson, Shelley. "Writing Whiteness: Contemporary Southern
  Literature in Black and White." Diss. U of Maryland, 2000.
  Print.

■ 71. Abstract of a dissertation

Chen, Shu-Ling. "Mothers and Daughters in Morrison, Tan, Marshall,
  and Kincaid." Diss. U of Washington, 2000. *DAI* 61.6 (2000):
  AAT 9975963. *ProQuest Dissertations and Theses*. Web.
  22 Feb. 2009.

■ 72. Published proceedings of a conference

Urgo, Joseph R., and Ann J. Abadie, eds. *Faulkner and Material
  Culture*. Proc. of Faulkner and Yoknapatawpha Conf., 25-29
  July 2004, U of Mississippi. Jackson: UP of Mississippi,
  2007. Print.

■ 73. Published interview

Simon, David. "Beyond the Choir: An Interview with David Simon."
  Film Quarterly 62.2 (2008/2009): 44-49.

Florida, Richard. "The Great Reset." Interview by Conor Clarke.
  Atlantic. Atlantic Monthly Group, Feb. 2009. Web. 28 Feb.
  2010.

■ 74. Personal interview

Akufo, Dautey. Personal interview. 11 Apr. 2010.

■ 75. Personal letter For the medium, use "MS" for "manuscript," or a handwritten letter; use "TS" for "type-script," or a typed letter.

Primak, Shoshana. Letter to the author. 6 May 2010. TS.

■ 76. Published letter

Wharton, Edith. Letter to Henry James. 28 Feb. 1915. *Henry James
  and Edith Wharton: Letters, 1900-1915*. Ed. Lyall H. Powers.
  New York: Scribner's, 1990. 323-26. Print.

33c MLA information notes (optional)

Researchers who use the MLA system of parenthetical documentation may also use information notes for one of two purposes:

1. to provide additional material that is important but might interrupt the flow of the paper
2. to refer to several sources that support a single point or to provide comments on sources

Information notes may be either footnotes or endnotes. Footnotes appear at the foot of the page; endnotes appear on a separate page at the end of the paper, just before the list of works cited. For either style, the notes are numbered consecutively throughout the paper. The text of the paper contains a raised arabic numeral that corresponds to the number of the note.

TEXT

In the past several years, employees have filed a number of lawsuits against employers because of online monitoring practices.[1]

NOTE

1. For a discussion of federal law applicable to electronic surveillance in the workplace, see Kesan 293.

34 MLA manuscript format; sample pages

The following guidelines are consistent with advice given in the *MLA Handbook for Writers of Research Papers*, 7th ed. (New York: MLA, 2009), and with typical requirements for student papers. For sample pages from MLA papers, see pages 159–62.

34a MLA manuscript format

Formatting the paper Papers written in MLA style should be formatted as follows.

Materials and font Use good-quality 8½" × 11" white paper. If your instructor does not require a specific font, choose one that is standard and easy to read (such as Times New Roman).

Title and identification MLA does not require a title page. On the first page of your paper, place your name, your instructor's name, the course title, and the date on separate lines against the left margin. Then center your title. (See pp. 159 and 161 for sample first pages.)

If your instructor requires a title page, ask for formatting guidelines. A format similar to the one on page 239 may be acceptable.

Pagination Put the page number preceded by your last name in the upper right corner of each page, one-half inch below the top edge. Use arabic numerals (1, 2, 3, and so on).

Margins, line spacing, and paragraph indents Leave margins of one inch on all sides of the page. Left-align the text.

Double-space throughout the paper. Do not add extra space above or below the title of the paper or between paragraphs.

Indent the first line of each paragraph one-half inch from the left margin.

Capitalization and italics In titles of works, capitalize all words except articles (*a, an, the*), prepositions (*to, from, between,* and so on), coordinating conjunctions (*and, but, or, nor, for, so, yet*), and the *to* in infinitives—unless they are the first or last word of the title or subtitle.

In the text of an MLA paper, when a complete sentence follows a colon, lowercase the first word following the colon unless the sentence is a direct quotation or a well-known expression or principle.

Italicize the titles of books, periodicals, and other long works, such as Web sites. Use quotation marks around the titles of periodical articles, short stories, poems, and other short works.

Long quotations When a quotation is longer than four typed lines of prose or three lines of verse, set it off from the text by indenting the entire quotation one inch from the left margin. Double-space the indented quotation and do not add extra space above or below it.

Do not use quotation marks when a quotation has been set off from the text by indenting. See page 159 for an example.

URLs (Web addresses)   When you need to break a URL at the end of a line in the text of your paper, break it only after a double slash or a slash and do not insert a hyphen. For MLA rules on dividing and formatting URLs in your list of works cited, see page 158.

Headings   MLA neither encourages nor discourages the use of headings and provides no guidelines for their use. If you would like to insert headings in a long essay or research paper, check first with your instructor.

Visuals   MLA classifies visuals as tables and figures (figures include graphs, charts, maps, photographs, and drawings). Label each table with an arabic numeral ("Table 1," "Table 2," and so on) and provide a clear caption that identifies the subject. The label and caption should appear on separate lines above the table, flush with the left margin.

For a table that you have borrowed or adapted, give the source below the table in a note like the following:

Source: David N. Greenfield and Richard A. Davis; "Lost in Cyberspace: The Web @ Work"; *CyberPsychology and Behavior* 5.4 (2002): 349; print.

For each figure, place the figure number (using the abbreviation "Fig.") and a caption below the figure, flush left.

Place visuals in the text, as close as possible to the sentences that relate to them, unless your instructor prefers that visuals appear in an appendix.

Preparing the list of works cited   Begin the list of works cited on a new page at the end of the paper. Center the title "Works Cited" about one inch from the top of the page. Double-space throughout. See pages 160 and 162 for sample lists of works cited.

Alphabetizing the list   Alphabetize the list by the last names of the authors (or editors); if a work has no author or editor, alphabetize by the first word of the title other than *A*, *An*, or *The*.

If your list includes two or more works by the same author, see item 6 on page 134.

Indenting Do not indent the first line of each works cited entry, but indent any additional lines one-half inch. See pages 160 and 162.

URLs (Web addresses) If you need to include a URL in a works cited entry and it must be divided across lines, break the URL only after a double slash or a slash. Do not insert a hyphen at the end of the line. Insert angle brackets around the URL. (See the note on p. 144.) If your word processing program automatically turns URLs into links (by underlining them and changing the color), turn off this feature.

34b Pages from two MLA papers

Following are excerpts from two MLA papers: a research paper written for a composition course and an analysis of a short story written for a literature class.

MODELS hackerhandbooks.com/pocket
> Model papers > MLA papers: Orlov; Houston; Daly; Levi
> MLA literature papers: Peel; Larson
> MLA annotated bibliography: Orlov

Sample MLA page: Research paper

Orlov 1

Anna Orlov

Professor Willis

English 101

17 March 2009

Online Monitoring:

A Threat to Employee Privacy in the Wired Workplace

Company policies on Internet usage have become as common as policies regarding vacation days or sexual harassment. A 2005 study by the American Management Association and ePolicy Institute found that **1** 76% of companies monitor employees' use of the Web, and the number of companies that block employees' access to certain Web sites has increased 27% since 2001 (1). Unlike other company rules, however, Internet usage policies raise questions about rights in the workplace. Although companies often have legitimate concerns that lead them **2** to monitor employees' Internet usage, the benefits of electronic surveillance are outweighed by its costs to employees' privacy and autonomy.

While surveillance of employees is not new, electronic surveillance allows employers to monitor workers with unprecedented efficiency. In *The Naked Employee*, Frederick Lane describes offline ways in which **3** employers have been permitted to intrude on employees' privacy for decades. The difference, Lane argues, between the old methods and electronic surveillance involves quantity:

> **4** Technology makes it possible for employers to gather enormous amounts of data about employees. . . . And the trends that drive technology—faster, smaller, cheaper— make it possible for larger and larger numbers of employers to gather ever-greater amounts of personal data. (3-4) **5**

1 Source provides background information. **2** Debatable thesis.
3 Signal phrase introduces quotation. **4** Long quotation indented
1"; quotation marks omitted. **5** Page numbers in parentheses
after the final period.

(Annotations indicate MLA-style formatting and effective writing.)

Sample MLA list of works cited

Orlov 5

1 Works Cited

2 Adams, Scott. *Dilbert and the Way of the Weasel*. New York:
Harper, 2002. Print.

American Management Association and ePolicy Institute. "2005
Electronic Monitoring and Surveillance Survey." *American
Management Association*. Amer. Management Assn., 2005.
Web. 15 Feb. 2009.

3 "Automatically Record Everything They Do Online! Spector Pro
4 5.0 FAQ's." *Netbus.org*. Netbus.Org, n.d. Web. 17 Feb.
2009.

5 Flynn, Nancy. "Internet Policies." *ePolicy Institute*. ePolicy
Inst., n.d. Web. 15 Feb. 2009.

Frauenheim, Ed. "Stop Reading This Headline and Get Back to
6 Work." *CNET News.com*. CNET Networks, 11 July 2005. Web.
17 Feb. 2009.

7 Gonsalves, Chris. "Wasting Away on the Web." *eWeek.com*. Ziff
Davis Enterprise Holdings, 8 Aug. 2005. Web. 16 Feb.
2009.

Kesan, Jay P. "Cyber-Working or Cyber-Shirking? A First
8 Principles Examination of Electronic Privacy in the
Workplace." *Florida Law Review* 54.2 (2002): 289-332.
Print.

Lane, Frederick S., III. *The Naked Employee: How Technology
Is Compromising Workplace Privacy*. New York: Amer.
Management Assn., 2003. Print.

9 Tam, Pui-Wing, et al. "Snooping E-Mail by Software Is Now a
Workplace Norm." *Wall Street Journal* 9 Mar. 2005: B1+.
Print.

1 Heading, centered. **2** Authors' names inverted; works
alphabetized by last names. **3** Work without author listed by
title. **4** Abbreviation "n.d." for online source with no update
date. **5** Short work from Web site. **6** First line of entry at left
margin; extra lines indented ½". **7** Article from online periodical.
8 Double-spacing throughout. **9** Four authors listed by first
author's name and the abbreviation "et al."

Sample MLA page: Literature paper

Dan Larson

Professor Duncan

English 102

19 April 2010

The Transformation of Mrs. Peters:

An Analysis of "A Jury of Her Peers"

1

In Susan Glaspell's 1917 short story "A Jury of Her Peers," two women accompany their husbands and a county attorney to an isolated house where a farmer named John Wright has been choked to death. The chief suspect is Wright's wife, Minnie, who is in jail awaiting trial. The sheriff's wife, Mrs. Peters, has come along to gather some items for Minnie, and Mrs. Hale has joined her. Initially, Mrs. Hale sympathizes with Minnie and objects to the male investigators "snoopin' round and criticizin' " her kitchen (191). But Mrs. Peters shows respect for the law, saying that the men are doing "no more than their duty" (191). By **2** the end of the story, however, Mrs. Peters has joined Mrs. Hale in lying to the men and committing a crime—hiding key evidence. What **3** causes this dramatic change?

One critic, Leonard Mustazza, argues that Mrs. Hale recruits Mrs. Peters "as a fellow 'juror' in the case, moving the sheriff's wife . . . towards identification with the accused wom[a]n" (494). However, Mrs. Peters also reaches insights on her own. Her observations in the **4** kitchen lead her to understand Minnie's plight:

> **5** The sheriff's wife had looked from the stove to the sink—to the pail of water which had been carried in from outside. . . . That look of seeing into things, of seeing through a thing to something else, was in the eyes of the sheriff's wife now. (194)

1 Title, centered. **2** Quotation from literary work followed by page number. **3** Writer's research question. **4** Debatable thesis. **5** Long quotation indented 1"; page number in parentheses after final period.

(Annotations indicate MLA-style formatting and effective writing.)

Sample MLA list of works cited

Works Cited

1 Ben-Zvi, Linda. " 'Murder, She Wrote': The Genesis of Susan
     Glaspell's *Trifles*." *Theatre Journal* 44.2 (1992): 141-62.
     Rpt. in *Susan Glaspell: Essays on Her Theater and Fiction*.
     Ed. Ben-Zvi. Ann Arbor: U of Michigan P, 1995. 19-48.
     Print.

Glaspell, Susan. "A Jury of Her Peers." *Literature and Its Writers:
     A Compact Introduction to Fiction, Poetry, and Drama*.
     Ed. Ann Charters and Samuel Charters. 5th ed. Boston:
     Bedford, 2010. 185-201. Print.

2 Hedges, Elaine. "Small Things Reconsidered: 'A Jury of Her
     Peers.' " *Women's Studies* 12.1 (1986): 89-110. Rpt. in
     Susan Glaspell: Essays on Her Theater and Fiction. Ed. Linda
     Ben-Zvi. Ann Arbor: U of Michigan P, 1995. 49-69. Print.

3 Mustazza, Leonard. "Generic Translation and Thematic Shift in
     Susan Glaspell's *Trifles* and 'A Jury of Her Peers.' " *Studies
     in Short Fiction* 26.4 (1989): 489-96. Print.

1 List alphabetized by last names. **2** Article reprinted in
anthology. **3** Article in journal.

APA Papers

Many writing assignments in the social sciences are either reports of original research or reviews of the literature (previously published research) on a particular topic. Often an original research report contains a "review of the literature" section that places the writer's project in the context of other researchers' findings.

Many social science instructors will ask you to document your sources with the American Psychological Association (APA) system of in-text citations and references described in 38. You face three main challenges when writing a social science paper that draws on sources: (1) supporting a thesis, (2) citing your sources and avoiding plagiarism, and (3) integrating quotations and other source material.

35 Supporting a thesis

Most assignments ask you to form a thesis and to support it with well-organized evidence. A thesis, which usually appears at the end of the introduction, is a one-sentence (or occasionally a two-sentence) statement of your central idea. In a paper reviewing the literature on a topic, the thesis analyzes the often competing conclusions drawn by a variety of researchers.

35a Forming a thesis

You will be reading articles and other sources that are related to your central research question. Your thesis will express your reasoned and informed answer to that question, given the current state of research in the field. Here are some examples.

RESEARCH QUESTION

Is medication the right treatment for the escalating problem of childhood obesity?

POSSIBLE THESIS

Understanding the limitations of medical treatments for children highlights the complexity of the childhood obesity problem in the United States and underscores the need for physicians, advocacy groups, and policymakers to search for other solutions.

PRACTICE hackerhandbooks.com/pocket
> APA > 35–1 and 35–2

RESEARCH QUESTION

How can a business improve employee motivation?

POSSIBLE THESIS

Setting clear expectations, sharing information in a timely fashion, and publicly offering appreciation to specific employees can help align individual motivation with corporate goals.

RESEARCH QUESTION

Why are boys diagnosed with ADHD more often than girls?

POSSIBLE THESIS

Recent studies have suggested that ADHD is diagnosed more often in boys than in girls because of personality differences between boys and girls as well as gender bias in referring adults, but an overlooked cause is that ADHD often coexists with other behavior disorders that exaggerate or mask gender differences.

Each of these thesis statements expresses a view on a debatable issue—an issue about which informed people might disagree. The writers will need to persuade readers to take their positions seriously.

35b Organizing your ideas

APA encourages the use of headings to help readers follow the organization of a paper. For an original research report, the major headings often follow a standard model: Method, Results, Discussion. For a review of the literature, headings will vary, depending on the topic. For examples of headings in APA papers, see pages 200 and 203.

35c Using sources to inform and support your argument

Sources can play several different roles as you develop your points.

Providing background information or context You can use facts and statistics to support generalizations or to establish the importance of your topic.

Explaining terms or concepts Explain words, phrases, or ideas that might be unfamiliar to your readers. Quoting or paraphrasing a source can help you define terms and concepts in accessible language.

Supporting your claims   Back up your assertions with facts, examples, and other evidence from your research.

Lending authority to your argument   Expert opinion can give weight to your argument. But don't rely on experts to make your argument for you. Construct your argument in your own words and cite authorities in the field to support your position.

Anticipating and countering other interpretations   Do not ignore sources that seem contrary to your position or that offer interpretations different from your own. Instead, use them to give voice to opposing ideas and interpretations before you counter them.

36   Avoiding plagiarism

Your research paper is a collaboration between you and your sources. To be fair and ethical, you must acknowledge your debt to the writers of those sources. When you acknowledge your sources, you avoid plagiarism, a serious academic offense.

Three different acts are considered plagiarism: (1) failing to cite quotations and borrowed ideas, (2) failing to enclose borrowed language in quotation marks, and (3) failing to put summaries and paraphrases in your own words.

36a   Citing quotations and borrowed ideas

When you cite sources, you give credit to writers from whom you've borrowed words and ideas. You also let your readers know where your information comes from, so that they can evaluate the original source.

You must cite anything you borrow from a source, including direct quotations; statistics and other specific facts; visuals such as cartoons, graphs, and diagrams; and any ideas you present in a summary or a paraphrase.

The only exception is common knowledge—information that your readers may know or could easily locate in general sources. For example, most general encyclopedias will tell readers that Sigmund Freud wrote *The Interpretation of Dreams* and that chimpanzees can learn American Sign Language. When you have seen certain information repeatedly in your reading, you don't need to cite it. However, when information has appeared in only a few sources, when it is highly specific (as with statistics), or when it is controversial, you should cite the source.

APA recommends an author-date style of citations. Here, briefly, is how the author-date system usually works. See 38 for a detailed discussion of variations.

1. The source is introduced by a signal phrase that includes the last name of the author followed by the date of publication in parentheses.
2. The material being cited is followed by a page number in parentheses.
3. At the end of the paper, an alphabetized list of references gives publication information for the source.

IN-TEXT CITATION

As researchers Yanovski and Yanovski (2002) have explained, obesity was once considered "either a moral failing or evidence of underlying psychopathology" (p. 592).

ENTRY IN THE LIST OF REFERENCES

Yanovski, S. Z., & Yanovski, J. A. (2002). Drug therapy: Obesity. *The New England Journal of Medicine, 346*, 591-602.

36b Enclosing borrowed language in quotation marks

To show that you are using a source's exact phrases or sentences, you must enclose them in quotation marks. To omit the quotation marks is to claim—falsely—that the language is your own. Such an omission is plagiarism even if you have cited the source.

ORIGINAL SOURCE

In an effort to seek the causes of this disturbing trend, experts have pointed to a range of important potential contributors to the rise in childhood obesity that are unrelated to media.

—Henry J. Kaiser Family Foundation, "The Role of Media in Childhood Obesity" (2004), p. 1

PLAGIARISM

According to the Henry J. Kaiser Family Foundation (2004), experts have pointed to a range of important potential contributors to the rise in childhood obesity that are unrelated to media (p. 1).

BORROWED LANGUAGE IN QUOTATION MARKS

According to the Henry J. Kaiser Family Foundation (2004), "experts have pointed to a range of important potential contributors to the rise in childhood obesity that are unrelated to media" (p. 1).

NOTE: When quoted sentences are set off from the text by indenting, quotation marks are not needed (see p. 170).

36c Putting summaries and paraphrases in your own words

A summary condenses information; a paraphrase conveys information in about the same number of words as in the original source. When you summarize or paraphrase, you must name the source and restate the source's meaning in your own words. You commit plagiarism if you half-copy the author's sentences—either by mixing the author's phrases with your own without using quotation marks or by plugging your own synonyms into the author's sentence structure. The following paraphrases are plagiarized—even though the source is cited—because their language and structure are too close to those of the source.

ORIGINAL SOURCE

> In an effort to seek the causes of this disturbing trend, experts have pointed to a range of important potential contributors to the rise in childhood obesity that are unrelated to media.
>> —Henry J. Kaiser Family Foundation, "The Role of Media in Childhood Obesity" (2004), p. 1

PLAGIARISM: UNACCEPTABLE BORROWING OF PHRASES

According to the Henry J. Kaiser Family Foundation (2004), experts have indicated a range of significant potential contributors to the rise in childhood obesity that are not linked to media (p. 1).

PLAGIARISM: UNACCEPTABLE BORROWING OF STRUCTURE

According to the Henry J. Kaiser Family Foundation (2004),
experts have identified a variety of significant factors causing
a rise in childhood obesity, factors that are not linked to media
(p. 1).

To avoid plagiarizing an author's language, don't look
at the source while you are summarizing or paraphrasing. After you've restated the author's ideas in your own
words, return to the source and check that you haven't
used the author's language or sentence structure or misrepresented the author's ideas.

ACCEPTABLE PARAPHRASE

A report by the Henry J. Kaiser Family Foundation (2004) described
sources other than media for the childhood obesity crisis (p. 1).

37 Integrating sources

Quotations, summaries, paraphrases, and facts will help
you develop your argument, but they cannot speak for
you. You can use several strategies to integrate information from research sources into your paper while maintaining your own voice.

37a Using quotations appropriately

Limiting your use of quotations   In your writing, keep
the emphasis on your own words. Do not quote excessively. It is not always necessary to quote full sentences
from a source. Often you can integrate words or phrases
from a source into your own sentence structure.

As researchers continue to face a number of unknowns about
obesity, it may be helpful to envision treating the disorder, as
Yanovski and Yanovski (2002) suggested, "in the same manner as
any other chronic disease" (p. 592).

Using the ellipsis mark   To condense a quoted passage,
you can use the ellipsis mark (three periods, with spaces

between) to indicate that you have omitted words. What remains must be grammatically complete.

Roman (2003) reported that "social factors are nearly as significant as individual metabolism in the formation of . . . dietary habits of adolescents" (p. 345).

The writer has omitted the words *both healthy and unhealthy* from the source.

When you want to omit a full sentence or more, use a period before the three ellipsis dots.

According to Sothern and Gordon (2003), "Environmental factors may contribute as much as 80% to the causes of childhood obesity. . . . Research suggests that obese children demonstrate decreased levels of physical activity and increased psychosocial problems" (p. 104).

Ordinarily, do not use an ellipsis mark at the beginning or at the end of a quotation. Readers will understand that the quoted material is taken from a longer passage. The only exception occurs when you have dropped words at the end of the final quoted sentence. In such cases, put three ellipsis dots before the closing quotation mark.

Using brackets Brackets allow you to insert your own words into quoted material to clarify a confusing reference or to make the quoted words fit grammatically into the context of your writing.

The cost of treating obesity currently totals $117 billion per year—a price, according to the surgeon general, "second only to the cost of [treating] tobacco use" (Carmona, 2004).

To indicate an error such as a misspelling in a quotation, insert [*sic*], italicized and with brackets around it, right after the error.

Setting off long quotations When you quote forty or more words, set off the quotation by indenting it one-half inch from the left margin. Use the normal right margin and do not single-space.

Long quotations should be introduced by an informative sentence, usually followed by a colon. Quotation marks are unnecessary because the indented format tells readers that the passage is taken from the source.

Yanovski and Yanovski (2002) have traced the history of treatments
for obesity:

> For many years, obesity was approached as if it were either
> a moral failing or evidence of underlying psychopathology.
> With the advent of behavioral treatments for obesity in the
> 1960s, hope arose that modification of maladaptive eating
> and exercise habits would lead to sustained weight loss, and
> that time-limited programs would produce permanent changes
> in weight. (p. 592)

At the end of the indented quotation, the parenthetical
citation goes outside the final punctuation mark.

37b Using signal phrases

Whenever you include a direct quotation, a paraphrase,
or a summary in your paper, prepare readers for it with a
signal phrase. A signal phrase usually names the author
of the source, gives the publication date in parentheses,
and often provides some context. It is generally acceptable in the social sciences to call authors by their last
name only, even on first mention. If your paper refers to
two authors with the same last name, use their initials
as well.

See the chart on page 172 for a list of verbs commonly
used in signal phrases.

Marking boundaries   Avoid dropping quotations into
your text without warning. Provide clear signal phrases,
including at least the author's name and the date of publication. Signal phrases mark the boundaries between
source material and your own words and ideas.

DROPPED QUOTATION

Obesity was once considered in a very different light. "For many
years, obesity was approached as if it were either a moral failing
or evidence of underlying psychopathology" (Yanovski & Yanovski,
2002, p. 592).

QUOTATION WITH SIGNAL PHRASE

As researchers Yanovski and Yanovski (2002) have explained,
obesity was once considered "either a moral failing or evidence of
underlying psychopathology" (p. 592).

Using signal phrases in APA papers

To avoid monotony, try to vary both the language and the placement of your signal phrases.

Model signal phrases

In the words of Carmona (2004), ". . ."

As Yanovski and Yanovski (2002) have noted, ". . ."

Hoppin and Taveras (2004), medical researchers, pointed out that ". . ."

". . .," claimed Critser (2003).

". . .," wrote Duenwald (2004), ". . ."

Researchers McDuffie et al. (2003) have offered a compelling argument for this view: ". . ."

Hilts (2002) answered these objections with the following analysis: ". . ."

Verbs in signal phrases

Are you providing background, explaining a concept, supporting a claim, lending authority, or refuting a belief? Choose a verb that is appropriate for the way you are using the source.

admitted	contended	reasoned
agreed	declared	refuted
argued	denied	rejected
asserted	emphasized	reported
believed	insisted	responded
claimed	noted	suggested
compared	observed	thought
confirmed	pointed out	wrote

NOTE: In APA style, use the past tense or present perfect tense to introduce quotations and other source material: *Davis (2005) noted* or *Davis (2005) has noted*, not *Davis (2005) notes*. Use the present tense only to discuss the results of an experiment (*the results show*) or knowledge that has clearly been established (*researchers agree*).

Putting source material in context Provide context for any source material that appears in your paper. A signal phrase can help you connect your own ideas with those of another writer by clarifying how the source will contribute to your paper. It's a good idea to embed source

material, especially long quotations, between sentences of
your own that interpret the source and link the source to
your argument.

QUOTATION WITH EFFECTIVE CONTEXT

A report by the Henry J. Kaiser Family Foundation (2004) outlined
trends that may have contributed to the childhood obesity crisis,
including food advertising for children as well as

> a reduction in physical education classes . . . , an increase
> in the availability of sodas and snacks in public schools,
> the growth in the number of fast-food outlets . . . , and the
> increasing number of highly processed high-calorie and high-
> fat grocery products. (p. 1)

Addressing each of these areas requires more than a doctor armed
with a prescription pad; it requires a broad mobilization not just
of doctors and concerned parents but of educators, food industry
executives, advertisers, and media representatives.

NOTE: When you bring other sources into a conversation
about your research topic, you are synthesizing sources.
For more on synthesis, see 31c.

Integrating statistics and other facts When you are
citing a statistic or another specific fact, a signal phrase
is often not necessary. In most cases, readers will understand that the citation refers to the statistic or fact (not
the whole paragraph).

In purely financial terms, the drugs cost more than $3 a day on
average (Duenwald, 2004).

There is nothing wrong, however, with using a signal
phrase.

Duenwald (2004) pointed out that in purely financial terms, the
drugs cost more than $3 a day on average.

38 APA documentation style

In most social science classes, you will be asked to use the
APA system for documenting sources, which is set forth in
the *Publication Manual of the American Psychological Association*, 6th ed. (Washington, DC: APA, 2010).

PRACTICE hackerhandbooks.com/pocket
> APA > 38–1 to 38–3

38a APA in-text citations

APA's in-text citations provide at least the author's last name and the year of publication. For direct quotations and some summaries and paraphrases, a page number is given as well. In the following models, the elements of the in-text citation are highlighted.

NOTE: APA style requires the use of the past tense or the present perfect tense in signal phrases introducing cited material: *Smith (2005) reported, Smith (2005) has argued.*

■ **1. A quotation** Ordinarily, introduce the quotation with a signal phrase that includes the author's last name followed by the year of publication in parentheses. Put the page number, preceded by "p." (or "pp." for more than one page), in parentheses after the quotation.

Critser (2003) noted that many health care providers still "remain either in ignorance or outright denial about the health danger to the poor and the young" (p. 5).

If the author is not named in the signal phrase, place the author's name, the year, and the page number in parentheses after the quotation: (Critser, 2003, p. 5). (See item 12 on p. 177 for citing parts of electronic sources.)

NOTE: Do not include a month, even if the entry in the reference list includes the month.

■ **2. A summary or a paraphrase** Include the author's last name and the year in a signal phrase introducing the material or in parentheses following it. Give a page number to help readers find the passage. For online sources without page numbers, see "No page numbers" on page 178.

Yanovski and Yanovski (2002) explained that sibutramine suppresses appetite by blocking the reuptake of the neurotransmitters serotonin and norepinephrine in the brain (p. 594).

Sibutramine suppresses appetite by blocking the reuptake of the neurotransmitters serotonin and norepinephrine in the brain (Yanovski & Yanovski, 2002, p. 594).

■ **3. Two authors** Name both authors in the signal phrase or in parentheses each time you cite the work. In the parentheses, use "&" between the authors' names; in the signal phrase, use "and."

According to Sothern and Gordon (2003), "Environmental factors may contribute as much as 80% to the causes of childhood obesity" (p. 104).

Obese children often engage in limited physical activity (Sothern & Gordon, 2003, p. 104).

■ **4. Three to five authors** Identify all authors in the signal phrase or in parentheses the first time you cite the source.

In 2003, Berkowitz, Wadden, Tershakovec, and Cronquist concluded that sibutramine "must be carefully monitored . . . to control increases in [blood pressure] and pulse rate" (p. 1811).

In subsequent citations, use the first author's name followed by "et al." in either the signal phrase or the parentheses.

As Berkowitz et al. (2003) advised, "Until more extensive safety and efficacy data are available, . . . weight-loss medications should be used only on an experimental basis for adolescents" (p. 1811).

■ **5. Six or more authors** Use the first author's name followed by "et al." in the signal phrase or in parentheses.

McDuffie et al. (2002) tested 20 adolescents, aged 12-16, over a three-month period and found that orlistat, combined with behavioral therapy, produced an average weight loss of 4.4 kg, or 9.7 pounds (p. 646).

■ **6. Unknown author** If the author is unknown, mention the work's title in the signal phrase or give the first word or two of the title in the parenthetical citation. Titles of short works such as articles and chapters are put in quotation marks; titles of long works such as books and reports are italicized.

Children struggling to control their weight must also struggle with the pressures of television advertising that, on the one hand, encourages the consumption of junk food and, on the other, celebrates thin celebrities ("Television," 2002).

NOTE: In the rare case when "Anonymous" is specified as the author, treat it as if it were a real name: (Anonymous, 2009). In the list of references, also use the name Anonymous as author.

■ **7. Organization as author** If the author is a government agency or another organization, name the organization in the signal phrase or in the parenthetical citation the first time you cite the source.

Obesity puts children at risk for a number of medical complications, including Type 2 diabetes, hypertension, sleep apnea, and orthopedic problems (Henry J. Kaiser Family Foundation, 2004, p. 1).

If the organization has a familiar abbreviation, you may include it in brackets the first time you cite the source and use the abbreviation alone in later citations.

FIRST CITATION   (National Institute of Mental Health [NIMH], 2010)
LATER CITATIONS   (NIMH, 2010)

■ **8. Authors with the same last name** To avoid confusion, use initials with the last names if your reference list includes two or more authors with the same last name.

Research by E. Smith (1989) revealed that. . . .

■ **9. Two or more works by the same author in the same year** When your list of references includes more than one work by the same author in the same year, use low-ercase letters ("a," "b," and so on) with the year to order the entries in the reference list. (See item 7 on p. 182.) Use those same letters with the year in the in-text citation.

Research by Durgin (2003b) has yielded new findings about the role of counseling in treating childhood obesity.

▓ **10. Two or more works in the same parentheses**   When your parenthetical citation names two or more works, put them in the same order that they appear in the reference list, separated with semicolons.

Researchers have indicated that studies of pharmacological treatments for childhood obesity are inconclusive (Berkowitz et al., 2003; McDuffie et al., 2002).

▓ **11. Personal communication**   Cite interviews, memos, letters, e-mail, and similar unpublished person-to-person communications in the text only, not in the reference list.

One of Atkinson's colleagues, who has studied the effect of the media on children's eating habits, has contended that advertisers for snack foods will need to design ads responsibly for their younger viewers (F. Johnson, personal communication, October 20, 2004).

▓ **12. Electronic source**   Cite electronic sources, includ-ing online sources, as you would any other sources, giving the author and the year when they are available.

Atkinson (2001) found that children who spent at least four hours a day watching TV were less likely to engage in adequate physical activity during the week.

Electronic sources may lack page numbers, authors' names, or dates. Here are APA's guidelines for handling sources without these details.

Unknown author

If no author is named in the source, mention the title of the source in a signal phrase or give the first word or two of the title in parentheses (see also item 6). (If an organi-zation serves as the author, see item 7.)

The body's basal metabolic rate, or BMR, is a measure of its at-rest energy requirement ("Exercise," 2003).

Unknown date

When the date is unknown, use the abbreviation "n.d." (for "no date").

Attempts to establish a definitive link between television programming and children's eating habits have been problematic (Magnus, n.d.).

No page numbers

APA ordinarily requires page numbers for quotations, summaries, and paraphrases. When an electronic source lacks stable numbered pages, include paragraph numbers or headings to help readers locate the passage being cited.

If the source has numbered paragraphs, use the paragraph number preceded by the abbreviation "para.": (Hall, 2009, para. 5). If the source contains headings, cite the appropriate heading in parentheses; you may also indicate which paragraph under that heading you are referring to.

Hoppin and Taveras (2004) pointed out that several other medications were classified by the Drug Enforcement Administration as having the "potential for abuse" (Weight-Loss Drugs section, para. 6).

NOTE: PDF documents often have stable page numbers. For such sources, give the page number in the parenthetical citation.

■ **13. Indirect source (source quoted in another source)**
If you use a source that was cited in another source (a secondary source), name the original source in your signal phrase. List the secondary source in your reference list and include it in your parenthetical citation, preceded by the words "as cited in." In the following example, Satcher is the original source; Critser is the secondary source, given in the reference list.

Former surgeon general Dr. David Satcher described "a nation of young people seriously at risk of starting out obese and dooming themselves to the difficult task of overcoming a tough illness" (as cited in Critser, 2003, p. 4).

38b APA references

In APA style, the alphabetical list of works cited, which appears at the end of the paper, is titled "References." For advice on preparing the list, see pages 197–98. For sample references lists, see pages 201, 204, and 206.

Alphabetize entries in the list of references by authors' last names; if a work has no author, alphabetize it by its title. The first element of each entry is important because citations in the text of the paper refer to it and readers will be looking for it in the alphabetized list. The date of publication appears immediately after the first element of the citation.

In APA references, titles of books are italicized; titles of articles are neither italicized nor put in quotation marks. (For rules on capitalization of titles, see p. 196.)

General guidelines for listing authors (print and online) In APA style, all authors' names are inverted (the last name comes first), and initials are used for all first and middle names.

NAME AND YEAR CITED IN TEXT

Duncan (2008) has reported that. . . .

BEGINNING OF ENTRY IN THE LIST OF REFERENCES

Duncan, B. (2008).

Directory to APA reference list models

■ 1. Single author

author: last name
+ initial(s)   year   title (book)

Egeland, J. (2008). *A billion lives: An eyewitness report from the*

place of
publication   publisher

frontlines of humanity. New York, NY: Simon & Schuster.

■ 2. Two to seven authors

List up to seven authors by last names followed by initials. Use an ampersand (&) before the name of the last author.

all authors:
last name + initial(s)   year   title (book)

Musick, M. A., & Wilson, J. (2007). *Volunteers: A social profile.*

place of
publication   publisher

Bloomington: Indiana University Press.

all authors:
last name + initial(s)

Diessner, R., Solom, R. C., Frost, N. K., Parsons, L., & Davidson, J.

year   title (article)

(2008). Engagement with beauty: Appreciating natural,

journal title

artistic, and moral beauty. *The Journal of Psychology,*

volume   page(s)

142, 303-329.

■ 3. Eight or more authors

List the first six authors followed by three ellipsis dots and the last author's name.

Mulvaney, S. A., Mudasiru, E., Schlundt, D. G., Baughman, C. L.,

Fleming, M., VanderWoude, A., . . . Rothman, R. (2008).

Self-management in Type 2 diabetes: The adolescent

perspective. *The Diabetes Educator, 34,* 118-127.

■ 4. Organization as author

author:
organization name   year   title (book)

American Psychiatric Association. (1994). *Diagnostic and statistical*

edition   place
number   of publication

manual of mental disorders (4th ed.). Washington, DC:

organization as author
and publisher

Author.

If the publisher is not the same as the author, give the publisher's name at the end as you would for any other source.

■ **5. Unknown author** Begin the entry with the work's title.

| title (book) | year | place of publication | publisher |

New concise world atlas. (2007). New York, NY: Oxford University

Press.

■ **6. Two or more works by the same author** Use the author's name for all entries. List the entries by year, the earliest first.

Barry, P. (2007, December 8). Putting tumors on pause. *Science News, 172*, 365.

Barry, P. (2008, August 2). Finding the golden genes. *Science News, 174*, 16-21.

■ **7. Two or more works by the same author in the same year** List the works alphabetically by title. In the parentheses, following the year add "a," "b," and so on. Use these same letters when giving the year in the in-text citation. (See also pp. 197–98.)

Elkind, D. (2008a, Spring). Can we play? *Greater Good, 4*(4), 14-17.

Elkind, D. (2008b, June 27). The price of hurrying children [Web log post]. Retrieved from http://blogs.psychologytoday.com /blog/digital-children

Articles in periodicals (print) Periodicals include journals, magazines, and newspapers. For a journal or a magazine, give only the volume number if the publication is paginated continuously throughout each volume; give the volume and issue numbers if each issue of the volume begins on page 1. Italicize the volume number and put the issue number, not italicized, in parentheses.

For all periodicals, when an article appears on consecutive pages, provide the range of pages. When an article does not appear on consecutive pages, list all pages on which the article appears: A1, A17.

Some print articles include a DOI (digital object identifier), often on the first page of the article. For such an article, give the DOI at the end of the reference list entry, following the print publication information. See item 8.

For an illustrated citation of an article in a print journal or magazine, see page 184.

8. Article in a journal paginated by volume

Holtug, N. (2010). Immigration and the politics of social cohesion. *Ethnicities, 10,* 435-451. doi:10.1177/1468796810378320

9. Article in a journal paginated by issue

Black, J. (2010). Big government: Good and bad. *The New Criterion, 28*(5), 24-27.

10. Article in a magazine Give the year and the month for monthly magazines; add the day for weekly magazines.

McKibben, B. (2007, October). Carbon's new math. *National Geographic, 212*(4), 32-37.

11. Article in a newspaper Use "p." (or "pp." for more than one page) before page numbers.

Svoboda, E. (2008, October 21). Deep in the rain forest, stalking the next pandemic. *The New York Times,* p. D5.

12. Letter to the editor

Park, T. (2008, August). Defining the line [Letter to the editor]. *Scientific American, 299*(2), 10.

13. Editorial or other unsigned article

The global justice movement [Editorial]. (2005). *Multinational Monitor, 26*(7/8), 6.

14. Review If the review has no author or title, use the material in brackets as the title.

Applebaum, A. (2008, February 14). A movie that matters [Review of the motion picture *Katyn,* 2007]. *The New York Review of Books, 55*(2), 13-15.

Agents of change. (2008, February 2). [Review of the book *The power of unreasonable people: How social entrepreneurs create markets that change the world,* by J. Elkington & P. Hartigan]. *The Economist, 386*(8565), 94.

Citation at a glance
Article in a journal or magazine (APA)

To cite an article in a print journal or magazine in APA style, include the following elements:

1. Author
2. Year of publication for journal; complete date for magazine
3. Title and subtitle of article
4. Name of journal or magazine
5. Volume number; issue number, if required (see p. 182)
6. Page number(s) of article
7. DOI, if there is one

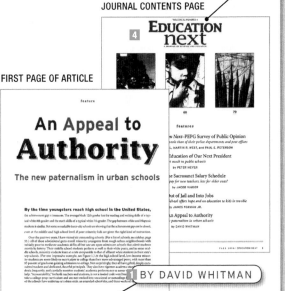

5 VOLUME 8, NUMBER 4

JOURNAL CONTENTS PAGE

EDUCATION next

4

FIRST PAGE OF ARTICLE

feature

An Appeal to Authority

The new paternalism in urban schools

By the time youngsters reach high school in the United States,

BY DAVID WHITMAN

1 BY DAVID WHITMAN

2   4

FALL 2008 / EDUCATION NEXT   53 — 6

REFERENCE LIST ENTRY FOR A JOURNAL OR MAGAZINE ARTICLE

1 ── 2 ── 3 ────────────
Whitman, D. (2008). An appeal to authority: The new
─────── 4 ──── 5 ─
paternalism in urban schools. *Education Next, 8*(4),
─ 6 ─
53-58.

For variations on citing articles in print journals or magazines in APA style, see pages 182 and 183.

Books (print)   Give the city and the state (abbreviated) for all US cities or the city and the country (not abbreviated) for all non-US cities; also include the province (not abbreviated) for Canadian cities. Do not give a state if the publisher's name includes it (as in many university presses). For an illustrated citation of a print book, see page 186.

▦ 15. Basic format for a book

McKenzie, F. R. (2008). *Theory and practice with adolescents: An applied approach*. Chicago, IL: Lyceum Books.

▦ 16. Book with an editor   Use the abbreviation "Ed." for one editor; use "Eds." for more than one.

Aronson, J., & Aronson, E. (Eds.). (2008). *Readings about the social animal* (10th ed.). New York, NY: Worth.

▦ 17. Book with an author and an editor   Use the abbreviation "Ed." for one editor; use "Eds." for more than one.

McLuhan, M. (2003). *Understanding me: Lectures and interviews* (S. McLuhan & D. Staine, Eds.). Toronto, Ontario, Canada: McClelland & Stewart.

▦ 18. Book with an author and a translator   Use "Trans." for one or more translators.

Steinberg, M. D. (2003). *Voices of revolution, 1917* (M. Schwartz, Trans.). New Haven, CT: Yale University Press. (Original work published 2001)

▦ 19. Edition other than the first

O'Brien, J. A. (Ed.). (2006). *The production of reality: Essays and readings on social interaction* (4th ed.). Thousand Oaks, CA: Pine Forge Press.

▦ 20. Article or chapter in an edited book or an anthology
Use the abbreviation "Ed." for one editor; use "Eds." for more than one.

Denton, N. A. (2006). Segregation and discrimination in housing. In R. G. Bratt, M. E. Stone, & C. Hartman (Eds.), *A right to housing: Foundation of a new social agenda* (pp. 61-81). Philadelphia, PA: Temple University Press.

Citation at a glance
Book (APA)

To cite a print book in APA style, include the following elements:

1 Author
2 Year of publication
3 Title and subtitle
4 Place of publication
5 Publisher

COPYRIGHT PAGE

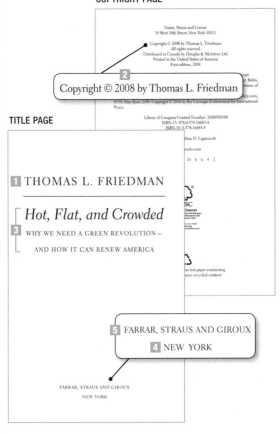

Farrar, Straus and Giroux
18 West 18th Street, New York 10011

Copyright © 2008 by Thomas L. Friedman
All rights reserved
Distributed in Canada by Douglas & McIntyre Ltd.
Printed in the United States of America
First edition, 2008

> 2
> Copyright © 2008 by Thomas L. Friedman

#154, May/June 2006, Copyright © 2006 by the Carnegie Endowment for International Peace.

Library of Congress Control Number: 2008930589
ISBN-13: 978-0-374-16685-4
ISBN-10: 0-374-16685-4

10 8 6 4 2

TITLE PAGE

1 THOMAS L. FRIEDMAN

Hot, Flat, and Crowded
3 WHY WE NEED A GREEN REVOLUTION—
AND HOW IT CAN RENEW AMERICA

> 5 FARRAR, STRAUS AND GIROUX
> 4 NEW YORK

FARRAR, STRAUS AND GIROUX
NEW YORK

REFERENCE LIST ENTRY FOR A PRINT BOOK

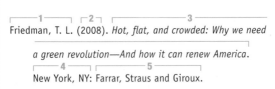

┌──1──┐ ┌─2─┐ ┌─────────3─────────
Friedman, T. L. (2008). *Hot, flat, and crowded: Why we need*

a green revolution—And how it can renew America.
┌───4───┐ ┌────5────┐
New York, NY: Farrar, Straus and Giroux.

For more on citing print books in APA style, see pages 185 and 187.

▥ 21. Multivolume work

Luo, J. (Ed.). (2005). *China today: An encyclopedia of life in the People's Republic* (Vols. 1-2). Westport, CT: Greenwood Press.

▥ 22. Book with a title in its title

If the book title contains another book title or an article title, neither italicize the internal title nor place it in quotation marks.

Marcus, L. (Ed.). (1999). *Sigmund Freud's* The interpretation of dreams*: New interdisciplinary essays.* Manchester, England: Manchester University Press.

Online sources Online articles and books sometimes include a DOI (digital object identifier). APA uses the DOI, when available, in place of a URL in reference list entries.

If a source has no publication date, use "n.d." (for "no date"). Use a retrieval date for an online source only if the content is likely to change. Most of the examples in this section do not show a retrieval date because the content of the sources is stable; if you are unsure about whether to use a retrieval date, consult your instructor.

▥ 23. Article in an online journal

author: last
name + initial(s) year article title

Whitmeyer, J. M. (2000). Power through appointment.

journal title volume page(s) DOI

Social Science Research, 29, 535-555. doi:10.1006

/ssre.2000.0680

If there is no DOI, include the URL for the journal's home page.

Ashe, D. D., & McCutcheon, L. E. (2001). Shyness, loneliness, and attitude toward celebrities. *Current Research in Social Psychology, 6,* 124-133. Retrieved from http://www.uiowa .edu/~grpproc/crisp/crisp.html

▥ 24. Article in an online magazine

Include the URL for the magazine's home page.

Shelburne, E. C. (2008, September). The great disruption. *The Atlantic, 302*(2). Retrieved from http://www.theatlantic.com/

Rupley, S. (2010, February 26). The myth of the benign monopoly. *Salon.* Retrieved from http://www.salon.com/

■ **25. Article in an online newspaper** Include the URL for the newspaper's home page.

Watson, P. (2008, October 19). Biofuel boom endangers orangutan
    habitat. *Los Angeles Times*. Retrieved from http://www
    .latimes.com/

■ **26. Article from a database** If the database gives a DOI for the article, use the DOI at the end. For an illustrated citation of an article from a database, see pages 190–91.

all authors:
last name + initial(s)   year   article title
Eskritt, M., & McLeod, K. (2008). Children's note taking as a

                                    journal title   volume
    mnemonic tool. *Journal of Experimental Child Psychology, 101,*

    page(s)   DOI
    52-74. doi:10.1016/jecp.2008.05.007

If there is no DOI, include the URL for the home page of the journal. If the URL is not included in the database entry, you can search for it on the Web.

Howard, K. R. (2007). Childhood overweight: Parental perceptions
    and readiness for change. *The Journal of School Nursing, 23,*
    73-79. Retrieved from http://jsn.sagepub.com/

■ **27. Online book**

Adams, B. (2004). *The theory of social revolutions*. Retrieved from
    http://www.gutenberg.org/catalog/world/readfile?fk
    _files=44092 (Original work published 1913)

■ **28. Chapter in an online book**

Clinton, S. J. (1999). What can be done to prevent childhood
    obesity? In *Understanding childhood obesity* (pp. 81-98).
    Retrieved from http://www.questia.com/

■ **29. Report or long document from a Web site**

Source with date

    all authors: online
    last name + initial(s)   publication date   document title
Cain, A., & Burris, M. (1999, April). *Investigation of the use of*

                                                    URL
    mobile phones while driving. Retrieved from http://www.cutr

    .usf.edu/pdf/mobile_phone_text.PDF

Source with no date

Archer, D. (n.d.). *Exploring nonverbal communication*. Retrieved
    from http://nonverbal.ucsc.edu

▓ 30. Section in a Web document

author (organization)   year

National Institute on Media and the Family. (2009). Mobile

title of section   title of Web document

    networking. In *Guide to social networking: Risks*. Retrieved

URL

    from http://www.mediafamily.org/network_pdf/MediaWise

    _Guide_to_Social_Networking_Risks_09.pdf

For an illustrated citation of a section in a Web document,
see pages 192–93.

▓ 31. Short work from a Web site

NATO statement endangers patients in Afghanistan. (2010,
    March 11). *Médecins sans frontières/Doctors without borders*.
    Retrieved from http://www.doctorswithoutborders.org/

▓ 32. Podcast

organization as producer   date of posting

National Academies (Producer). (2007, June 6). Progress in

podcast title

    preventing childhood obesity: How do we measure up?

descriptive label   series title

    [Audio podcast]. *The sounds of science podcast*.

URL

    Retrieved from http://media.nap.edu/podcasts/

writer/
presenter   date of posting   podcast title

Chesney, M. (2007, September 13). Gender differences in the use

podcast number

    of complementary and alternative medicine (No. 12827)

descriptive label   Web site hosting podcast

    [Audio podcast]. Retrieved from University of California

URL

    Television website: http://www.uctv.tv/ondemand

Citation at a glance
Article from a database (APA)

To cite an article from a database in APA style, include the following elements:

1 Author(s)
2 Date of publication
3 Title of article
4 Name of periodical
5 Volume number; issue number, if required (see p. 182)
6 Page number(s)
7 DOI (digital object identifier)
8 URL for journal's home page (if there is no DOI)

ON-SCREEN VIEW OF DATABASE RECORD

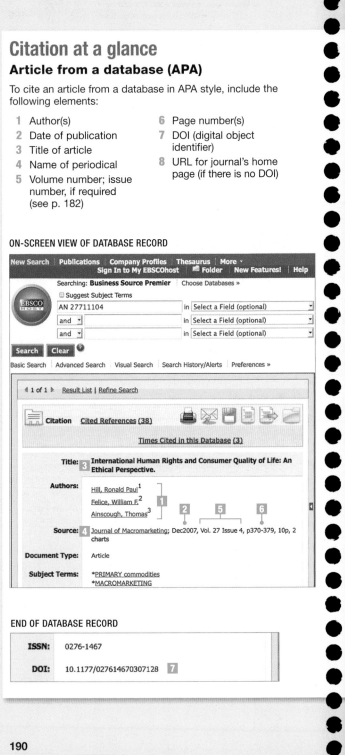

END OF DATABASE RECORD

ISSN:	0276-1467
DOI:	10.1177/027614670307128 7

33. Blog (Weblog) post Give the writer's name, the
date of the post, the subject, the label "Web log post" in
brackets, and the URL. For a response to a post, use the
label "Web log comment."

Kellermann, M. (2007, May 23). Disclosing clinical trials [Web log
    post]. Retrieved from http://www.iq.harvard.edu/blog/sss
    /archives/2007/05

34. Online audio or video file

Chomsky, N. (n.d.). The new imperialism [Audio file]. Retrieved
    from http://www.rhapsody.com/noamchomsky

Zakaria, F. (Host), & McCullough, C. (Writer). (2007, March 6). In
    focus: American teens, Rwandan truths [Video file]. Retrieved
    from http://www.pulitzercenter.org/showproject.cfm?id=26

35. Entry in a wiki Include the date of retrieval; wiki
content can change frequently. If an author or an editor is
identified, include that name at the beginning of the entry.

Ethnomethodology. (n.d.). Retrieved June 18, 2010, from http://
    stswiki.org/index.php?title/Ethnomethodology

36. Data set or graphic representation

U.S. Department of Agriculture, Economic Research Service. (2009).
    Eating and health module (ATUS): 2007 data [Data set].
    Retrieved from http://www.ers.usda.gov/Data/ATUS
    /Data/2007/2007data.htm

Gallup. (2008, October 23). *No increase in proportion of first-time
    voters* [Graphs]. Retrieved from http://www.gallup.com
    /poll/111331/No-Increase-Proportion-First-Time-Voters.aspx

Citation at a glance
Section in a Web document (APA)

To cite a section in a Web document in APA style, include the following elements:

1 Author
2 Date of publication or most recent update
3 Title of section
4 Title of document
5 URL of section or of document

BROWSER PRINTOUT OF WEB SITE

2008 Minnesota Health Statistics Annual Summary – Minnesota Dept. of Health

Minnesota Department of Health
Protecting, maintaining and improving the health of all Minnesotans

MDH

4 2008 Minnesota Health Statistics Annual Summary

The Minnesota "Annual Summary" or "Minnesota Health Statistics" is a report published yearly. The most recent version of this report is **2008 Minnesota Health Statistics**, published January 2010. This report provides statistical data on the following subjects for the state of Minnesota.

To view the PDF files, you will need Adobe Acrobat R
site).

published January 2010.

- Introduction, Technical Notes, Definitions (PDF: 42KB/7 pages)
- Overview of 2008 Annual Summary (PDF: 66KB/11 pages)
- Live Births (PDF: 196KB/21 pages)
- Fertility (PDF: 26KB/2 pages) • 3
- Infant Mortality and Fetal Deaths (PDF: 188KB/15 pages)
- General Mortality (PDF: 333KB/40 pages)
- Marriage/Dissolution of Marriage Divorce (PDF: 25KB/2 pages)
- Population (PDF: 73KB/12 pages)

Note: Induced abortion statistics previously reported in this publication are now published separately.
See Report to the Legislature: Induced Abortions in Minnesota

See also Minnesota Health Statistics Annual Summary Main Page

For further information about the Annual Summary, please contact:

Center for Health Statistics
Minnesota Department of Health
Golden Rule Building, 3rd Floor
85 East Seventh Place

http://www.health.state.mn.us/divs/chs/annsum/08annsum/index.html   Page 1 of 2

5

`http://www.health.state.mn.us/divs/chs/annsum/08annsum/Fertility08.pdf`

ON-SCREEN VIEW OF DOCUMENT

`http://www.health.state.mn.us/divs/chs/annsum/08annsum/Fertility08.pdf`

Fertility Table 1
Total Reported Pregnancies by Outcome and Rate
Minnesota Residents, 1980 - 2008

Year	Total Reported Pregnancies*	Live Births	Induced Abortions	Fetal Deaths	Female Population Ages 15-44	Pregnancy Rate**
1980	84,782	67,843	16,490	449	958,773	88.4
1981	84,934	68,652	15,821	461	967,087	87.8
1982	84,500	68,512	15,559	429	977,905	86.4
1983	80,530	65,559	14,514	457	981,287	82.1
1984	82,736	66,715	15,556	465	985,608	83.9
1985	83,853	67,412	16,002	439	994,249	84.3
1986	81,882	65,766	15,716	400	997,501	82.1
1987	81,318	65,168	15,746	404	1,004,801	80.9
1988	83,335	66,745	16,124	466	1,020,209	81.7
1989	83,426	67,490	15,506	430	1,024,576	81.4
1990	83,714	67,985	15,280	449	1,025,919	81.6
1991	81,904	67,037	14,441	426	1,036,146	79.0
1992	79,844	65,591	13,846	407	1,049,175	76.1
1993	77,939	64,646	12,955	338	1,060,396	73.5

REFERENCE LIST ENTRY FOR A SECTION IN A WEB DOCUMENT

— 1 — — 2 — — 3 —
Minnesota Department of Health. (2010, January). Fertility.

— 4 —
In *2008 Minnesota health statistics annual summary.*

— 5 —
Retrieved from http://www.health.state.mn.us/divs

/chs/annsum/08annsum/Fertility08.pdf

For more on citing documents from Web sites in APA style,
see pages 188–91.

■ **37. E-mail** E-mail messages, letters, and other personal communications are not included in the list of references. (See item 11 on p. 177 for citing these sources in
the text of your paper.)

■ **38. Online posting**

McKinney, J. (2006, December 19). Adult education-healthcare

partnerships [Electronic mailing list message]. Retrieved from

http://www.nifl.gov/pipermail/healthliteracy/2006

/000524.html

Other sources (including online versions)

39. Dissertation from a database

Hymel, K. M. (2009). *Essays in urban economics* (Doctoral
dissertation). Available from ProQuest Dissertations and
Theses database. (AAT 3355930)

40. Government document

U.S. Census Bureau. (2006). *Statistical abstract of the United States.*
Washington, DC: Government Printing Office.

U.S. Census Bureau, Bureau of Economic Analysis. (2008, August).
U.S. international trade in goods and services (Report No.
CB08-121, BEA08-37, FT-900). Retrieved from http://
www.census.gov/foreign-trade/Press-Release/2008pr
/06/ftdpress.pdf

41. Report from a private organization   If the report has
a number, put it in parentheses following the title. (See
also item 4 on pp. 181–82.)

Ford Foundation. (n.d.). *Helping citizens to understand and influence
state budgets.* Retrieved from http://www.fordfound.org/pdfs
/impact/evaluations/state_fiscal_initiative.pdf

42. Conference proceedings

Stahl, G. (Ed.). (2002). *Proceedings of CSCL '02: Computer support for
collaborative learning.* Hillsdale, NJ: Erlbaum.

43. Map, chart, or illustration

Ukraine [Map]. (2008). Retrieved from the University of Texas
at Austin Perry-Castañeda Library Map Collection website:
http://www.lib.utexas.edu/maps/cia08/ukraine_sm
_2008.gif

44. Advertisement

Xbox 360 [Advertisement]. (2007, February). *Wired, 15*(2), 71.

45. Lecture, speech, or address

Fox, V. (2008, March 5). *Economic growth, poverty, and democracy
in Latin America: A president's perspective.* Address at the
Freeman Spogli Institute, Stanford University, Stanford, CA.

■ 46. Brochure, pamphlet, or fact sheet

National Council of State Boards of Nursing. (n.d.).
Professional boundaries [Brochure]. Retrieved from
https://www.ncsbn.org/Professional_Boundaries
_2007_Web.pdf

World Health Organization. (2007, October). *Health of indigenous
peoples* (No. 326) [Fact sheet]. Retrieved from http://
www.who.int/mediacentre/factsheets/fs326/en
/index.html

■ 47. Film or video (motion picture)

Guggenheim, D. (Director), & Bender, L. (Producer). (2006). *An
inconvenient truth* [DVD]. United States: Paramount Home
Entertainment.

Spurlock, M. (Director). (2004). *Super size me* [Motion picture].
Available from IDP Films, 1133 Broadway, Suite 926, New York,
NY 10010

■ 48. Television program

Pratt, C. (Executive producer). (2008, October 5). *Face the nation*
[Television broadcast]. Washington, DC: CBS News.

Smith, M. (Writer/producer). (2008). Heat [Television series episode].
In D. Fanning (Executive producer), *Frontline*. Boston, MA:
WGBH.

■ 49. Computer software or video game

Sims 2 [Computer software]. (2005). New York, NY: Maxis.

39 APA manuscript format; sample pages

The American Psychological Association makes a number
of recommendations for formatting a paper and preparing a list of references. The following guidelines are consistent with advice given in the *Publication Manual of the
American Psychological Association*, 6th ed. (Washington,
DC: APA, 2010).

39a APA manuscript format

Formatting the paper The explanations and examples in 39a and 39b for formatting student papers in the social sciences are consistent with APA's guidelines for papers prepared for publication and with typical requirements for undergraduate papers.

Title page Most instructors will want you to include a title page. See pages 199 and 202.

Page numbers and running head Number all pages with arabic numerals (1, 2, 3, and so on) in the upper right corner about one-half inch from the top of the page. Flush with the left margin and on the same line as the page number, type a running head consisting of the title of the paper (shortened to no more than fifty characters) in all capital letters. (See pp. 200–01 and 203–04.) On the title page only, include the words "Running head" followed by a colon before the title. (See pp. 199 and 202.)

Margins and line spacing Use margins of one inch on all sides of the page. Left-align the text. Double-space throughout the paper.

Capitalization, italics, and quotation marks Capitalize all words of four letters or more in titles of works and in headings that appear in the text of the paper. Capitalize the first word after a colon if the word begins a complete sentence.

Italicize the titles of books, periodicals, and other long works, such as Web sites. Use quotation marks around the titles of periodical articles, short stories, poems, and other short works.

NOTE: APA has different requirements for titles in the reference list. See page 198.

Long quotations and footnotes See page 170 for APA's guidelines for formatting long quotations. Place footnotes at the bottom of the page on which the text reference occurs. Begin each note with the superscript arabic numeral that corresponds to the number in the text. Indent the first line one-half inch. See page 200.

Abstract If your instructor requires one, include an abstract on its own page after the title page. Center the word "Abstract" one inch from the top of the page.

An abstract is a 100-to-150-word overview of your
essay. It should express your main idea and key points; it
might also suggest any implications or applications of the
research you discuss in the paper.

Headings Although headings are not always necessary,
their use is encouraged in the social sciences. For college
papers, one level of heading is usually sufficient.

In APA style, major headings are centered and boldface.
Second-level headings, if any, are flush left and boldface. Capitalize the first word of the heading, along with
all other words except articles, short prepositions, and
coordinating conjunctions.

Visuals APA classifies visuals as tables and figures (figures
include graphs, charts, drawings, and photographs).

Label each table with an arabic numeral (Table 1,
Table 2) and provide a clear title. The label and title should
appear on separate lines above the table, flush left and
double-spaced. Below the table, give its source in a note.

Note. From "Innovation Roles: From Souls of Fire to Devil's
Advocates," by M. Meyer, 2000, *The Journal of Business
Communication, 37*, p. 338.

For each figure, place a label and a caption below the
figure, flush left and double-spaced. They need not appear
on separate lines.

Preparing the list of references Begin your list of references on a new page at the end of the paper. Center
the title "References" one inch from the top of the page.
Double-space throughout. For sample reference lists, see
pages 201, 204, and 206.

Indenting entries Type the first line of each entry flush
left and indent any additional lines one-half inch, as
shown on pages 201, 204, and 206.

Alphabetizing the list Alphabetize the reference list by
the last names of the authors (or editors); when a work
has no author or editor, alphabetize by the first word of
the title other than *A*, *An*, or *The*.

If you list two or more works by the same author,
arrange the entries by year, the earliest first. If you
include two or more works by the same author in the
same year, arrange them alphabetically by title. Add the

letters "a," "b," and so on in the parentheses after the year. For journal articles, use only the year and the letter: (2009a). For articles in magazines and newspapers, use the full date and the letter in the reference list: (2009a, July 17); use only the year and the letter in in-text citations.

Authors' names Invert all authors' names and use initials instead of first names. Separate the names with commas. With two to seven authors, use an ampersand (&) before the last author's name. If there are eight or more authors, give the first six authors, three ellipsis dots, and the last author (see item 3, p. 181).

Titles of books and articles Italicize the titles and subtitles of books. Do not italicize or use quotation marks around the titles of articles. Capitalize only the first word of the title and subtitle (and all proper nouns). Capitalize names of periodicals as you would capitalize them normally (see 22c).

Abbreviations for page numbers Abbreviations for "page" and "pages" ("p." and "pp.") are used before page numbers of newspaper articles and articles in edited books (see item 11 on p. 183 and item 20 on p. 185) but not before page numbers of articles in magazines and scholarly journals (see items 8–10 on p. 183).

Breaking a URL or DOI When a URL or a DOI (digital object identifier) must be divided, break it after a double slash or before any other mark of punctuation. Do not insert a hyphen, and do not add a period at the end.

39b Sample APA pages

On the following pages are excerpts from a review of the literature paper written for a psychology class, a nursing practice paper, and a paper written for a business class.

MODELS hackerhandbooks.com/pocket
  > Model papers > APA papers: Mirano
                  > APA annotated bibliography: Haddad
                  > APA nursing practice paper: Riss
                  > APA business proposal: Ratajczak

Sample APA title page

[1] Running head: CAN MEDICATION CURE OBESITY IN CHILDREN?   1 [2]

Can Medication Cure Obesity in Children?

A Review of the Literature

[3] Luisa Mirano

Northwest-Shoals Community College

Author Note

[4]   This paper was prepared for Psychology 108, Section B, taught by
Professor Kang.

[1] Short title in all capital letters on all pages; words "Running
head" on title page only. [2] Arabic page number on all pages.
[3] Full title and writer's name and affiliation, centered.
[4] Author's note (optional) for extra information.

(Annotations indicate APA-style formatting and effective writing.)

Sample APA page

Can Medication Cure Obesity in Children?
1
A Review of the Literature

In March 2004, U.S. Surgeon General Richard Carmona called attention to a health problem in the United States that, until recently, has been overlooked: childhood obesity. Carmona said that **2** the "astounding" 15% child obesity rate constitutes an "epidemic." Since the early 1980s, that rate has "doubled in children and tripled in adolescents." Now more than 9 million children are classified as obese.[1] This literature review considers whether the use of medication is a promising approach for solving the childhood obesity problem by responding to the following questions:

3
1. What are the implications of childhood obesity?
2. Is medication effective at treating childhood obesity?
3. Is medication safe for children?
4. Is medication the best solution?

4 Understanding the limitations of medical treatments for children highlights the complexity of the childhood obesity problem in the United States and underscores the need for physicians, advocacy groups, and policymakers to search for other solutions.

5   **What Are the Implications of Childhood Obesity?**

Obesity can be a devastating problem from both an individual and a societal perspective. Obesity puts children at risk for a number of medical complications, including Type 2 diabetes, hypertension,

6   [1]Obesity is measured in terms of body-mass index (BMI): weight in kilograms divided by square of height in meters. An adolescent with a BMI in the 95th percentile for his or her age and gender is considered obese.

---

1 Full title, centered. **2** Signal phrase introduces source.
3 Questions provide organization. **4** Paper's thesis.
5 First-level heading, boldface and centered. **6** Footnote defines essential term without interrupting text.

Sample APA list of references

CAN MEDICATION CURE OBESITY IN CHILDREN?   9

1 References

2 Berkowitz, R. I., Wadden, T. A., Tershakovec, A. M., & Cronquist, J. L.
(2003). Behavior therapy and sibutramine for the treatment
of adolescent obesity. *Journal of the American Medical
Association, 289,* 1805-1812.

Carmona, R. H. (2004, March 2). *The growing epidemic of childhood
3 obesity.* Testimony before the Subcommittee on Competition,
Foreign Commerce, and Infrastructure of the U.S. Senate
Committee on Commerce, Science, and Transportation.
Retrieved from http://www.hhs.gov/asl/testify/t040302.html

Critser, G. (2003). *Fat land.* Boston, MA: Houghton Mifflin.

Duenwald, M. (2004, January 6). Slim pickings: Looking beyond ephedra.
The New York Times, p. F1. Retrieved from http://nytimes.com/

4 Henry J. Kaiser Family Foundation. (2004, February). *The role of
media in childhood obesity.* Retrieved from http://www.kff.org
/entmedia/7030.cfm

Hilts, P. J. (2002, March 20). Petition asks for removal of diet drug
from market. *The New York Times,* p. A26. Retrieved from http://
nytimes.com/

Hoppin, A. G., & Taveras, E. M. (2004, June 25). Assessment and
management of childhood and adolescent obesity. *Clinical
Update.* Retrieved from http://www.medscape.com/viewarticle
/481633

McDuffie, J. R., Calis, K. A., Uwaifo, G. I., Sebring, N. G., Fallon,
E. M., Hubbard, V. S., & Yanovski, J. A. (2002). Three-month
tolerability of orlistat in adolescents with obesity-related
comorbid conditions. *Obesity Research, 10,* 642-650.

1 Reference list on new page, heading centered.
2 Authors' names inverted and alphabetized. **3** First line of entry
flush left, subsequent lines indented ½". **4** Double-spaced
throughout.

Sample APA title page

[1] Running head: ALL AND HTN IN ONE CLIENT   1 [2]

Acute Lymphoblastic Leukemia and Hypertension in One Client:

A Nursing Practice Paper

[3]   Julie Riss

George Mason University

Author Note

[4]   This paper was prepared for Nursing 451, taught by Professor

Durham. The author wishes to thank the nursing staff of Milltown

General Hospital for help in understanding client care and diagnosis.

[1] Short title in all capital letters on all pages; words "Running head" on title page only. [2] Arabic page number on all pages. [3] Full title and writer's name and affiliation, centered. [4] Author's note (optional) for extra information.

(Annotations indicate APA-style formatting and effective writing.)

Sample APA page

1 Acute Lymphoblastic Leukemia and Hypertension in One Client:
A Nursing Practice Paper

2 **Historical and Physical Assessment**

3 **Physical History**

E.B. is a 16-year-old white male 5'10" tall weighing 190 lb. He was
admitted to the hospital on April 14, 2006, due to decreased platelets
and a need for a PRBC transfusion. He was diagnosed in October 2005
with T-cell acute lymphoblastic leukemia (ALL), after a 2-week **4**
period of decreased energy, decreased oral intake, easy bruising, and
petechia. The client had experienced a 20-lb weight loss in the previous
6 months. At the time of diagnosis, his CBC showed a WBC count of
32, an H & H of 13/38, and a platelet count of 34,000. He began
induction chemotherapy on October 12, 2005, receiving vincristine,
6-mercaptopurine, doxorubicin, intrathecal methotrexate, and then high-
dose methotrexate per protocol. During his hospital stay he required
packed red cells and platelets on two different occasions. He was
diagnosed with hypertension (HTN) due to systolic blood pressure
readings consistently ranging between 130s and 150s and was started
on nifedipine. E.B. has a history of mild ADHD, migraines, and deep
vein thrombosis (DVT). He has tolerated the induction and consolidation
phases of chemotherapy well and is now in the maintenance phase.

5 **Psychosocial History**

There is a possibility of a depressive episode a year previously
when he would not attend school. He got into serious trouble and was
sent to a shelter for 1 month. He currently lives with his mother, father,
and 14-year-old sister.

Family History

Paternal: prostate cancer and hypertension in grandfather

---

1 Full title, centered. **2** First-level heading, boldface and
centered. **3** Second-level heading, boldface and flush left.
4 Writer's summary of client's medical history. **5** Headings guide
readers and define sections.

Sample APA list of references

ALL AND HTN IN ONE CLIENT   10

1 References

2 Hockenberry, M. (2003). *Wong's nursing care of infants and children.*
St. Louis, MO: Mosby.

3 Lemone, P., & Burke, K. (2004). *Medical surgical nursing: Critical* **4**
thinking in client care. Upper Saddle River, NJ: Pearson   **5**
Education.

1 Reference list on new page, heading centered.
2 Authors' names inverted and alphabetized. **3** First line of entry
flush left, subsequent lines indented ½". **4** Ampersand used with
multiple authors. **5** Double-spaced throughout.

Sample proposal, APA style

1 MEMORANDUM

To: Jay Crosson, Senior Vice President, Human Resources

From: Kelly Ratajczak, Intern, Purchasing Department

Subject: Proposal to Add a Wellness Program

Date: April 24, 2006

Health care costs are rising. In the long run, implementing a wellness **2** program in our corporate culture will decrease the company's health care costs.

Research indicates that nearly 70% of health care costs are from common illnesses related to high blood pressure, overweight, lack of exercise, high cholesterol, stress, poor nutrition, and other preventable health **3** issues (Hall, 2006). Health care costs are a major expense for most businesses, and they do not reflect costs due to the loss of productivity or absenteeism. A wellness program would address most, if not all, of these health care issues and related costs.

Benefits of Healthier Employees **4**

Not only would a wellness program substantially reduce costs associated with employee health care, but our company would prosper through many other benefits. Businesses that have wellness programs show a lower cost in production, fewer sick days, and healthier employees ("Workplace Health," 2006). Our healthier employees will help to cut not only our production and absenteeism costs but also potential costs such as higher turnover because of low employee morale.

Implementing the Program

Implementing a good wellness program means making small changes to the work environment, starting with a series of information sessions.

1 First page in memo format. **2** Clear point in first paragraph. **3** Introduction provides background information. **4** Headings define sections.

(Annotations indicate typical business-style formatting and effective writing.)

Sample APA list of references

1 References

2 Hall, B. (2006). Good health pays off! Fundamentals of health promotion incentives. *Journal of Deferred Compensation 11*(2), 16-26. Retrieved from http://www.aspenpublishers.com/

3 Springer, D. (2005, October 28). Key to business success? *La Crosse Tribune*. Retrieved from http://lacrossetribune.com/

4 Workplace health and productivity programs lower absenteeism, costs. (2006). *Managing benefit plans 6*(2), 1-4. Retrieved from http://www.ioma.com/

1 Reference list on new page, heading centered.
2 Authors' names inverted and alphabetized. **3** First line of entry flush left, subsequent lines indented ½". **4** Work with no author listed by title.

Chicago Papers

Many history instructors and some humanities instructors require the *Chicago*-style footnotes or endnotes explained in section 43. When you write a paper using sources, you face three main challenges in addition to documenting those sources: (1) supporting a thesis, (2) avoiding plagiarism, and (3) integrating quotations and other source material.

40 Supporting a thesis

Most assignments ask you to form a thesis, or main idea, and to support that thesis with well-organized evidence.

40a Forming a thesis

A thesis is a one-sentence (or occasionally a two-sentence) statement of your central idea. Usually your thesis will appear at the end of the first paragraph (see the example on p. 240).

The thesis of your paper will be your reasoned and informed answer to the central research question you pose, as in the following examples.

RESEARCH QUESTION

To what extent was Confederate Major General Nathan Bedford Forrest responsible for the massacre of Union troops at Fort Pillow?

POSSIBLE THESIS

Although we will never know whether Nathan Bedford Forrest directly ordered the massacre of Union troops at Fort Pillow, evidence suggests that he was responsible for it.

RESEARCH QUESTION

How did the 365-day combat tour affect soldiers' experiences of the Vietnam War?

POSSIBLE THESIS

Letters and diaries written by combat soldiers in Vietnam reveal that when soldiers' tours of duty were shortened, their investment in the war shifted from fighting for victory to fighting for survival.

PRACTICE hackerhandbooks.com/pocket
> *Chicago* > 40–1 and 40–2

Each of these thesis statements expresses a view on a debatable issue—an issue about which intelligent, well-meaning people might disagree. The writer's job is to convince such readers that this view is worth taking seriously.

40b Organizing your ideas

The body of your paper will consist of evidence in support of your thesis. To get started, sketch an informal plan that organizes your evidence. The student who wrote about Fort Pillow used a simple list of questions as the blueprint for his paper. These questions became headings that help readers follow the writer's line of argument.

What happened at Fort Pillow?

Did Forrest order the massacre?

Can Forrest be held responsible for the massacre?

40c Using sources to inform and support your argument

Sources can play several different roles as you develop your points.

Providing background information or context   You can use facts and statistics to support generalizations or to establish the importance of your topic.

Explaining terms or concepts   Explain words, phrases, or ideas important to your topic that may be unfamiliar to readers. Quoting or paraphrasing a source can help you define terms and concepts in accessible language.

Supporting your claims   Back up your assertions with facts, examples, and other evidence from your research.

Lending authority to your argument   Expert opinion can give weight to your argument. But don't rely on experts to make your argument for you. Construct your argument in your own words and cite authorities in the field to support your position.

Anticipating and countering objections   Do not ignore sources that seem contrary to your position or that offer arguments different from your own. Instead, use them to raise opposing ideas and interpretations before you counter them.

41 Avoiding plagiarism

Your research paper is a collaboration between you and your sources. To be fair and ethical, you must acknowledge your debt to the writers of those sources. When you acknowledge your sources, you avoid plagiarism, a serious academic offense.

Three different acts are considered plagiarism: (1) failing to cite quotations and borrowed ideas, (2) failing to enclose borrowed language in quotation marks, and (3) failing to put summaries and paraphrases in your own words.

41a Citing quotations and borrowed ideas

When you cite sources, you give credit to writers from whom you've borrowed words and ideas. You also let your readers know where your information comes from so that they can evaluate the original source.

You must cite anything you borrow from a source, including direct quotations; statistics and other specific facts; visuals such as cartoons, graphs, and diagrams; and any ideas you present in a summary or a paraphrase.

The only exception is common knowledge—information your readers could easily locate. For example, most encyclopedias will tell readers that the Korean War ended in 1953 and that President Theodore Roosevelt was the first American to receive a Nobel Prize. When you have seen certain general information repeatedly in your reading, you don't need to cite it. However, when information has appeared in only a few sources, when it is highly specific (as with statistics), or when it is controversial, you should cite it.

Chicago citations consist of superscript numbers in the text of the paper that refer readers to notes with corresponding numbers either at the foot of the page (footnotes) or at the end of the paper (endnotes).

TEXT

Governor John Andrew was not allowed to recruit black soldiers
from out of state. "Ostensibly," writes Peter Burchard, "no
recruiting was done outside Massachusetts, but it was an open
secret that Andrew's agents were working far and wide."[1]

NOTE

  1. Peter Burchard, *One Gallant Rush: Robert Gould Shaw and
His Brave Black Regiment* (New York: St. Martin's, 1965), 85.

For detailed advice on using *Chicago* notes, see 43a.
When you use footnotes or endnotes, you will usually
need to provide a bibliography as well (see 43b).

41b Enclosing borrowed language in quotation marks

To show that you are using a source's exact phrases or
sentences, you must enclose them in quotation marks.
To omit the quotation marks is to claim—falsely—that
the language is your own. Such an omission is plagiarism
even if you have cited the source.

ORIGINAL SOURCE

> For many Southerners it was psychologically impossible
> to see a black man bearing arms as anything but an
> incipient slave uprising complete with arson, murder,
> pillage, and rapine.
> —Dudley Taylor Cornish, *The Sable Arm: Negro
> Troops in the Union Army, 1861–1865*, p. 158

PLAGIARISM

According to Civil War historian Dudley Taylor Cornish, for many
Southerners it was psychologically impossible to see a black man
bearing arms as anything but an incipient slave uprising complete
with arson, murder, pillage, and rapine.[2]

BORROWED LANGUAGE IN QUOTATION MARKS

According to Civil War historian Dudley Taylor Cornish, "For many
Southerners it was psychologically impossible to see a black man
bearing arms as anything but an incipient slave uprising complete
with arson, murder, pillage, and rapine."[2]

NOTE: When quoted sentences are set off from the text by
indenting, quotation marks are not needed (see p. 214).

41c Putting summaries and paraphrases in your own words

A summary condenses information; a paraphrase conveys information in about the same number of words as in the original source. When you summarize or paraphrase, you must name the source and restate the source's meaning in your own words.

In the following example, the paraphrase is plagiarized—even though the source is cited—because too much of its language is borrowed from the source without quotation marks. The underlined phrases have been copied exactly (without quotation marks). In addition, the writer has closely followed the sentence structure of the original source, merely making a few substitutions (such as *Fifty percent* for *Half* and *angered and perhaps frightened* for *enraged and perhaps terrified*).

ORIGINAL SOURCE

> Half of the force holding Fort Pillow were Negroes, former slaves now enrolled in the Union Army. Toward them Forrest's troops had the fierce, bitter animosity of men who had been educated to regard the colored race as inferior and who for the first time had encountered that race armed and fighting against white men. The sight enraged and perhaps terrified many of the Confederates and aroused in them the ugly spirit of a lynching mob.
>
> —Albert Castel, "The Fort Pillow Massacre," pp. 46–47

PLAGIARISM: UNACCEPTABLE BORROWING

Albert Castel suggests that much of the brutality at Fort Pillow can be traced to racial attitudes. Fifty percent of the troops <u>holding Fort Pillow were Negroes, former slaves</u> who had joined <u>the Union Army. Toward them Forrest's</u> soldiers displayed the savage hatred <u>of men who had been</u> taught the inferiority of blacks <u>and who for the first time had</u> confronted them <u>armed and fighting against white men.</u> The vision angered and perhaps frightened <u>the Confederates and aroused in them the ugly spirit of a lynching mob.</u>[3]

To avoid plagiarizing an author's language, don't look at the source while you are summarizing or paraphrasing. After you've restated the author's idea in your own words, return to the source and check that you haven't used the author's language or sentence structure or misrepresented the author's ideas.

ACCEPTABLE PARAPHRASE

Albert Castel suggests that much of the brutality at Fort Pillow
can be traced to racial attitudes. Nearly half of the Union troops
were blacks, men whom the Confederates had been raised to
consider their inferiors. The shock and perhaps fear of facing armed
ex-slaves in battle for the first time may well have unleashed the
fury that led to the massacre.[3]

42 Integrating sources

Quotations, summaries, paraphrases, and facts will support your argument, but they cannot speak for you. You
can use several strategies to integrate information from
research sources into your paper while maintaining your
own voice.

42a Using quotations appropriately

Limiting your use of quotations   In your writing, keep
the emphasis on your own words. Do not quote excessively. It is not always necessary to quote full sentences
from a source. Often you can integrate words or phrases
from a source into your own sentence structure.

As Hurst has pointed out, until "an outcry erupted in the Northern
press," even the Confederates did not deny that there had been a
massacre at Fort Pillow.[4]

Union surgeon Dr. Charles Fitch testified that after he was in
custody he "saw" Confederate soldiers "kill every negro that
made his appearance dressed in Federal uniform."[5]

Using the ellipsis mark   You can use the ellipsis mark
(three periods, with spaces between) to condense a quoted
passage and indicate that you have omitted words. What
remains must be grammatically complete.

Union surgeon Fitch's testimony that all women and children had
been evacuated from Fort Pillow before the attack conflicts with
Forrest's report: "We captured . . . about 40 negro women and
children."[6]

The writer has omitted several words not relevant to the issue at hand: *164 Federals, 75 negro troops, and.*

When you want to omit a full sentence or more, use a period before the three ellipsis dots. For an example, see the long quotation at the bottom of this page.

You do not need an ellipsis mark at the beginning or at the end of a quotation. Readers will understand that the quoted material is taken from a longer passage.

Using brackets Brackets allow you to insert your own words into quoted material to clarify a confusing reference or to make the quoted words fit grammatically into the context of your writing.

According to Albert Castel, "It can be reasonably argued that he [Forrest] was justified in believing that the approaching steamships intended to aid the garrison [at Fort Pillow]."[7]

NOTE: Use [*sic*], italicized and with brackets around it, to indicate that an error in a quoted sentence appears in the original source. (See the example below.)

Setting off long quotations *Chicago* style allows you to set off a long quotation or run it into your text. For emphasis, you may want to set off a quotation of more than five lines; you should always set off quotations of ten lines or more. To set off a quotation, indent it one-half inch from the left margin and keep the standard right margin. Double-space the quotation.

Introduce long quotations with an informative sentence, usually ending in a colon. Because the indented format tells readers that the words are taken directly from the source, you don't need quotation marks.

In a letter home, Confederate officer Achilles V. Clark recounted what happened at Fort Pillow:

> Words cannot describe the scene. The poor deluded negroes would run up to our men fall upon their knees and with uplifted hands scream for mercy but they were ordered to their feet and then shot down. The whitte [*sic*] men fared but little better. . . . I with several others tried to stop the butchery and at one time had partially succeeded, but Gen. Forrest ordered them shot down like dogs, and the carnage continued.[8]

42b Using signal phrases

Whenever you include a direct quotation, a paraphrase, or a summary in your paper, prepare readers for it with a *signal phrase*. A signal phrase usually names the author of the source and often provides some context for the source material. The first time you mention an author, use the full name: *Shelby Foote argues*. . . . When you refer to the author again, you may use the last name only: *Foote raises an important question.*

See the chart on page 216 for a list of verbs commonly used in signal phrases. Note that *Chicago* style calls for verbs in the present tense or present perfect tense (*points out* or *has pointed out*) to introduce source material unless you include a date that specifies the time of the original author's writing.

Marking boundaries Avoid dropping quotations into your text without warning. Provide clear signal phrases, including at least the author's name. A signal phrase indicates the boundary between your words and the source's words.

DROPPED QUOTATION

Unionists claimed that their troops had abandoned their arms and were in full retreat. "The Confederates, however, all agreed that the Union troops retreated to the river with arms in their hands."[9]

QUOTATION WITH SIGNAL PHRASE

Unionists claimed that their troops had abandoned their arms and were in full retreat. "The Confederates, however," writes historian Albert Castel, "all agreed that the Union troops retreated to the river with arms in their hands."[9]

Introducing summaries and paraphrases Introduce most summaries and paraphrases with a signal phrase that mentions the author and places the material in context. Readers will then understand where the summary or paraphrase begins.

The signal phrase (highlighted) in the following example shows that the whole paragraph, not just the last sentence, is based on the source.

According to Jack Hurst, official Confederate policy was that black soldiers were to be treated as runaway slaves; in addition,

Using signal phrases in *Chicago* papers

To avoid monotony, try to vary both the language and the placement of your signal phrases.

Model signal phrases

In the words of historian James M. McPherson, ". . ."[1]

As Dudley Taylor Cornish has argued, ". . ."[2]

In a letter to his wife, a Confederate soldier who witnessed the massacre wrote that ". . ."[3]

". . .," claims Benjamin Quarles.[4]

". . .," writes Albert Castel, ". . ."[5]

Shelby Foote offers an intriguing interpretation: ". . ."[6]

Verbs in signal phrases

Are you providing background, explaining a concept, supporting a claim, lending authority, or refuting a belief? Choose a verb that is appropriate for the way you are using the source.

admits	contends	reasons
agrees	declares	refutes
argues	denies	rejects
asserts	emphasizes	reports
believes	insists	responds
claims	notes	suggests
compares	observes	thinks
confirms	points out	writes

NOTE: In *Chicago* style, use the present tense or present perfect tense to introduce quotations or other material from nonfiction sources: *Foote points out* or *Foote has pointed out*. Use the past tense only to emphasize that the author's language or opinion was articulated in the past.

the Confederate Congress decreed that white Union officers commanding black troops be killed. Confederate Lieutenant General Kirby Smith went one step further, declaring that he would kill all captured black troops. Smith's policy never met with strong opposition from the Richmond government.[10]

Putting source material in context Provide context for any source material that appears in your paper. A signal phrase can help you connect your own ideas with those of another writer by clarifying how the source will contribute to your paper. It's a good idea to embed source material, especially long quotations, between sentences of your own that interpret the source and link the source to your argument.

QUOTATION WITH EFFECTIVE CONTEXT

In a respected biography of Nathan Bedford Forrest, Hurst suggests that the temperamental Forrest "may have ragingly ordered a massacre and even intended to carry it out — until he rode inside the fort and viewed the horrifying result" and ordered it stopped.[11] While this is an intriguing interpretation of events, even Hurst would probably admit that it is merely speculation.

NOTE: When you bring other sources into a conversation about your research topic, you are synthesizing sources. For more on synthesis, see 31c.

Integrating statistics and other facts   When you cite a statistic or another specific fact, a signal phrase is often not necessary. In most cases, readers will understand that the citation refers to the statistic or fact (not the whole paragraph).

Of 295 white troops garrisoned at Fort Pillow, 168 were taken prisoner. Black troops fared worse, with only 58 of 262 captured and most of the rest presumably killed or wounded.[12]

There is nothing wrong, however, with using a signal phrase.

43   *Chicago* documentation style (notes and bibliography)

In history and some humanities courses, you may be asked to use the documentation system set forth in *The Chicago Manual of Style*, 16th ed. (Chicago: University of Chicago Press, 2010). In *Chicago* style, superscript numbers in the text of the paper refer readers to notes with corresponding numbers either at the bottom of the page (footnotes) or at the end of the paper (endnotes). A bibliography is often required as well.

PRACTICE   hackerhandbooks.com/pocket
   > *Chicago* > 43–1 to 43–8

43a First and subsequent notes for a source

The first time you cite a source, the note should include publication information for that work as well as the page number on which the passage you cite may be found.

> 1. Peter Burchard, *One Gallant Rush: Robert Gould Shaw and His Brave Black Regiment* (New York: St. Martin's, 1965), 85.

For subsequent references to a source you have already cited, you may simply give the author's last name, a short form of the title, and the page or pages cited. A short form of the title of a book is italicized; a short form of the title of an article is put in quotation marks.

> 4. Burchard, *One Gallant Rush*, 31.

When you have two consecutive notes from the same source, you may use "Ibid." (meaning "in the same place") and the page number for the second note. Use "Ibid." alone if the page number is the same.

> 5. Jack Hurst, *Nathan Bedford Forrest: A Biography* (New York: Knopf, 1993), 8.
>
> 6. Ibid., 174.

43b *Chicago*-style bibliography

A bibliography, which appears at the end of your paper, lists every work you have cited in your notes; in addition, it may include works that you consulted but did not cite. For advice on constructing the list, see pages 237–38. A sample bibliography appears on page 242.

NOTE: If you include a bibliography, *The Chicago Manual of Style* suggests that you shorten all notes, including the first reference to a source, as described in 43a. Check with your instructor, however, to see whether using a shortened note for a first reference to a source is acceptable.

43c Model notes and bibliography entries

The following models are consistent with guidelines in *The Chicago Manual of Style*, 16th ed. For each type of source, a note appears first, followed by a bibliography entry. The note shows the format you should use when citing a source for the first time. For subsequent citations of a source, use shortened notes (see 43a).

Some online sources, especially periodical articles, contain a permanent locator called a digital object identifier (DOI). Use the DOI, when available, in place of a URL in citations of online sources.

Books (print and online)

■ 1. Basic format for a print book

1. Mary N. Woods, *Beyond the Architect's Eye: Photographs and the American Built Environment* (Philadelphia: University of Pennsylvania Press, 2009), 45.

Woods, Mary N. *Beyond the Architect's Eye: Photographs and the American Built Environment*. Philadelphia: University of Pennsylvania Press, 2009.

For an illustrated citation of a print book, see page 221.

■ 2. Basic format for an online book

2. John Dewey, *Democracy and Education* (1916; ILT Digital Classics, 1994), chap. 4, http://www.ilt.columbia.edu/publications/dewey.html.

Dewey, John. *Democracy and Education*. 1916. ILT Digital Classics, 1994. http://www.ilt.columbia.edu/publications/dewey.html.

■ 3. Basic format for an e-book (electronic book)

3. Leo Tolstoy, *War and Peace*, trans. Richard Pevear and Larissa Volokhonsky (New York: Knopf, 2007), Kindle edition, vol. 1, pt. 1, chap. 3.

Tolstoy, Leo. *War and Peace*. Translated by Richard Pevear and Larissa Volokhonsky. New York: Knopf, 2007. Kindle edition.

Citation at a glance
Book (*Chicago*)

To cite a print book in *Chicago* style, include the following elements:

1 Author
2 Title and subtitle
3 City of publication
4 Publisher
5 Year of publication
6 Page number(s) cited (for notes)

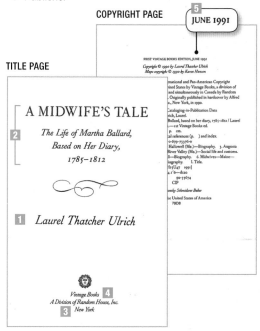

COPYRIGHT PAGE

5 JUNE 1991

FIRST VINTAGE BOOKS EDITION, JUNE 1991

Copyright © 1990 by Laurel Thatcher Ulrich
Maps copyright © 1990 by Karen Hansen

...national and Pan-American Copyright
...nited States by Vintage Books, a division of
...and simultaneously in Canada by Random
... Originally published in hardcover by Alfred
..., New York, in 1990.

...Cataloging-in-Publication Data
...rich, Laurel.
...Ballard, based on her diary, 1785–1812 / Laurel
...—1st Vintage Books ed.
... p.   cm.
...al references (p.   ) and index.
...0-679-73376-0
...Hallowell (Me.)—Biography.   3. Augusta
...River Valley (Me.)—Social life and customs.
...ll—Biography.   6. Midwives—Maine—
...iography.   I. Title.
...815U47   1991]
...4.1'6—dc20
...   90-55674
...   CIP

...nsky Schneidaw Baker

...he United States of America
...   7908

TITLE PAGE

A MIDWIFE'S TALE

2 *The Life of Martha Ballard,*
Based on Her Diary,
1785–1812

1 *Laurel Thatcher Ulrich*

Vintage Books **4**
A Division of Random House, Inc.
3 *New York*

NOTE

┌──────1──────┐ ┌──────2──────
1. Laurel Thatcher Ulrich, *A Midwife's Tale: The Life of*

────────────────────────┐ ┌─3─┐
Martha Ballard, Based on Her Diary, 1785-1812 (New York:
┌──4──┐ ┌─5─┐ ┌─6─┐
Vintage, 1991), 174.

BIBLIOGRAPHY

┌────────1────────┐ ┌────────2────────
Ulrich, Laurel Thatcher. *A Midwife's Tale: The Life of Martha*

──────────────┐ ┌─3─┐
Ballard, Based on Her Diary, 1785-1812. New York:
┌──4──┐ ┌─5─┐
Vintage, 1991.

For more on citing print books in *Chicago* style, see pages 220–26.

4. Two or three authors

4. Chris Stringer and Peter Andrews, *The Complete World of Human Evolution* (London: Thames and Hudson, 2005), 45.

Stringer, Chris, and Peter Andrews. *The Complete World of Human Evolution*. London: Thames and Hudson, 2005.

5. Four or more authors
In the note, give the first author's name followed by "et al." (for "and others"); in the bibliography entry, list all authors' names.

5. Lynn Hunt et al., *The Making of the West: Peoples and Cultures,* 3rd ed. (Boston: Bedford/St. Martin's, 2009), 541.

Hunt, Lynn, Thomas R. Martin, Barbara H. Rosenwein, R. Po-chia Hsia, and Bonnie G. Smith. *The Making of the West: Peoples and Cultures*. 3rd ed. Boston: Bedford/St. Martin's, 2009.

6. Unknown author

6. *The Men's League Handbook on Women's Suffrage* (London, 1912), 23.

The Men's League Handbook on Women's Suffrage. London, 1912.

7. Multiple works by the same author
In the bibliography, use six hyphens in place of the author's name in the second and subsequent entries. Arrange the entries alphabetically by title.

Harper, Raymond L. *A History of Chesapeake, Virginia*. Charleston, SC: History Press, 2008.

------. *South Norfolk, Virginia, 1661-2005*. Charleston, SC: History Press, 2005.

8. Edited work without an author

8. Jack Beatty, ed., *Colossus: How the Corporation Changed America* (New York: Broadway Books, 2001), 127.

Beatty, Jack, ed. *Colossus: How the Corporation Changed America*. New York: Broadway Books, 2001.

9. Edited work with an author

9. Ted Poston, *A First Draft of History*, ed. Kathleen A. Hauke (Athens: University of Georgia Press, 2000), 46.

Poston, Ted. *A First Draft of History*. Edited by Kathleen A. Hauke. Athens: University of Georgia Press, 2000.

■ 10. Translated work

10. Tonino Guerra, *Abandoned Places*, trans. Adria Bernardi
(Barcelona: Guernica, 1999), 71.

Guerra, Tonino. *Abandoned Places*. Translated by Adria Bernardi.
     Barcelona: Guernica, 1999.

■ 11. Edition other than the first

11. Walter Muir Whitehill and Lawrence W. Kennedy, *Boston:
A Topographical History*, 3rd ed. (Cambridge, MA: Belknap Press of
Harvard University Press, 2000), 58.

Whitehill, Walter Muir, and Lawrence W. Kennedy. *Boston: A
     Topographical History*. 3rd ed. Cambridge, MA: Belknap Press
     of Harvard University Press, 2000.

■ 12. Volume in a multivolume work

12. Charles Reagan Wilson, ed., *Myth, Manner, and Memory*,
vol. 4 of *The New Encyclopedia of Southern Culture* (Chapel Hill:
University of North Carolina Press, 2006), 198.

Wilson, Charles Reagan, ed. *Myth, Manner, and Memory*. Vol. 4
     of *The New Encyclopedia of Southern Culture*. Chapel Hill:
     University of North Carolina Press, 2006.

■ 13. Selection in an anthology   Begin with the author
and title of the selection and then give the title and editor
(if any) of the anthology.

13. Zora Neale Hurston, "From *Dust Tracks on a Road*,"
in *The Norton Book of American Autobiography*, ed. Jay Parini
(New York: Norton, 1999), 336.

Hurston, Zora Neale. "From *Dust Tracks on a Road*." In *The
     Norton Book of American Autobiography*, edited by Jay Parini,
     333-43. New York: Norton, 1999.

■ 14. Letter in a published collection   If the letter writer's
name is part of the book title, begin the note with the writer's last name but begin the bibliography entry with the full
name. (For an illustrated citation of a letter in a published
collection, see pp. 224–25.)

14. Mitford to Esmond Romilly, 29 July 1940, in *Decca: The
Letters of Jessica Mitford*, ed. Peter Y. Sussman (New York: Knopf,
2006), 55-56.

Mitford, Jessica. *Decca: The Letters of Jessica Mitford*. Edited by
     Peter Y. Sussman. New York: Knopf, 2006.

Citation at a glance
Letter in a published collection (*Chicago*)

To cite a letter in a published collection in *Chicago* style, include the following elements:

1. Author of letter
2. Recipient of letter
3. Date of letter
4. Title of collection
5. Editor of collection
6. City of publication
7. Publisher
8. Year of publication
9. Page number(s) cited (for notes); page range of letter (for bibliography)

TITLE PAGE

> # TO HIS EXCELLENCY THOMAS JEFFERSON [4]
>
> .... *Letters to a President* ....
>
> ### JACK McLAUGHLIN [5]
>
> AVON BOOKS [7] • NEW YORK [6]

COPYRIGHT PAGE

Copyright © 1991 [8]

AVON BOOKS
A division of
The Hearst Corporation
1350 Avenue of the Americas
New York, New York 10019

Copyright © 1991 by Jack McLaughlin
Cover painting by Giraudon/Art Resource, New York
Published by arrangement with W.W. Norton & Company, Inc.
Library of Congress Catalog Card Number: 90-27824
ISBN: 0-380-71964-9

The W.W. Norton & Company, Inc. edition contains the following Library of Congress Cataloging in Publication Data:
McLaughlin, Jack.
  To his excellency Thomas Jefferson : Letters to a president/ selected and edited by Jack McLaughlin.
  p. cm.
Includes bibliographical references and index. 1. Jefferson, Thomas, 1743–1826—Correspondence. 2. Working class—United States—Correspondence. 3. Presidents—United States—Correspondence. I. Jefferson, Thomas, 1743–1826. II. Title.
E332.86 1991
973.4'6' 092—dc20   90-27824

First Avon Trade Books Printing: July 1993

AVON TRADEMARK REG. U.S. PAT. OFF. AND IN OTHER COUNTRIES, MARCA REGISTRADA, HECHO EN U.S.A.

Printed in the U.S.A.

FIRST AND LAST PAGES OF LETTER

Washington 30th. Oct 1805 **3**

His Excellency Ths. Jefferson **2**

Sɪʀ,

I have not the honor to be personally known to your Excellency therefore you will no doubt think it strange to receive this letter from a person of whom you have not the smallest knowledge. But in order to state to your Excellency in as few words as possible the purport of this address, I am a young man, a Roman Catholic who had been born and partly educated in Ireland but finding like many others who had been compelled to Migrate from that Kingdom in consequence of the late troubles which had almost overwhelmed that unhappy Nation That it was impossible for me to do anything in my Native Country. I came into this Country a few years since as an adventurer but having had the [m]isfortune not to be bred to any particular profession which

Patronage *6 1* **9**

your Excellency this very prolix letter which should it please your Excellency to give me some little Office or appointment in that extensive Country of Louisiana It should be my constant endeavour to merit the same by fidelity and an indefatigable attention to whatever business I should be assigned. May I have the satisfaction in whatsoever Country or situation [I] may be in to hear of your Excellencies long continuence of your Natural powers unempaired to conduct the Helm of this Extensive Country which are the sincere wishes of your Excellencies Mo. Obt. Hum. Servt.

1 Jᴏʜɴ O'Nᴇɪʟʟ

NOTE

┌——1——┐ ┌———2———┐ ┌———3———┐
1. John O'Neill to Thomas Jefferson, 30 October 1805,
┌————————4————————┐
in *To His Excellency Thomas Jefferson: Letters to a President,*
┌——5——┐ ┌——6——┐ ┌——7——┐ ┌—8—┐ ┌9┐
ed. Jack McLaughlin (New York: Avon Books, 1991), 61.

BIBLIOGRAPHY

┌——1——┐ ┌——1——┐ ┌———2———┐ ┌——3——┐
O'Neill, John. John O'Neill to Thomas Jefferson, 30 October
┌——┐ ┌————————4————————┐
1805. In *To His Excellency Thomas Jefferson: Letters to*
┌————5————┐ ┌9┐ ┌——6——┐
a President, edited by Jack McLaughlin, 59-61. New York:
┌——7——┐ ┌8┐
Avon Books, 1991.

For another citation of a letter in *Chicago* style, see item 14.

■ **15. Work in a series**

15. R. Keith Schoppa, *The Columbia Guide to Modern Chinese History*, Columbia Guides to Asian History (New York: Columbia University Press, 2000), 256-58.

Schoppa, R. Keith. *The Columbia Guide to Modern Chinese History*. Columbia Guides to Asian History. New York: Columbia University Press, 2000.

■ **16. Encyclopedia or dictionary entry**

16. *Encyclopaedia Britannica*, 15th ed., s.v. "Monroe Doctrine."

The abbreviation "s.v." is for the Latin *sub verbo* ("under the word"). Reference works are usually not included in the bibliography.

■ **17. Sacred text**

17. Matt. 20:4-9 (Revised Standard Version).

17. Qur'an 18:1-3.

Sacred texts are usually not included in the bibliography.

■ **18. Source quoted in another source**

18. Ron Grossman and Charles Leroux, "A Local Outpost of Democracy," *Chicago Tribune,* March 5, 1996, quoted in William Julius Wilson and Richard P. Taub, *There Goes the Neighborhood: Racial, Ethnic, and Class Tensions in Four Chicago Neighborhoods and Their Meaning for America* (New York: Knopf, 2006), 18.

Grossman, Ron, and Charles Leroux. "A Local Outpost of Democracy." *Chicago Tribune,* March 5, 1996. Quoted in William Julius Wilson and Richard P. Taub, *There Goes the Neighborhood: Racial, Ethnic, and Class Tensions in Four Chicago Neighborhoods and Their Meaning for America* (New York: Knopf, 2006), 18.

Articles in periodicals (print and online)

■ **19. Article in a print journal**   Include the volume and issue numbers and the date; end the bibliography entry with the page range of the article. (For an illustrated cita-tion of an article in a print journal, see p. 227.)

19. T. H. Breen, "Will American Consumers Buy a Second American Revolution?," *Journal of American History* 93, no. 2 (2006): 405.

Breen, T. H. "Will American Consumers Buy a Second American Revolution?" *Journal of American History* 93, no. 2 (2006): 404-8.

Citation at a glance
Article in a journal (*Chicago*)

To cite an article in a print journal in *Chicago* style, include the following elements:

1. Author
2. Title of article
3. Title of journal
4. Volume and issue numbers
5. Date of publication
6. Page number(s) cited (for notes); page range of article (for bibliography)

4 **5**

VOLUME 113 · NUMBER 2 · APRIL 2008

TITLE PAGE OF JOURNAL

FIRST PAGE OF ARTICLE

3 The American Historical Review

AMERICAN HISTORICAL ASSOCIATION

VOLUME 113 · NUMBER 2 · APRIL 2008

2 An Age of Imperial Revolutions

1 JEREMY ADELMAN

WHEN THE VENEZUELAN CREOLE FRANCISCO DE MIRANDA led an expeditionary force to the shores of his native land to liberate it from Spanish rule in the summer of 1806, he brought with him a new weapon for making revolutions: a printing press. He hoped that his band of white, black, and mulatto patriots would start a revolt to free a continent with an alliance of swords and ideas. After dawdling for ten days, Miranda learned that royal troops (also white, black, and mulatto) were marching from Caracas. He withdrew before the two multiracial forces could clash. Consider Miranda's reasons for retreat: The nation he sought to free from its chains was not, in his opinion, a nation at all. While Venezuelans yearned for "Civil Liberty," they did not know how to grasp and protect it. They needed a liberation that would tutor them in the ways of liberty and fraternity, to create a nation of virtuous citizens out of a colony of subjects. This was why Miranda treated the printing press, a portable factory of words about liberty and sovereignty, as part of the arsenal of change: he wanted to create public opinion where there was none. But faced with the prospect of a violent clash and a scourge of "opposition and internal divisions," of a war waged mainly with swords, he preferred to pull out and bide his time.¹

Miranda's dilemma—whether or not to move forward knowing how revolutions worked in imperial settings when their protagonists did not presume that their cause was self-evidently bound to triumph—evokes questions about the embedded politics of what we might now call, with a wince, "regime change." As empires gave way to successor states, those regimes began to call themselves nations not in order to cause imperial crises, but as the result of such crises. The study of imperial crises and the study of the origins of nationalism in colonial societies should inform each other more than they do. Bringing these two separate fields of scholarship together, and questioning the tacit and not-so-tacit beliefs upon which they rest, can help us reframe the complex passages from empires to successor states, free

I want to extend my thanks to Howard Adelman, Steve Aron, Tom Bender, Graham Burnett, Josep Cskárates-Esguerra, Josep Pradera, Roy Hora, Dina Khapaeva, and Rafe Blaufarb for their suggestions on this article, and to the *AHR*'s thoughtful reviewers and editors. Versions of this essay were presented as papers at the Universidad San Andrés in Buenos Aires, Smolny College in St. Petersburg, Russia, and the University of Texas at Austin.

¹ Archivo General de Indias (Seville) [hereafter AGI], Gobierno, Caracas, Legajo 458, September 13, 1806, Manuel de Guevara Vasconcelos to Príncipe de la Paz; September 5, 1806, Francisco Cavallero Sarmiento to Príncipe de la Paz; Estudo/Caracas, 719, November 6, 1808, "Informe de Secretaría á S.M. sobre el asunto de Miranda"; Francisco de Miranda, "Todo pende de nuestra voluntad," in Miranda, *América espera* (Caracas, 1982), 356; Karen Racine, *Francisco de Miranda: A Transatlantic Life in the Age of Revolution* (Wilmington, Del., 2003).

6 319

NOTE

1 **2**
1. Jeremy Adelman, "An Age of Imperial Revolutions,"
3 **4** **5** **6**
American Historical Review 113, no. 2 (2008): 321.

BIBLIOGRAPHY

1 **2** **3**
Adelman, Jeremy. "An Age of Imperial Revolutions." *American*
4 **5** **6**
Historical Review 113, no. 2 (2008): 319-40.

For more on citing articles from journals in *Chicago* style, see pages 226–29.

Citation at a glance
Journal article from a database (*Chicago*)

To cite a journal article from a database in *Chicago* style, include the following elements:

1 Author
2 Title of article
3 Title of journal
4 Volume and issue numbers
5 Year of publication

6 Page number(s) cited (for notes); page range of article (for bibliography)
7 DOI; *or* database name and article number; *or* "stable" or "persistent" URL for article

ON-SCREEN VIEW OF DATABASE RECORD

NOTE

┌──1──┐ ┌────────2────────┐
1. Lillian Guerra, "The Promise and Disillusion of

Americanization: Surveying the Socioeconomic Terrain of
                                        ┌────3────┐
Early-Twentieth-Century Puerto Rico," *Centro Journal*
┌──4──┐ ┌─5─┐ ┌6┐ ┌────────7────────┐
11, no. 1 (1999): 10. Academic Search Premier (10672276).

BIBLIOGRAPHY

┌──1──┐ ┌────────2────────┐
Guerra, Lillian. "The Promise and Disillusion of Americanization:

Surveying the Socioeconomic Terrain of Early-Twentieth-
            ┌───3───┐ ┌──4──┐ ┌─5─┐
Century Puerto Rico." *Centro Journal* 11, no. 1 (1999):
┌6┐ ┌────────7────────┐
8-31. Academic Search Premier (10672276).

For more on citing journal, magazine, and newspaper articles
from databases in *Chicago* style, see items 21, 24, and 27.

■ **20. Article in an online journal**   Give the DOI if the article has one; if there is no DOI, give the URL for the article.

20. Brian Lennon, "New Media Critical Homologies,"
Postmodern Culture 19, no. 2 (2009), http://pmc.iath.virginia.edu
/text-only/issue.109/19.2lennon.txt.

Lennon, Brian. "New Media Critical Homologies." *Postmodern
    Culture* 19, no. 2 (2009). http://pmc.iath.virginia.edu
    /text-only/issue.109/19.2lennon.txt.

■ **21. Journal article from a database**   Give whatever identifying information is available in the database listing: a DOI for the article; or the name of the database and the number assigned by the database; or a "stable" or "persistent" URL for the article. (For an illustrated citation of a journal article from a database, see pp. 228–29.)

21. Constant Leung, "Language and Content in Bilingual
Education," *Linguistics and Education* 16, no. 2 (2005): 239,
doi:10.1016/j.linged.2006.01.004.

Leung, Constant. "Language and Content in Bilingual Education."
    Linguistics and Education 16, no. 2 (2005): 238-52.
    doi:10.1016/j.linged.2006.01.004.

■ 22. Article in a print magazine

22. Tom Bissell, "Improvised, Explosive, and Divisive," *Harper's*, January 2006, 42.

Bissell, Tom. "Improvised, Explosive, and Divisive." *Harper's*, January 2006, 41-54.

■ 23. Article in an online magazine   Include the URL for the article.

23. Katharine Mieszkowski, "A Deluge Waiting to Happen," *Salon*, July 3, 2008, http://www.salon.com/news/feature/2008/07/03/floods/index.html.

Mieszkowski, Katharine. "A Deluge Waiting to Happen." *Salon*, July 3, 2008. http://www.salon.com/news/feature/2008/07/03/floods/index.html.

■ 24. Magazine article from a database   Give whatever identifying information is available in the database listing: a DOI for the article; or the name of the database and the number assigned by the database; or a "stable" or "persistent" URL for the article.

24. "Facing Facts in Afghanistan," *National Review*, November 2, 2009, 14, Expanded Academic ASAP (A209905060).

"Facing Facts in Afghanistan." *National Review*, November 2, 2009, 14. Expanded Academic ASAP (A209905060).

■ 25. Article in a print newspaper   Page numbers are not necessary; a section letter or number, if available, is sufficient.

25. Randal C. Archibold, "These Neighbors Are Good Ones without a New Fence," *New York Times*, October 22, 2008, sec. A.

Archibold, Randal C. "These Neighbors Are Good Ones without a New Fence." *New York Times*, October 22, 2008, sec. A.

■ 26. Article in an online newspaper   Include the URL for the article; if the URL is very long, use the URL for the newspaper's home page. Omit page numbers, even if the source provides them.

26. Doyle McManus, "The Candor War," *Chicago Tribune*, July 29, 2010, http://www.chicagotribune.com/.

McManus, Doyle. "The Candor War." *Chicago Tribune*, July 29, 2010. http://www.chicagotribune.com/.

■ **27. Newspaper article from a database**   Give whatever identifying information is available in the database listing: a DOI for the article; or the name of the database and the number assigned by the database; or a "stable" or "persistent" URL for the article.

27. Clifford J. Levy, "In Kyrgyzstan, Failure to Act Adds to Crisis," *New York Times*, June 18, 2010, General OneFile (A229196045).

Levy, Clifford J. "In Kyrgyzstan, Failure to Act Adds to Crisis." *New York Times*, June 18, 2010. General OneFile (A229196045).

■ **28. Unsigned newspaper article**   Begin the note with the title of the article; begin the bibliography entry with the name of the newspaper.

28. "Renewable Energy Rules," *Boston Globe*, August 11, 2003, sec. A.

Boston Globe. "Renewable Energy Rules." August 11, 2003, sec. A.

■ **29. Book review**

29. Benjamin Wittes, "Remember the Titan," review of *Louis D. Brandeis: A Life*, by Melvin T. Urofsky, *Wilson Quarterly* 33, no. 4 (2009): 100.

Wittes, Benjamin. "Remember the Titan." Review of *Louis D. Brandeis: A Life*, by Melvin T. Urofsky. *Wilson Quarterly* 33, no. 4 (2009): 100-101.

Online sources   For most Web sites, include an author if a site has one, the title of the site, the sponsor, the date the site was last modified or updated, and the site's URL. Do not italicize a Web site title unless the site is an online book or periodical. Use quotation marks for the titles of sections or pages in a Web site. If a site does not have a date, give the date you accessed the site ("accessed January 3, 2011").

■ **30. Web site**

30. Chesapeake and Ohio Canal National Historical Park, National Park Service, last modified April 9, 2010, http://www.nps.gov/choh/index.htm.

Chesapeake and Ohio Canal National Historical Park. National Park Service. Last modified April 9, 2010. http://www.nps.gov/choh/index.htm.

Citation at a glance

Primary source from a Web site (*Chicago*)

To cite a primary source (or another document) from a Web site in *Chicago* style, include as many of the following elements as are available:

1 Author
2 Title of document
3 Title of site
4 Sponsor of site

5 Update or modified date (date of access if none)
6 URL of document

6 http://memory.loc.gov/ammem/alhtml/almss/dep001.html

FIRST PAGE OF DOCUMENT

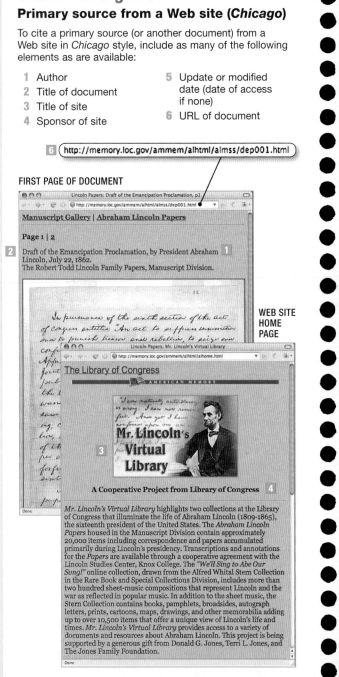

Manuscript Gallery | Abraham Lincoln Papers

Page 1 | 2

2 Draft of the Emancipation Proclamation, by President Abraham Lincoln, July 22, 1862. 1
The Robert Todd Lincoln Family Papers, Manuscript Division.

WEB SITE HOME PAGE

The Library of Congress
AMERICAN MEMORY

3 Mr. Lincoln's Virtual Library

A Cooperative Project from Library of Congress 4

Mr. Lincoln's Virtual Library highlights two collections at the Library of Congress that illuminate the life of Abraham Lincoln (1809–1865), the sixteenth president of the United States. The *Abraham Lincoln Papers* housed in the Manuscript Division contain approximately 20,000 items including correspondence and papers accumulated primarily during Lincoln's presidency. Transcriptions and annotations for the *Papers* are available through a cooperative agreement with the Lincoln Studies Center, Knox College. The *"We'll Sing to Abe Our Song!"* online collection, drawn from the Alfred Whital Stern Collection in the Rare Book and Special Collections Division, includes more than two hundred sheet-music compositions that represent Lincoln and the war as reflected in popular music. In addition to the sheet music, the Stern Collection contains books, pamphlets, broadsides, autograph letters, prints, cartoons, maps, drawings, and other memorabilia adding up to over 10,500 items that offer a unique view of Lincoln's life and times. *Mr. Lincoln's Virtual Library* provides access to a variety of documents and resources about Abraham Lincoln. This project is being supported by a generous gift from Donald G. Jones, Terri L. Jones, and The Jones Family Foundation.

■ **31. Short work from a Web site**

    31. George P. Landow, "Victorian and Victorianism," Victorian Web, last modified August 2, 2009, http://victorianweb.org/vn /victor4.html.

Landow, George P. "Victorian and Victorianism." Victorian Web. Last modified August 2, 2009. http://victorianweb.org/vn /victor4.html.

(For an illustrated citation of a primary source from a Web site, see pp. 232–33.)

■ **32. Online posting or e-mail** E-mails that are not part of an online discussion are treated as personal communications (see item 38). Online postings and e-mails are not included in the bibliography.

    32. Susanna J. Sturgis to Copyediting-L discussion list, July 17, 2010, http://listserv.indiana.edu/archives/copyediting-l.html.

■ **33. Blog (Weblog) post** Treat as a short work from a Web site (item 31). Put the title of the posting in quotation marks; italicize the name of the blog. Insert the word "blog" in parentheses after the name if it is not part of the name.

33. Miland Brown, "The Flawed Montevideo Convention of 1933," *World History Blog*, May 31, 2008, http://www.worldhistoryblog.com /2008/05/flawed-montevideo-convention-of-1933.html.

Brown, Miland. "The Flawed Montevideo Convention of 1933." *World History Blog*. May 31, 2008. http://www .worldhistoryblog.com/2008/05/flawed-montevideo -convention-of-1933.html.

■ **34. Podcast** Treat as a short work from a Web site (item 31), including the following, if available: the author's (or speaker's) name; the title of the podcast, in quotation marks; an identifying number, if any; the title of the site on which the podcast appears; the sponsor of the site; and the URL. Before the URL, identify the type of podcast or file format and the date of posting or your date of access.

34. Paul Tiyambe Zeleza, "Africa's Global Past," Episode 40, Africa Past and Present, African Online Digital Library, podcast audio, April 29, 2010, http://afripod.aodl.org/.

Zeleza, Paul Tiyambe. "Africa's Global Past." Episode 40. Africa Past and Present. African Online Digital Library. Podcast audio. April 29, 2010. http://afripod.aodl.org/.

■ **35. Online audio or video** Cite as a short work from a Web site (see item 31). If the source is a downloadable file, identify the file format or medium before the URL.

35. Richard B. Freeman, "Global Capitalism, Labor Markets, and Inequality," Institute of International Studies, University of California at Berkeley, October 31, 2007, http://www.youtube.com /watch?v=cgNCFsXGUa0.

Freeman, Richard B. "Global Capitalism, Labor Markets, and Inequality." Institute of International Studies, University of California at Berkeley. October 31, 2007. http://www.youtube .com/watch?v=cgNCFsXGUa0.

Other sources (including online versions)

■ **36. Government document**

36. U.S. Department of State, *Foreign Relations of the United States: Diplomatic Papers, 1943* (Washington, DC: GPO, 1965), 562.

U.S. Department of State. *Foreign Relations of the United States: Diplomatic Papers, 1943*. Washington, DC: GPO, 1965.

▓ 37. Unpublished dissertation

37. Stephanie Lynn Budin, "The Origins of Aphrodite" (PhD diss., University of Pennsylvania, 2000), 301-2, ProQuest (AAT 9976404).

Budin, Stephanie Lynn. "The Origins of Aphrodite." PhD diss., University of Pennsylvania, 2000. ProQuest (AAT 9976404).

▓ 38. Personal communication

38. Sara Lehman, e-mail message to author, August 13, 2003.

Personal communications are not included in the bibliography.

▓ 39. Published or broadcast interview

39. Robert Downey Jr., interview by Graham Norton, *The Graham Norton Show*, BBC America, December 14, 2009.

Downey, Robert, Jr. Interview by Graham Norton. *The Graham Norton Show*. BBC America, December 14, 2009.

▓ 40. Video (DVD, Blu-ray Disc)

40. *The Secret of Roan Inish*, directed by John Sayles (1993; Culver City, CA: Columbia TriStar Home Video, 2000), DVD.

The Secret of Roan Inish. Directed by John Sayles. 1993; Culver City, CA: Columbia TriStar Home Video, 2000. DVD.

▓ 41. Sound recording

41. Gustav Holst, *The Planets*, Royal Philharmonic Orchestra, conducted by André Previn, Telarc 80133, compact disc.

Holst, Gustav. *The Planets*. Royal Philharmonic Orchestra. Conducted by André Previn. Telarc 80133. Compact disc.

44 *Chicago* manuscript format; sample pages

44a *Chicago* manuscript format

The guidelines in this section for formatting a *Chicago* paper and preparing endnotes and a bibliography are based on *The Chicago Manual of Style*, 16th ed. (Chicago:

University of Chicago Press, 2010). For pages from a sample paper, see 44b.

Formatting the paper

Title page   Include the full title of your paper, your name, the course title, the instructor's name, and the date. Do not number the title page but count it in the manuscript numbering; that is, the first page of the text will be numbered 2. See page 239 for a sample title page.

Pagination   Using arabic numerals, number all pages except the title page in the upper right corner. You may also place your last name to the left of the page number.

Margins and line spacing   Leave margins of at least one inch at the top, bottom, and sides of the page. Double-space the entire manuscript, including long, indented quotations. (For line spacing in notes and the bibliography, see pp. 237 and 238.) Left-align the text.

Long quotations   See page 214 for *Chicago* guidelines for setting off long quotations from the text.

Capitalization and italics   In titles of works, capitalize all words except articles (*a, an, the*), prepositions (*at, from, between,* and so on), coordinating conjunctions (*and, but, or, nor, for, so, yet*), and *to* and *as*—unless one of these words is first or last in the title or subtitle.

Lowercase the first word following a colon even if the word begins a complete sentence. When the colon introduces a series of sentences or questions, capitalize all sentences in the series, including the first.

Italicize the titles of books, periodicals, and other long works. Use quotation marks around the titles of periodical articles, short stories, poems, and other short works.

Visuals   Visuals are tables and figures, which include drawings, photographs, maps, and charts.

Label each table with an arabic numeral (Table 1, Table 2, and so on) and provide a clear title that identifies the subject. The label and title should appear on separate lines above the table, flush left. Below the table, give its source in a note like this one:

Source: Edna Bonacich and Richard P. Appelbaum, *Behind the Label* (Berkeley: University of California Press, 2000), 145.

For each figure, place a label and a caption below the figure, flush left. The label and caption need not appear on separate lines. The word "Figure" may be abbreviated as "Fig."

Place visuals as close as possible to the sentences that relate to them unless your instructor prefers that visuals appear in an appendix.

URLs (Web addresses)   When a URL must be divided at the end of a line, do not insert a hyphen or break at a hyphen if the URL contains one. Instead, break the URL after a colon or a double slash or before any other mark of punctuation. If your word processing program automatically turns URLs into links (by underlining them and changing the color), turn off this feature.

Headings   *Chicago* does not provide guidelines for the use of headings in student papers. If you would like to insert headings in a long essay or research paper, check first with your instructor. See page 240 for typical placement and formatting of headings.

Preparing the endnotes   Begin the endnotes on a new page at the end of the paper. Center the title "Notes" about one inch from the top of the page, and number the pages consecutively with the rest of the manuscript. See page 241 for an example.

Indenting and numbering   Indent the first line of each note one-half inch from the left margin; do not indent additional lines. Begin the note with the arabic numeral that corresponds to the number in the text. Put a period after the number.

Line spacing   Single-space each note and double-space between notes (unless your instructor prefers double-spacing throughout).

Preparing the bibliography   Typically, the notes in *Chicago* papers are followed by a bibliography, an alphabetically arranged list of all the works cited or consulted. Center the title "Bibliography" about one inch from the top of the page. Number bibliography pages consecutively with the rest of the paper. See page 242 for an example.

Alphabetizing the list   Alphabetize the bibliography by the last names of the authors (or editors); when a work has no author or editor, alphabetize by the first word of the title other than *A*, *An*, or *The*.

If your list includes two or more works by the same author, use six hyphens instead of the author's name in all entries after the first. Arrange the entries alphabetically by title. See item 7 on page 222.

Indenting and line spacing   Begin each entry at the left margin, and indent any additional lines one-half inch. Single-space each entry and double-space between entries (unless your instructor prefers double-spacing throughout).

44b Sample pages from a *Chicago* paper

On the following pages is an excerpt from a research paper written for a history class.

Sample *Chicago* title page

The Massacre at Fort Pillow: **1**
Holding Nathan Bedford Forrest Accountable

Ned Bishop **2**

History 214 **3**
Professor Citro
March 22, 2008

1 Paper title, centered. **2** Writer's name. **3** Course title, instructor's name, date.

(Annotations indicate *Chicago*-style formatting and effective writing.)

Bishop 2

Although Northern newspapers of the time no doubt exaggerated some of the Confederate atrocities at Fort Pillow, most modern sources agree that a massacre of Union troops took place there on April 12, 1864. It seems clear that Union soldiers, particularly black soldiers, were killed after they had stopped fighting or had surrendered or were being held prisoner. Less clear is the role played by Major General Nathan Bedford Forrest in leading his troops. Although we will never know whether Forrest directly ordered the massacre, evidence suggests that he was responsible for it.   **1**

What happened at Fort Pillow?   **2**

Fort Pillow, Tennessee, which sat on a bluff overlooking the Mississippi River, had been held by the Union for two years. It was garrisoned by 580 men, 292 of them from United States Colored Heavy and Light Artillery regiments, 285 from the white Thirteenth Tennessee Cavalry. Nathan Bedford Forrest commanded about 1,500 troops.[1]

The Confederates attacked Fort Pillow on April 12, 1864, and had virtually surrounded the fort by the time Forrest arrived on the battlefield. At 3:30 p.m., Forrest demanded the surrender of the Union forces: "The conduct of the officers and men garrisoning Fort Pillow has been such as to entitle them to being treated as prisoners of war. . . . Should my demand be refused, I cannot be responsible for the fate of your command."[2] Union Major William Bradford, who had replaced   **3** Major Booth, killed earlier by sharpshooters, asked for an hour to consider the demand. Forrest, worried that vessels in the river were bringing in more Union troops, "shortened the time to twenty minutes."[3] Bradford refused to surrender, and Forrest quickly ordered the attack.

The Confederates charged to the fort, scaled the parapet, and fired on

1 Writer's thesis. **2** Headings (centered) guide readers.
3 Quotation cited with endnote.

Sample *Chicago* endnotes

Bishop 8

Notes

1   1. John Cimprich and Robert C. Mainfort Jr., eds., "Fort Pillow Revisited: New Evidence about an Old Controversy," *Civil War History* 28, no. 4 (1982): 293-94.

2   2. Quoted in Brian Steel Wills, *A Battle from the Start: The Life of Nathan Bedford Forrest* (New York: HarperCollins, 1992), 182.

3. Ibid., 183.

4. Shelby Foote, *The Civil War, a Narrative: Red River to Appomattox* (New York: Vintage, 1986), 110.

5. Nathan Bedford Forrest, "Report of Maj. Gen. Nathan B. Forrest, C. S. Army, Commanding Cavalry, of the Capture of Fort Pillow," Shotgun's Home of the American Civil War, accessed March 6, 2008, http://www.civilwarhome.com/forrest.htm.

3   6. Jack Hurst, *Nathan Bedford Forrest: A Biography* (New York: Knopf, 1993), 174.

7. Foote, *Civil War*, 111.

4   8. Cimprich and Mainfort, "Fort Pillow," 295.

9. Ibid., 305.

10. Ibid., 299.

11. Foote, *Civil War*, 110.

12. Quoted in Wills, *Battle from the Start*, 187.

5   13. Albert Castel, "The Fort Pillow Massacre: A Fresh Examination of the Evidence," *Civil War History* 4, no. 1 (1958): 44-45.

14. Cimprich and Mainfort, "Fort Pillow," 300.

1 First line of note indented ½". **2** Note number not raised, followed by period. **3** Authors' names not inverted. **4** Last names and shortened title refer to earlier note by same authors. **5** Single-space notes; double-space between them.

Sample *Chicago* bibliography

Bibliography

1 Castel, Albert. "The Fort Pillow Massacre: A Fresh Examination of the Evidence." *Civil War History* 4, no. 1 (1958): 37-50.

Cimprich, John, and Robert C. Mainfort Jr., eds. "Fort Pillow Revisited: New Evidence about an Old Controversy." *Civil War History* 28, no. 4 (1982): 293-306.

2 Cornish, Dudley Taylor. *The Sable Arm: Black Troops in the Union Army, 1861-1865*. Lawrence: University Press of Kansas, 1987.

Foote, Shelby. *The Civil War, a Narrative: Red River to Appomattox*. New York: Vintage, 1986.

Forrest, Nathan Bedford. "Report of Maj. Gen. Nathan B. Forrest, C. S. Army, Commanding Cavalry, of the Capture of Fort Pillow." Shotgun's Home of the American Civil War. Accessed March 6, 2008. http://www.civilwarhome.com/forrest.htm.

3 Hurst, Jack. *Nathan Bedford Forrest: A Biography*. New York: Knopf, 1993.

McPherson, James M. *Battle Cry of Freedom: The Civil War Era*. New York: Oxford University Press, 1988.

Wills, Brian Steel. *A Battle from the Start: The Life of Nathan Bedford Forrest*. New York: HarperCollins, 1992.

1 Alphabetize by authors' last names. **2** First line of each entry at left margin; additional lines indented ½". **3** Single-space entries; double-space between them.

CSE Papers

45 CSE documentation style

In many science classes, you may be asked to use one of three systems of documentation recommended by the Council of Science Editors (CSE) in *Scientific Style and Format: The CSE Manual for Authors, Editors, and Publishers*, 7th ed. (Reston: CSE, 2006).

45a CSE documentation systems

The three CSE documentation systems specify the ways that sources are cited in the text of the paper and in the reference list at the end of the paper.

In the citation-sequence system, each source is given a superscript number the first time it appears in the paper. Any subsequent references to that source are marked with the same number. At the end of the paper, a list of references provides full publication information for each numbered source. Entries in the reference list are numbered in the order in which they are mentioned in the paper.

In the citation-name system, the list of references is created first, with entries alphabetized by authors' last names. The entries are numbered according to their alphabetical order, and the numbers are used in the text to cite the sources from the list.

In the name-year system, the author of the source is named in the text or in parentheses, and the date is given in parentheses. The reference list at the end of the paper is arranged alphabetically by authors' last names.

Sections 45b and 45c describe formatting of in-text citations and the reference list, respectively, in all three systems.

45b CSE in-text citations

In-text citations in all three CSE systems refer readers to
the reference list at the end of the paper. The reference
list is organized differently in the three systems (see 45c).

▓ 1. Basic format

Citation-sequence or citation-name system

Scientists are beginning to question the validity of linking genes to
a number of human traits and disorders [1].

Name-year

Scientists are beginning to question the validity of linking genes to
a number of human traits and disorders (Allen 2009).

▓ 2. Author named in the text

Citation-sequence or citation-name

Smith [2], studying three species of tree frogs, identified variations
in coloring over a small geographic area.

Name-year

Smith (2010), studying three species of tree frogs, identified
variations in coloring over a small geographic area.

▓ 3. Specific part of source

Citation-sequence or citation-name

Our data differed markedly from Markam's study [3(Figs. 2,7)] on the
same species in North Dakota.

Researchers observed an immune response in "19 of 20 people who
ate a potato vaccine aimed at the Norwalk virus," according to
Langridge [4(p. 68)].

Name-year

Our data differed markedly from Markam's study (2010, Figs. 2, 7)
on the same species in North Dakota.

Researchers observed an immune response in "19 of 20 people who
ate a potato vaccine aimed at the Norwalk virus," according to
Langridge (2009, p. 68).

▓ 4. Work by two authors

Citation-sequence or citation-name

Follow item 1, 2, or 3, depending on the way you are
using the source in your paper.

Name-year

Self-organization plays a complex role in the evolution of biological systems (Johnson and Lam 2010).

Johnson and Lam (2010) explored the complex role of self-organization in evolution.

■ 5. Work by three or more authors

Citation-sequence or citation-name

Follow item 1, 2, or 3 on page 245, depending on the way you are using the source in your paper.

Name-year

Orchid seed banking is a promising method of conservation to preserve species in situ (Seaton et al. 2010).

Seaton et al. (2010) provided a range of in situ techniques for orchid seed banking as a method of conservation of species.

■ 6. Multiple works by one author

Citation-sequence or citation-name

Gawande's work [4,5,6] deals not just with the practice of modern medicine but more broadly with the way we rely on human expertise in every aspect of society.

Name-year: works in different years

Gawande's work (2003, 2007, 2009) deals not just with the practice of modern medicine but more broadly with the way we rely on human expertise in every aspect of society.

Name-year: works in the same year

The works are arranged in the reference list in chronological order, the earliest first. The letters "a," "b," and so on are added after the year, in both the reference list and the in-text citation. (See also the name-year model at the top of p. 250.)

Scientists have investigated the role of follicle stimulating hormone (FSH) in the growth of cancer cells beyond the ovaries and testes (Seppa 2010a).

■ 7. Organization as author

Citation-sequence or citation-name

Follow item 1, 2, or 3 on page 245, depending on the way you are using the source in your paper.

Name-year

Developing standards for handling and processing biospecimens is
essential to ensure the validity of cancer research and, ultimately,
treatment (OBBR 2010).

The reference list entry gives the abbreviation for the
organization's name, followed by the full name of the
organization (Office of Biorepositories and Biospecimen
Research); only the abbreviation is used in the in-text
citation. (See item 3 on pp. 248–49.)

Directory to CSE reference list models

45c CSE references

In the citation-sequence system, entries in the reference list are numbered in the order in which they appear in the text of the paper. In the citation-name system, entries in the reference list are put into alphabetical order and then numbered in that order. In the name-year system, entries are listed alphabetically in the reference list; they are not numbered. See 45b for examples of in-text citations using all three systems. See 46b for details about formatting the reference list.

Basic guidelines

▓ 1. Single author

Citation-sequence or citation-name

1. Bliss M. The making of modern medicine: turning points in the treatment of disease. Chicago: University of Chicago Press; 2011.

Name-year

Bliss M. 2011. The making of modern medicine: turning points in the treatment of disease. Chicago: University of Chicago Press.

▓ 2. Two or more authors
For a source with two to ten authors, list all authors' names; for a source with more than ten authors, list the first ten authors followed by a comma and "et al." (for "and others").

Citation-sequence or citation-name

2. Seaton PT, Hong H, Perner H, Pritchard HW. Ex situ conservation of orchids in a warming world. Bot Rev. 2010;76(2):193-203.

Name-year

Seaton PT, Hong H, Perner H, Pritchard HW. 2010. Ex situ conservation of orchids in a warming world. Bot Rev. 76(2):193-203.

▓ 3. Organization as author

Citation-sequence or citation-name

3. American Cancer Society. Cancer facts and figures for African Americans 2005-2006. Report. Atlanta (GA): The Society; 2005.

Name-year

Give the abbreviation of the organization name in brackets at the beginning of the entry; alphabetize the entry by

the first word of the full name. (For an in-text citation, see
the name-year model at the top of p. 247.)

[ACS] American Cancer Society. 2005. Cancer facts and figures for
African Americans 2005-2006. Report. Atlanta (GA): The Society.

■ 4. Two or more works by the same author

Citation-sequence or citation-name
In the citation-sequence system, list the works in the order
in which they appear in the paper. In the citation-name
system, order the works alphabetically by title. (The following examples are presented in the citation-name system.)

4. Gawande A. Better: a surgeon's notes on performance. New York:
Metropolitan; 2007.

5. Gawande A. The checklist manifesto: how to get things right.
New York: Metropolitan; 2009.

6. Gawande A. Complications: a surgeon's notes on an imperfect
science. New York: Picador; 2003.

Name-year
List the works chronologically, the earliest first.

Gawande A. 2003. Complications: a surgeon's notes on an imperfect
science. New York: Picador.

Gawande A. 2007. Better: a surgeon's notes on performance. New
York: Metropolitan.

Gawande A. 2009. The checklist manifesto: how to get things right.
New York: Metropolitan.

■ 5. Two or more works by the same author in the same year

Citation-sequence or citation-name
In the citation-sequence system, list the works in the order
in which they appear in the paper. In the citation-name
system, order the works alphabetically by title. (The following examples are presented in the citation-sequence
system.)

5. Seppa N. Protein implicated in many cancers. Sci News
[Internet]. 2010 Oct 20 [cited 2011 Jan 22]; [11 paragraphs].
Available from: http://www.sciencenews.org/view/generic/id/64426

8. Seppa N. Anticancer protein might combat HIV. Sci News. 2010
Nov 20;178(11):9.

Name-year

List the works in chronological order, the earliest first, and add the letters "a," "b," and so on after the year. If the works have only a year but not exact dates, arrange the entries alphabetically by title.

Seppa N. 2010a. Fish oil may fend off breast cancer: other supplements studied show no signs of protection. Sci News. Jul 31;178(3):13.

Seppa N. 2010b. Ovary removal boosts survival: procedure shown to benefit women with BRCA mutations. Sci News. Sep 25;178(7):12.

Books

■ 6. Print book

Citation-sequence or citation-name

6. Tobin M. Endangered: biodiversity on the brink. Golden (CO): Fulcrum; 2010.

Name-year

Tobin M. 2010. Endangered: biodiversity on the brink. Golden (CO): Fulcrum.

■ 7. Online book

Citation-sequence or citation-name

7. Wilson DE, Reeder DM, editors. Mammal species of the world [Internet]. Washington (DC): Smithsonian Institution; 3rd ed. Baltimore (MD): Johns Hopkins University Press; c2005 [cited 2010 Oct 14]; [about 200 screens]. Available from: http:// vertebrates.si.edu/mammals/msw/.

Name-year

Wilson DE, Reeder DM, editors. c2005. Mammal species of the world [Internet]. Washington (DC): Smithsonian Institution; 3rd ed. Baltimore (MD): Johns Hopkins University Press; [cited 2010 Oct 14]; [about 200 screens]. Available from: http:// vertebrates.si.edu/mammals/msw/.

■ 8. Book with an editor

Citation-sequence or citation-name

8. Kurimoto N, Fielding D, Musani A, editors. Endobronchial ultrasonography. New York: Wiley-Blackwell; 2011.

Name-year

Kurimoto N, Fielding D, Musani A, editors. 2011. Endobronchial
    ultrasonography. New York: Wiley-Blackwell.

▓ 9. Edition other than the first

Citation-sequence or citation-name

9. Mai J, Paxinos G, Assheuer J. Atlas of the human brain. 2nd ed.
Burlington (MA): Elsevier; 2004.

Name-year

Mai J, Paxinos G, Assheuer J. 2004. Atlas of the human brain. 2nd ed.
    Burlington (MA): Elsevier.

▓ 10. Article or chapter in an edited volume

Citation-sequence or citation-name

10. Underwood AJ, Chapman MG. Intertidal ecosystems. In:
Levin SA, editor. Encyclopedia of biodiversity. Vol. 3. San Diego:
Academic Press; 2000. p. 485-499.

Name-year

Underwood AJ, Chapman MG. 2000. Intertidal ecosystems. In: Levin
    SA, editor. Encyclopedia of biodiversity. Vol. 3. San Diego:
    Academic Press; p. 485-499.

Articles

▓ 11. Article in a print journal

Citation-sequence or citation-name

11. Wasserman EA, Blumberg MS. Designing minds: how should we
explain the origins of novel behaviors. Am Sci. 2010;98(3):183-185.

Name-year

Wasserman EA, Blumberg MS. 2010. Designing minds: how
    should we explain the origins of novel behaviors. Am Sci.
    98(3):183-185.

▓ 12. Article in an online journal

Citation-sequence or citation-name

12. Leslie M. The power of one. Science [Internet]. 2011 Jan 7
[cited 2011 Feb 3];331(6013):24-26. Available from: http://
www.sciencemag.org/content/331/6013/24.1.summary doi:10.1126/
science.331.6013.24-a

Name-year

Leslie M. The power of one. Science [Internet]. 2011 Jan 7
    [cited 2011 Feb 3];331(6013):24-26. Available from: http://
    www.sciencemag.org/content/331/6013/24.1.summary
    doi:10.1126/science.331.6013.24-a

■ 13. Article in a print magazine

Citation-sequence or citation-name

13. Quammen D. Great migrations. Natl Geogr. 2010 Nov:31-51.

Name-year

Quammen D. 2010 Nov. Great migrations. Natl Geogr. 31-51.

■ 14. Article in an online magazine

Citation-sequence or citation-name

14. Matson J. Twisted light could enable black hole detection. Sci
Am [Internet]. 2011 Feb 14 [cited 2011 Feb 28]; [8 paragraphs]. Available
from: http://www.scientificamerican.com/article.cfm?id=twisting-light-oam

Name-year

Matson J. 2011 Feb 14. Twisted light could enable black hole
    detection. Sci Am [Internet]. [cited 2011 Feb 28]; [8
    paragraphs]. Available from: http://
    www.scientificamerican.com/
    article.cfm?id=twisting-light-oam

■ 15. Article in a print newspaper

Citation-sequence or citation-name

15. Wald M. Scientists call for new sources of critical elements.
New York Times (New York Ed.). 2011 Feb 19;B5 (col. 1).

Name-year

Wald M. 2011 Feb 19. Scientists call for new sources of critical
    elements. New York Times (New York Ed.). B5 (col. 1).

■ 16. Article in an online newspaper

Citation-sequence or citation-name

16. Wade N. Human DNA contamination seen in genome databases.
New York Times [Internet]. 2011 Feb 16; [17 paragraphs]. Available
from: http://www.nytimes.com/2011/02/17/science/
17genome.html?ref=science

Name-year

Wade N. 2011 Feb 16. Human DNA contamination seen in genome databases. New York Times [Internet]. [17 paragraphs]. Available from: http://www.nytimes.com/2011/02/17/science/17genome.html?ref=science

■ 17. Article from a database

Citation-sequence or citation-name

17. Logan CA. A review of ocean acidification and America's response. BioScience [Internet]. 2010 [cited 2011 Jun 17];60(10):819-828. General OneFile. Available from: http://find.galegroup.com.ezproxy.bpl.org/. Document No.: A241952492.

Name-year

Logan CA. 2010. A review of ocean acidification and America's response. BioScience [Internet]. [cited 2011 Jun 17];60(10):819-828. General OneFile. Available from: http://find.galegroup.com.ezproxy.bpl.org/. Document No.: A241952492.

Other sources

■ 18. Home page of a Web site

Citation-sequence or citation-name

18. American Society of Gene and Cell Therapy [Internet]. Milwaukee (WI): The Society; c2000-2011 [cited 2011 Jan 16]. Available from: http://www.asgt.org/.

Name-year

[ASGCT] American Society of Gene and Cell Therapy [Internet]. c2000-2011. Milwaukee (WI): The Society; [cited 2010 Jan 16]. Available from: http://www.asgt.org/.

■ 19. Short work from a Web site

Citation-sequence or citation-name

19. Cleveland Clinic [Internet]. Cleveland (OH): The Clinic; c1995-2011. Diabetes and smoking; [cited 2010 Feb 8]; [8 paragraphs]. Available from: http://my.clevelandclinic.org/tobacco/diabetes_and_smoking.aspx

Name-year

Cleveland Clinic [Internet]. c1995-2011. Cleveland (OH): The Clinic.
Diabetes and smoking; [cited 2010 Feb 8]; [8 paragraphs].
Available from: http://my.clevelandclinic.org/tobacco/
diabetes_and_smoking.aspx

■ 20. Report from a government agency (print and online)

Citation-sequence or citation-name

20. National Institute on Drug Abuse (US). Inhalant abuse.
Bethesda (MD): National Institutes of Health (US); 2010 Jul.
NIH Pub. No.: 10-3818. Available from: National Clearinghouse on
Alcohol and Drug Information, Rockville, MD 20852.

20. National Institute on Drug Abuse (US). Inhalant abuse
[Internet]. Bethesda (MD): National Institutes of Health (US);
[revised 2010 Jul; cited 2011 Jan 23]; [about 13 pages]. NIH
Pub. No.: 10-3818. Available from: http://www.drugabuse.gov/
ResearchReports/Inhalants/inhalants.html

Name-year

[NIDA] National Institute on Drug Abuse (US). 2010 Jul. Inhalant
abuse. Bethesda (MD): National Institutes of Health (US). NIH
Pub. No.: 10-3818. Available from: National Clearinghouse on
Alcohol and Drug Information, Rockville, MD 20852.

[NIDA] National Institute on Drug Abuse (US). 2010 Jul. Inhalant
abuse [Internet]. Bethesda (MD): National Institutes of
Health (US); [cited 2010 Jan 23]; [about 13 pages]. NIH Pub.
No.: 10-3818. Available from: http://www.drugabuse.gov/
ResearchReports/Inhalants/inhalants.html

■ 21. Conference presentation (print and online)

Citation-sequence or citation-name

21. Pendleton L. The cost of beach water monitoring errors in
southern California. In: Proceedings of the 2004 National Beaches
Conference; 2004 Oct 13-15; San Diego, CA. Washington (DC):
Environmental Protection Agency (US); 2005 Mar. p. 104-110.

21. Pendleton L. The cost of beach water monitoring errors in
southern California [conference presentation on the Internet]. In:
Proceedings of the 2004 National Beaches Conference [Internet];
2004 Oct 13-15; San Diego, CA. Washington (DC): Environmental

Protection Agency (US); 2005 Mar [cited 2011 Jan 30]. p. 104-110.
Available from: http://water.epa.gov/type/oceb/beaches/
upload/2008_10_28_beaches_meetings_2004_part1.pdf

Name-year

Pendleton L. 2005 Mar. The cost of beach water monitoring errors
in southern California. In: Proceedings of the 2004 National
Beaches Conference; 2004 Oct 13-15; San Diego, CA. Washington
(DC): Environmental Protection Agency (US). p. 104-110.

Pendleton L. 2005 Mar. The cost of beach water monitoring errors
in southern California [conference presentation on the
Internet]. In: Proceedings of the 2004 National Beaches
Conference [Internet]; 2004 Oct 13-15; San Diego, CA.
Washington (DC): Environmental Protection Agency (US);
[cited 2011 Jan 30]. p. 104-110. Available from: http://
water.epa.gov/type/oceb/beaches/upload/
2008_10_28_beaches_meetings_2004_part1.pdf

■ 22. DVD or Blu-ray Disc (BD)

Citation-sequence or citation-name

22. NOVA: secrets beneath the ice [DVD]. Seifferlein B, editor;
Hochman G, producer. Boston: WGBH Educational Foundation; 2010.
1 DVD: 52 min., sound, color.

Name-year

NOVA: secrets beneath the ice [DVD]. 2010. Seifferlein B, editor;
Hochman G, producer. Boston: WGBH Educational Foundation.
1 DVD: 52 min., sound, color.

■ 23. Online video

Citation-sequence or citation-name

23. Life: creatures of the deep: nemertean worms and sea stars
[video on the Internet]. Gunton M, executive producer; Holmes M,
series producer. [place unknown]: Discovery Channel/BBC; 2010
Mar 21 [cited 2011 Feb 4]. 2:55 min. Available from: http://
dsc.discovery.com/videos/life-the-series-videos/?bcid=73073289001

Name-year

Life: creatures of the deep: nemertean worms and sea stars
[video on the Internet]. 2010 Mar 21. Gunton M, executive
producer; Holmes M, series producer. [place unknown]:

Discovery Channel/BBC; [cited 2011 Feb 4]. 2:55 min.
Available from: http://dsc.discovery.com/videos/
life-the-series-videos/?bcid=73073289001

■ 24. Podcast

Citation-sequence or citation-name

24. The spirit of innovation: from high school to the moon [podcast
on the Internet]. Mirsky S, host; Conrad N, interviewee. New York:
Scientific American; 2011 Feb 17 [cited 2011 Feb 27]. 19:26 min.
Available from: http://www.scientificamerican.com/podcast/
episode.cfm?id=from-high-school-innovation-to-the-11-02-17

Name-year

The spirit of innovation: from high school to the moon [podcast
     on the Internet]. 2011 Feb 17. Mirsky S, host; Conrad N,
     interviewee. New York: Scientific American; [cited 2011
     Feb 27]. 19:26 min. Available from: http://
     www.scientificamerican.com/podcast/
     episode.cfm?id=from-high-school-innovation-to-the-11-02-17

■ **25. E-mail** CSE recommends not including personal
communications such as e-mail in the reference list.
A parenthetical note in the text usually suffices: (2010
e-mail to me; unreferenced).

46 CSE manuscript format

The guidelines in this section are adapted from advice
given in *Scientific Style and Format: The CSE Manual for
Authors, Editors, and Publishers*, 7th ed. (Reston: CSE,
2006). When in doubt about the formatting required in
your course, check with your instructor.

46a Formatting the paper

Materials and typeface Use good-quality 8½″ × 11″ white
paper. If your instructor does not require a specific font,
choose one that is standard and easy to read (such as
Times New Roman).

Title page   Center all information on the title page: the title of your paper, your name, the course name, and the date.

Pagination   The title page is counted as page 1, although a number does not appear. Number the first page of the text of the paper as page 2. Type a shortened form of the title followed by the page number in the top right corner of each page.

Margins, spacing, and indentation   Leave margins of at least one inch on all sides of the page. Double-space throughout the paper. Indent the first line of each paragraph one-half inch. When a quotation is set off from the text, indent the entire quotation one-half inch from the left margin.

Abstract   An abstract is a single paragraph at the beginning of the paper that summarizes the paper and might include your research methods, findings, and conclusions. Do not include bibliographic references in the abstract.

Headings   CSE encourages the use of headings to help readers follow the organization of a paper. Common headings for papers reporting research are Introduction, Methods, Results, and Discussion.

Visuals   A visual, such as a table, figure, or chart, should be placed as close as possible to the text that discusses it. In general, try to place visuals at the top of a page.

Appendixes   Appendixes may be used for relevant information that is too long to include in the body of the paper. Label each appendix and give it a title (for example, Appendix 1: Methodologies of Previous Researchers).

Acknowledgments   An acknowledgments section is common in scientific writing because research is often conducted with help from others. Place the acknowledgments at the end of the paper before the reference list.

46b Formatting the reference list

Basic format   Center the title "References" and then list the works you have cited in the paper. Double-space throughout.

Organization of the list   In the citation-sequence system, number the entries in the order in which they appear in the text. In the citation-name system, first alphabetize all the entries by authors' last names (or by organization name or by title for works with no author, ignoring any initial *A*, *An*, or *The*); for two or more works by the same author, arrange the entries alphabetically by title. Then number the entries in the order in which they appear in the list. Make the entire entry flush with the left margin. In both systems, use the number from the reference list whenever you refer to the source in the text of the paper.

In the name-year system, alphabetize the entries by authors' last names (or by organization name or by title for works with no author, ignoring any initial *A*, *An*, or *The*). Place the year after the last author's name, followed by a period. For two or more works by the same author, arrange the entries by year, the earliest first. For two or more works by the same author in the same year, see item 5 at the top of page 250. Unless your instructor prefers otherwise, type the first line of each entry flush left, and indent any additional lines one-half inch.

Authors' names   Give the last name first; use initials for first and middle names, with no periods after the initials and no space between them. Do not use a comma between the last name and the initials. For a work with up to ten authors, use all authors' names; for a work with eleven or more authors, list the first ten names followed by a comma and "et al." (for "and others").

Titles of books and articles   Capitalize only the first word and all proper nouns in the title of a book or an article. Do not underline or italicize titles of books; do not place titles of articles in quotation marks.

Titles of journals   Abbreviate titles of journals that consist of more than one word. Omit the words *the* and *of* and apostrophes. Capitalize all the words or abbreviated words in the title; do not underline or italicize the title: Science, Sci Am, N Engl J Med, Womens Health.

Page ranges   Do not abbreviate page ranges for articles in journals or periodicals or for chapters in edited volumes. When an article appears on discontinuous pages, list all pages or page ranges, separated by commas: 145-149, 162-174. For chapters in edited volumes, use the abbreviation "p." before the numbers (p. 63-90).

Breaking a URL or DOI   When a URL or a DOI (digital object identifier) must be divided, break it only after a double slash or a slash. Do not insert a hyphen, and do not add a period at the end unless a URL ends in a slash.

Glossaries

47 Glossary of usage

This glossary includes words commonly confused, words commonly misused, and words that are nonstandard. It also lists colloquialisms that may be appropriate in informal speech but are inappropriate in formal writing.

a, an   Use *an* before a vowel sound, *a* before a consonant sound: *an apple, a peach.* Problems sometimes arise with words beginning with *h* or *u.* If the *h* is silent, the word begins with a vowel sound, so use *an: an hour, an heir, an honest senator.* If the *h* is pronounced, the word begins with a consonant sound, so use *a: a hospital, a historian, a hotel.* Words such as *university* and *union* begin with a consonant sound, so use *a: a union.* Words such as *uncle* and *umbrella* begin with a vowel sound, so use *an: an underground well.* When an abbreviation or acronym begins with a vowel sound, use *an: an EKG, an MRI.*

accept, except   *Accept* is a verb meaning "to receive." *Except* is usually a preposition meaning "excluding." *I will accept all the packages except that one. Except* is also a verb meaning "to exclude." *Please except that item from the list.*

adapt, adopt   *Adapt* means "to adjust or become accustomed"; it is usually followed by *to. Adopt* means "to take as one's own." *Our family adopted a Vietnamese child, who quickly adapted to his new life.*

adverse, averse   *Adverse* means "unfavorable." *Averse* means "opposed" or "reluctant"; it is usually followed by *to. I am averse to your proposal because it could have an adverse impact on the economy.*

advice, advise   *Advice* is a noun, *advise* a verb. *We advise you to follow John's advice.*

affect, effect   *Affect* is usually a verb meaning "to influence." *Effect* is usually a noun meaning "result." *The drug did not affect the disease, and it had adverse side effects. Effect* can also be a verb meaning "to bring about." *Only the president can effect such a change.*

all ready, already   *All ready* means "completely prepared." *Already* means "previously." *Susan was all ready for the concert, but her friends had already left.*

all right   *All right,* written as two words, is correct. *Alright* is nonstandard.

all together, altogether   *All together* means "everyone gathered." *Altogether* means "entirely." *We were not altogether sure that we could bring the family all together for the reunion.*

allusion, illusion An *allusion* is an indirect reference; an *illusion* is a misconception or false impression. *Did you catch my allusion to Shakespeare? Mirrors give the room an illusion of depth.*

a lot *A lot* is two words. Do not write *alot*.

among, between Ordinarily, use *among* with three or more entities, *between* with two. *The prize was divided among several contestants. You have a choice between carrots and beans.*

amoral, immoral *Amoral* means "neither moral nor immoral"; it also means "not caring about moral judgments." *Immoral* means "morally wrong." *Many business courses are taught from an amoral perspective. Murder is immoral.*

amount, number Use *amount* with quantities that cannot be counted; use *number* with those that can. *This recipe calls for a large amount of sugar. We have a large number of toads in our garden.*

an See *a, an*.

and/or Avoid *and/or* except in technical or legal documents.

anxious *Anxious* means "worried" or "apprehensive." In formal writing, avoid using *anxious* to mean "eager." *We are eager* (not *anxious*) *to see your new house.*

anybody, anyone See pages 21 and 31.

anyone, any one *Anyone*, an indefinite pronoun, means "any person at all." *Any one* refers to a particular person or thing in a group. *Anyone in the class may choose any one of the books to read.*

anyways, anywheres *Anyways* and *anywheres* are nonstandard for *anyway* and *anywhere*.

as *As* is sometimes used to mean "because." But do not use it if there is any chance of ambiguity. *We canceled the picnic because* (not *as*) *it began raining. As* here could mean "because" or "when."

as, like See *like, as*.

averse See *adverse, averse*.

awful The adjective *awful* and the adverb *awfully* are too colloquial for formal writing.

awhile, a while *Awhile* is an adverb; it can modify a verb, but it cannot be the object of a preposition such as *for*. The two-word form *a while* is a noun preceded by an article and therefore can be the object of a preposition. *Stay awhile. Stay for a while.*

back up, backup *Back up* is a verb phrase. *Back up the car carefully. Be sure to back up your hard drive. Backup* is a noun often meaning "duplicate of electronically stored data." *Keep your backup in a safe place. Backup* can also be used as an adjective. *I regularly create backup disks.*

bad, badly *Bad* is an adjective, *badly* an adverb. *They felt bad about being early and ruining the surprise. Her arm hurt badly after she slid into second.* See section 13.

being as, being that *Being as* and *being that* are non-standard expressions. Write *because* instead.

beside, besides *Beside* is a preposition meaning "at the side of" or "next to." *Annie sleeps with a flashlight beside her bed. Besides* is a preposition meaning "except" or "in addition to." *No one besides Terrie can have that ice cream. Besides* is also an adverb meaning "in addition." *I'm not hungry; besides, I don't like ice cream.*

between See *among, between*.

bring, take Use *bring* when an object is being transported toward you, *take* when it is being moved away. *Please bring me a glass of water. Please take these magazines to Mr. Scott.*

can, may *Can* is traditionally reserved for ability, *may* for permission. *Can you speak French? May I help you?*

capital, capitol *Capital* refers to a city, *capitol* to a building where lawmakers meet. *The residents of the state capital protested the development plans. The capitol has undergone extensive renovations. Capital* also refers to wealth or resources.

censor, censure *Censor* means "to remove or suppress material considered objectionable." *Censure* means "to criticize severely." *The school's policy of censoring books has been censured by the media.*

cite, site *Cite* means "to quote as an authority or example." *Site* is usually a noun meaning "a particular place." *He cited the zoning law in his argument against the proposed site of the gas station.* Locations on the Internet are usually referred to as *sites*.

coarse, course *Coarse* means "crude" or "rough in texture." *The hand-knit sweater had a coarse weave. Course* usually refers to a path, a playing field, or a unit of study. *I plan to take a course in car repair this summer.* The expression *of course* means "certainly."

complement, compliment *Complement* is a verb meaning "to go with or complete" or a noun meaning "something that completes." As a verb, *compliment* means "to flatter"; as a noun, it means "flattering remark." *Her skill at rushing the net complements his skill at volleying. Sheiying's music arrangements receive many compliments.*

conscience, conscious *Conscience* is a noun meaning "moral principles"; *conscious* is an adjective meaning "aware or alert." *Let your conscience be your guide. Were you conscious of his love for you?*

continual, continuous *Continual* means "repeated regularly and frequently." *She grew weary of the continual telephone calls. Continuous* means "extended or prolonged without interruption." *The broken siren made a continuous wail.*

could care less *Could care less* is a nonstandard expression. Write *couldn't care less* instead.

could of *Could of* is nonstandard for *could have.*

council, counsel A *council* is a deliberative body, and a *councilor* is a member of such a body. *Counsel* usually means "advice" and can also mean "lawyer"; a *counselor* is one who gives advice or guidance. *The councilors met to draft the council's position paper. The pastor offered wise counsel to the troubled teenager.*

criteria *Criteria* is the plural of *criterion*, which means "a standard, rule, or test on which a judgment or decision can be based." *The only criterion for the scholarship is ability.*

data *Data* is a plural noun meaning "facts or results." But *data* is increasingly being accepted as a singular noun. *The new data suggest* (or *suggests*) *that our theory is correct.* (The singular *datum* is rarely used.)

different from, different than Ordinarily, write *different from. Your sense of style is different from Jim's.* However, *different than* is acceptable to avoid an awkward construction. *Please let me know if your plans are different than* (to avoid *from what*) *they were six weeks ago.*

don't *Don't* is the contraction for *do not. I don't want milk. Don't* should not be used as the contraction for *does not*, which is *doesn't. He doesn't* (not *don't*) *want milk.*

due to *Due to* is an adjective phrase and should not be used as a preposition meaning "because of." *The trip was canceled because of* (not *due to*) *lack of interest. Due to* is acceptable as a subject complement and usually follows a form of the verb *be. His success was due to hard work.*

each See pages 21 and 31.

effect See *affect, effect.*

either See pages 21 and 31.

elicit, illicit   *Elicit* is a verb meaning "to bring out" or "to evoke." *Illicit* is an adjective meaning "unlawful." *The reporter was unable to elicit any information from the police about illicit drug traffic.*

emigrate from, immigrate to   *Emigrate* means "to leave one place to settle in another." *My great-grandfather emigrated from Russia to escape the religious pogroms. Immigrate* means "to enter another place and reside there." *Thousands of Bosnians immigrated to the United States in the 1990s.*

enthused   As an adjective, *enthusiastic* is preferred. *The children were enthusiastic* (not *enthused*) *about going to the circus.*

etc.   Avoid ending a list with *etc.* It is more emphatic to end with an example, and usually readers will understand that the list is not exhaustive. When you don't wish to end with an example, *and so on* is more graceful than *etc.*

everybody, everyone   See pages 21 and 31.

everyone, every one   *Everyone* is an indefinite pronoun. *Everyone wanted to go. Every one*, the pronoun *one* preceded by the adjective *every*, means "each individual or thing in a particular group." *Every one* is usually followed by *of. Every one of the missing books was found.*

except   See *accept, except.*

farther, further   *Farther* describes distances. *Further* suggests quantity or degree. *Detroit is farther from Miami than I thought. You extended the curfew further than necessary.*

fewer, less   *Fewer* refers to items that can be counted; *less* refers to items that cannot be counted. *Fewer people are living in the city. Please put less sugar in my tea.*

firstly   *Firstly* sounds pretentious, and it leads to the ungainly series *firstly, secondly, thirdly, fourthly*, and so on. Write *first, second, third* instead.

further   See *farther, further.*

good, well   See page 39.

graduate   Both of the following uses of *graduate* are standard: *My sister was graduated from UCLA last year. My sister graduated from UCLA last year.* It is nonstandard to drop the word *from*: *My sister graduated UCLA last year.*

grow   Phrases such as *to grow a business* are jargon. Usually the verb *grow* is intransitive (it does not take a direct object). *Our business has grown very quickly.* When *grow* is used in a transitive sense, with a direct object, it means "to cultivate" or "to allow to grow." *We plan to grow tomatoes. John is growing a beard.* (See also pp. 272 and 276.)

hanged, hung *Hanged* is the past-tense and past-participle form of the verb *hang*, meaning "to execute." *The prisoner was hanged at dawn.* *Hung* is the past-tense and past-participle form of the verb *hang*, meaning "to fasten or suspend." *The stockings were hung by the chimney with care.*

hardly Avoid expressions such as *can't hardly* and *not hardly*, which are considered double negatives. *I can (not can't) hardly describe my elation at getting the job.*

he At one time *he* was used to mean "he or she." Today such usage is inappropriate. See pages 17 and 31 for alternative constructions.

hisself *Hisself* is nonstandard. Use *himself*.

hopefully *Hopefully* means "in a hopeful manner." *We looked hopefully to the future.* Some usage experts object to the use of *hopefully* as a sentence adverb, apparently on grounds of clarity. To be safe, avoid using *hopefully* in sentences such as the following: *Hopefully, your son will recover soon.* Instead, indicate who is doing the hoping: *I hope that your son will recover soon.*

however Some writers object to *however* at the beginning of a sentence, but experts advise placing the word according to the meaning and emphasis intended. Any of the following sentences is correct, depending on the intended contrast. *Pam decided, however, to attend the lecture.* *However, Pam decided to attend the lecture.* (She had been considering other activities.) *Pam, however, decided to attend the lecture.* (Unlike someone else, Pam opted for the lecture.)

hung See *hanged, hung.*

illusion See *allusion, illusion.*

immigrate See *emigrate from, immigrate to.*

immoral See *amoral, immoral.*

imply, infer *Imply* means "to suggest or state indirectly"; *infer* means "to draw a conclusion." *John implied that he knew all about computers, but the interviewer inferred that John was inexperienced.*

in, into *In* indicates location or condition; *into* indicates movement or a change in condition. *They found the lost letters in a box after moving into the house.*

in regards to Use either *in regard to* or *as regards*. *In regard to* (or *As regards*) *the contract, ignore the first clause.*

USAGE **hackerhandbooks.com/pocket**
> Language Debates > Sexist language
> *however* at the beginning of
a sentence

irregardless *Irregardless* is nonstandard. Use *regardless.*

is when, is where See section 6c.

its, it's *Its* is a possessive pronoun; *it's* is a contraction for *it is. It's always fun to watch a dog chase its tail.*

kind of, sort of Avoid using *kind of* or *sort of* to mean "somewhat." *The movie was a little* (not *kind of*) *boring.* Do not put *a* after either phrase. *That kind of* (not *kind of a*) *salesclerk annoys me.*

lay, lie See page 25.

lead, led *Lead* is a metallic element; it is a noun. *Led* is the past tense of the verb *lead. He led me to the treasure.*

learn, teach *Learn* means "to gain knowledge"; *teach* means "to impart knowledge." *I must teach* (not *learn*) *my sister to read.*

leave, let *Leave* means "to exit." Avoid using it with the nonstandard meaning "to permit." *Let* (not *Leave*) *me help you with the dishes.*

less See *fewer, less.*

let, leave See *leave, let.*

liable *Liable* means "obligated" or "responsible." Do not use it to mean "likely." *You're likely* (not *liable*) *to trip if you don't tie your shoelaces.*

lie, lay See page 25.

like, as *Like* is a preposition, not a subordinating conjunction. It should be followed only by a noun or a noun phrase. *As* is a subordinating conjunction that introduces a subordinate clause. In casual speech, you may say *She looks like she has not slept.* But in formal writing, use *as. She looks as if she has not slept.*

loose, lose *Loose* is an adjective meaning "not securely fastened." *Lose* is a verb meaning "to misplace" or "to not win." *Did you lose your only loose pair of work pants?*

may See *can, may.*

maybe, may be *Maybe* is an adverb meaning "possibly"; *may be* is a verb phrase. *Maybe the sun will shine tomorrow. Tomorrow may be a brighter day.*

may of, might of *May of* and *might of* are nonstandard for *may have* and *might have.*

media, medium *Media* is the plural of *medium. Of all the media that cover the Olympics, television is the medium that best captures the spectacle of the events.*

must of *Must of* is nonstandard for *must have.*

myself *Myself* is a reflexive or intensive pronoun. Reflexive: *I cut myself.* Intensive: *I will drive you myself.* Do not use *myself* in place of *I* or *me*: *He gave the plants to Melinda and me* (not *myself*).

neither See pages 21 and 31.

none See page 21.

nowheres *Nowheres* is nonstandard for *nowhere.*

number See *amount, number.*

off of *Off* is sufficient. Omit *of.*

passed, past *Passed* is the past tense of the verb *pass. Emily passed me a slice of cake. Past* usually means "belonging to a former time" or "beyond a time or place." *Our past president spoke until past 10:00. The hotel is just past the station.*

plus *Plus* should not be used to join independent clauses. *This raincoat is dirty; moreover* (not *plus*), *it has a hole in it.*

precede, proceed *Precede* means "to come before." *Proceed* means "to go forward." *As we proceeded up the mountain, we saw evidence that some hikers had preceded us.*

principal, principle *Principal* is a noun meaning "the head of a school or an organization" or "a sum of money." It is also an adjective meaning "most important." *Principle* is a noun meaning "a basic truth or law." *The principal expelled her for three principal reasons. We believe in the principle of equal justice for all.*

proceed, precede See *precede, proceed.*

quote, quotation *Quote* is a verb; *quotation* is a noun. Avoid using *quote* as a shortened form of *quotation. Her quotations* (not *quotes*) *from Shakespeare intrigued us.*

real, really *Real* is an adjective; *really* is an adverb. *Real* is sometimes used informally as an adverb, but avoid this use in formal writing. *She was really* (not *real*) *angry.* See also section 13.

reason . . . is because See section 6c.

reason why The expression *reason why* is redundant. *The reason* (not *The reason why*) *Jones lost the election is clear.*

respectfully, respectively *Respectfully* means "showing or marked by respect." *He respectfully submitted his opinion. Respectively* means "each in the order given." *John, Tom, and Larry were a butcher, a baker, and a lawyer, respectively.*

sensual, sensuous *Sensual* means "gratifying the physical senses," especially those associated with sexual pleasure. *Sensuous* means "pleasing to the senses," especially involving art, music, and nature. *The sensuous music and balmy air led the dancers to more sensual movements.*

set, sit *Set* means "to put" or "to place"; *sit* means "to be seated." *She set the dough in a warm corner of the kitchen. The cat sits in the warmest part of the room.*

should of *Should of* is nonstandard for *should have.*

since Do not use *since* to mean "because" if there is any chance of ambiguity. *Because* (not *Since*) *we won the game, we have been celebrating with a pitcher of root beer. Since* here could mean "because" or "from the time that."

sit See *set, sit.*

site, cite See *cite, site.*

somebody, someone, something See pages 21 and 31.

suppose to Write *supposed to.*

sure and *Sure and* is nonstandard for *sure to. Be sure to* (not *sure and*) *bring a gift for the host.*

take See *bring, take.*

than, then *Than* is a conjunction used in comparisons; *then* is an adverb denoting time. *That pizza is more than I can eat. Tom laughed, and then we recognized him.*

that See *who, which, that.*

that, which Many writers reserve *that* for restrictive clauses, *which* for nonrestrictive clauses. (See pp. 57–58.)

theirselves *Theirselves* is nonstandard for *themselves.*

them The use of *them* in place of *those* is nonstandard. *Please send those* (not *them*) *letters to the sponsors.*

then See *than, then.*

there, their, they're *There* is an adverb specifying place; it is also an expletive (placeholder). Adverb: *Sylvia is sitting there patiently.* Expletive: *There are two plums left.* (See also p. 272.) *Their* is a possessive pronoun. *Fred and Jane finally washed their car. They're* is a contraction of *they are. They're late today.*

to, too, two *To* is a preposition; *too* is an adverb; *two* is a number. *Too many of your shots slice to the left, but the last two were right on the mark.*

toward, towards   *Toward* and *towards* are generally inter-changeable, although *toward* is preferred in American English.

try and   *Try and* is nonstandard for *try to*. *I will try to* (not *try and*) *be better about writing to you.*

unique   See page 40.

use to   Write *used to*. *We used to live in an apartment.*

utilize   *Utilize* is often a pretentious substitute for *use*; in most cases, *use* is sufficient. *I used* (not *utilized*) *the best workers to get the job done fast.*

wait for, wait on   *Wait for* means "to be in readiness for" or "await." *Wait on* means "to serve." *We're waiting for* (not *waiting on*) *Ruth before we can leave.*

ways   *Ways* is colloquial when used in place of *way* to mean "distance." *The city is a long way* (not *ways*) *from here.*

weather, whether   The noun *weather* refers to the state of the atmosphere. *Whether* is a conjunction indicating a choice between alternatives. *We wondered whether the weather would clear up in time for our picnic.*

well, good   See page 39.

where   Do not use *where* in place of *that*. *I heard that* (not *where*) *the crime rate is increasing.*

which   See *that, which* and *who, which, that.*

while   Avoid using *while* to mean "although" or "whereas" if there is any chance of ambiguity. *Although* (not *While*) *Gloria lost money in the slot machine, Tom won it at roulette.* Here *While* could mean either "although" or "at the same time that."

who, which, that   Use *who*, not *which*, to refer to persons. Generally, use *that* to refer to things or, occasionally, to a group or class of people. *The player who* (not *that* or *which*) *made the basket at the buzzer was named MVP. The team that scores the most points in this game will win the tournament.*

who, whom   See section 12d.

who's, whose   *Who's* is a contraction of *who is; whose* is a possessive pronoun. *Who's ready for more popcorn? Whose coat is this?*

would of   *Would of* is nonstandard for *would have.*

USAGE   hackerhandbooks.com/pocket
  > Language Debates > Absolute concepts such
                            as *unique*
                    > *who* versus *which* or *that*
                    > *who* versus *whom*

you   See pages 33–34.

your, you're   *Your* is a possessive pronoun; *you're* is a contraction of *you are*. *Is that your bike? You're in the finals.*

48 Glossary of grammatical terms

This glossary gives definitions for parts of speech, such as nouns; parts of sentences, such as subjects; and types of sentences, clauses, and phrases.

   If you are looking up the name of an error (sentence fragment, for example), consult the index or the table of contents instead.

absolute phrase   A word group that modifies a whole clause or sentence, usually consisting of a noun followed by a participle or participial phrase: *Her words echoing in the large arena*, the senator mesmerized the crowd.

active vs. passive voice   When a verb is in the active voice, the subject of the sentence does the action: *Hernando caught the ball.* In the passive voice, the subject receives the action: *The ball was caught by Hernando.* Often the actor does not appear in a passive-voice sentence: *The ball was caught.* See also section 2.

adjective   A word used to modify (describe) a noun or pronoun: the *frisky* horse, *rare old* stamps, *sixteen* candles. Adjectives usually answer one of these questions: Which one? What kind of? How many or how much? See also section 13.

adjective clause   A subordinate clause that modifies a noun or pronoun. An adjective clause begins with a relative pronoun (*who, whom, whose, which, that*) or a relative adverb (*when, where*) and usually appears right after the word it modifies: The book *that goes unread* is a writer's worst nightmare.

adverb   A word used to modify a verb, an adjective, or another adverb: rides *smoothly*, *unusually* attractive, *very* slowly. An adverb usually answers one of these questions: When? Where? How? Why? Under what conditions? To what degree? See also section 13.

adverb clause   A subordinate clause that modifies a verb (or occasionally an adjective or adverb). An adverb clause begins with a subordinating conjunction such as *although, because, if, unless,* or *when* and usually appears at the beginning or the end of a sentence: *When the sun went down*, the hikers prepared their camp. See also *subordinate clause; subordinating conjunction*.

agreement   See sections 10 and 12.

antecedent   A noun or pronoun to which a pronoun refers: When the *battery* wears down, we recharge *it*. The noun *battery* is the antecedent of the pronoun *it*.

appositive   A noun or noun phrase that renames a nearby noun or pronoun: Bloggers, *conversationalists at heart*, are the online equivalent of talk show hosts.

article   The word *a, an,* or *the,* used to mark a noun. Also see 16b.

case   See sections 12c and 12d.

clause   A word group containing a subject, a verb, and any objects, complements, or modifiers. See *independent clause; subordinate clause*.

collective noun   See sections 10e and 12a.

common noun   See section 22a.

complement   See *object complement; subject complement*.

complex sentence   A sentence consisting of one independent clause and one or more subordinate clauses. In the following example, the subordinate clause is italicized: We walked along the river *until we came to the bridge*.

compound-complex sentence   A sentence consisting of at least two independent clauses and at least one subordinate clause: *Jan dictated a story, and the children wrote whatever he said*. In the preceding sentence, the subordinate clause is *whatever he said*. The two independent clauses are *Jan dictated a story* and *the children wrote whatever he said*.

compound sentence   A sentence consisting of two independent clauses. The clauses are usually joined with a comma and a coordinating conjunction (*and, but, or, nor, for, so, yet*) or with a semicolon: *The car broke down,* but *a rescue van arrived within minutes. A shark was spotted near shore; people left the water immediately*.

conjunction   A joining word. See *conjunctive adverb; coordinating conjunction; correlative conjunction; subordinating conjunction*.

conjunctive adverb   An adverb used with a semicolon to connect independent clauses: The bus was stuck in traffic; *therefore*, the team was late for the game. The most commonly used conjunctive adverbs are *consequently, furthermore, however, moreover, nevertheless, then, therefore,* and *thus*. See page 62 for a longer list.

coordinating conjunction One of the following words, used to join elements of equal grammatical rank: *and, but, or, nor, for, so, yet.*

correlative conjunction A pair of conjunctions connecting grammatically equal elements: *either . . . or, neither . . . nor, whether . . . or, not only . . . but also,* and *both . . . and.* See also 3b.

count noun See pages 48–49.

demonstrative pronoun A pronoun used to identify or point to a noun: *this, that, these, those. This* is my favorite chair.

direct object A word or word group that receives the action of the verb: The hungry cat clawed *the bag of dry food.* The complete direct object is *the bag of dry food.* The simple direct object is always a noun or a pronoun, in this case *bag.*

expletive The word *there* or *it* when used at the beginning of a sentence to delay the subject: *There* are eight planes waiting to take off. *It* is healthy to eat breakfast every day. The delayed subjects are the noun *planes* and the infinitive phrase *to eat breakfast every day.*

gerund A verb form ending in *-ing* used as a noun: *Reading* aloud helps children appreciate language. The gerund *reading* is used as the subject of the verb *helps.*

gerund phrase A gerund and its objects, complements, or modifiers. A gerund phrase always functions as a noun, usually as a subject, a subject complement, or a direct object. In the following example, the phrase functions as a direct object: We tried *planting tulips.*

helping verb One of the following words, when used with a main verb: *be, am, is, are, was, were, being, been; has, have, had; do, does, did; can, will, shall, should, could, would, may, might, must.* Helping verbs always precede main verbs: *will work, is working, had worked.* See also *modal verb.*

indefinite pronoun A pronoun that refers to a nonspecific person or thing: *Something* is burning. The most common indefinite pronouns are *all, another, any, anybody, anyone, anything, both, each, either, everybody, everyone, everything, few, many, neither, nobody, none, no one, nothing, one, some, somebody, someone, something.* See also pages 21 and 31.

independent clause A word group containing a subject and a verb that can or does stand alone as a sentence. In addition to at least one independent clause, many sentences contain subordinate clauses that function as adjectives, adverbs, or nouns. See also *clause; subordinate clause.*

indirect object A noun or pronoun that names to whom or for whom the action of a sentence is done: We gave *her* some leftover yarn. An indirect object always precedes a direct object, in this case *some leftover yarn.*

infinitive The word *to* followed by the base form of a verb: *to think, to dream.*

infinitive phrase An infinitive and its objects, complements, or modifiers. An infinitive phrase can function as a noun, an adjective, or an adverb. Noun: *To live without health insurance* is risky. Adjective: The Nineteenth Amendment gave women the right *to vote.* Adverb: Volunteers knocked on doors *to rescue people from the flood.*

intensive or reflexive pronoun A pronoun ending in *-self* (or *-selves*): *myself, yourself, himself, herself, itself, ourselves, yourselves, themselves.* An intensive pronoun emphasizes a noun or another pronoun: I *myself* don't have a job. A reflexive pronoun names a receiver of an action identical with the doer of the action: Did Paula cut *herself*?

interjection A word expressing surprise or emotion: *Oh! Wow! Hey! Hooray!*

interrogative pronoun A pronoun used to introduce a question: *who, whom, whose, which, what. What* does history teach us?

intransitive verb See *transitive and intransitive verbs.*

irregular verb See *regular and irregular verbs.* See also section 11a.

linking verb A verb that links a subject to a subject complement, a word or word group that renames or describes the subject: The winner *was* a teacher. The cherries *taste* sour. The most common linking verbs are forms of *be*: *be, am, is, are, was, were, being, been.* The following sometimes function as linking verbs: *appear, become, feel, grow, look, make, seem, smell, sound, taste.* See also *subject complement.*

modal verb A helping verb that cannot be used as a main verb. There are nine modals: *can, could, may, might, must, shall, should, will,* and *would*: We *must* shut the windows before the storm. The verb phrase *ought to* is often classified as a modal as well. See also *helping verb.*

modifier A word, phrase, or clause that describes or qualifies the meaning of a word. Modifiers include adjectives, adverbs, prepositional phrases, participial phrases, some infinitive phrases, and adjective and adverb clauses.

mood See section 11c.

noncount noun See pages 49–50.

noun The name of a person, place, thing, or concept (*freedom*): The *lion* in the *cage* growled at the *zookeeper.*

noun clause   A subordinate clause that functions as a noun, usually as a subject, a subject complement, or a direct object. In the following sentence, the italicized noun clause functions as the subject: *Whoever leaves the house last* must lock the door. Noun clauses usually begin with *how, who, whom, whoever, that, what, whatever, whether,* or *why*.

noun equivalent   A word or word group that functions like a noun: a pronoun, a noun and its modifiers, a gerund phrase, some infinitive phrases, or a noun clause.

object   See *direct object; indirect object.*

object complement   A word or word group that renames or describes a direct object. It always appears after the direct object: The kiln makes clay *firm and strong.*

object of a preposition   See *prepositional phrase.*

participial phrase   A present or past participle and its objects, complements, or modifiers. A participial phrase always functions as an adjective describing a noun or pronoun. Usually it appears before or after the word it modifies: *Being a weight-bearing joint,* the knee is often injured. Plants *kept in moist soil* will thrive.

participle, past   A verb form usually ending in *-d, -ed, -n, -en,* or *-t: asked, stolen, fought.* Past participles are used with helping verbs to form perfect tenses (had *spoken*) and the passive voice (were *required*). They are also used as adjectives (the *stolen* car).

participle, present   A verb form ending in *-ing.* Present participles are used with helping verbs in progressive forms (is *rising,* has been *walking*). They are also used as adjectives (the *rising* tide).

parts of speech   A system for classifying words. Many words can function as more than one part of speech. See *adjective, adverb, conjunction, interjection, noun, preposition, pronoun, verb.*

passive voice   See *active vs. passive voice.*

personal pronoun   One of the following pronouns, used to refer to a specific person or thing: *I, me, you, she, her, he, him, it, we, us, they, them.* After Julia won the award, *she* gave half of the prize money to a literacy program. See also *antecedent.*

phrase   A word group that lacks a subject, a verb, or both. Most phrases function within sentences as adjectives, as adverbs, or as nouns. See *absolute phrase; appositive; gerund phrase; infinitive phrase; participial phrase; prepositional phrase.*

possessive case   See section 19a.

possessive pronoun   A pronoun used to indicate ownership: *my, mine, your, yours, her, hers, his, its, our, ours, your, yours, their, theirs*. The guest made *his* own breakfast.

predicate   A verb and any objects, complements, and modifiers that go with it: The horses *exercise in the corral every day*.

preposition   A word placed before a noun or noun equivalent to form a phrase modifying another word in the sentence. The preposition indicates the relation between the noun (or noun equivalent) and the word the phrase modifies. The most common prepositions are *about, above, across, after, against, along, among, around, at, before, behind, below, beside, besides, between, beyond, by, down, during, except, for, from, in, inside, into, like, near, of, off, on, onto, out, outside, over, past, since, than, through, to, toward, under, unlike, until, up, with, within,* and *without*.

prepositional phrase   A phrase beginning with a preposition and ending with a noun or noun equivalent (called the *object of the preposition*). Most prepositional phrases function as adjectives or adverbs. Adjective phrases usually come right after the noun or pronoun they modify: The road *to the summit* was treacherous. Adverb phrases usually appear at the beginning or the end of the sentence: *To the hikers*, the brief shower was a welcome relief. The brief shower was a welcome relief *to the hikers*.

progressive verb forms   See pages 28–29 and 46–47.

pronoun   A word used in place of a noun. Usually the pronoun substitutes for a specific noun, known as the pronoun's *antecedent*. In the following example, *alarm* is the antecedent of the pronoun *it*: When the *alarm* rang, I reached over and turned *it* off. See also *demonstrative pronoun; indefinite pronoun; intensive or reflexive pronoun; interrogative pronoun; personal pronoun; possessive pronoun; relative pronoun*.

proper noun   See section 22a.

regular and irregular verbs   When a verb is regular, both the past tense and the past participle are formed by adding *-ed* or *-d* to the base form of the verb: *walk, walked, walked*. The past tense and past participle of irregular verbs are formed in a variety of other ways: *ride, rode, ridden; begin, began, begun; go, went, gone;* and so on. Also see 11a.

relative adverb   The word *when* or *where*, when used to introduce an adjective clause. See also *adjective clause*.

relative pronoun   One of the following words, when used to introduce an adjective clause: *who, whom, whose, which, that*. The writer *who* won the award refused to accept it.

sentence A word group consisting of at least one independent clause. See also *complex sentence*; *compound sentence*; *compound-complex sentence*; *simple sentence*.

simple sentence A sentence consisting of one independent clause and no subordinate clauses: *Without a passport, Eva could not visit her parents in Poland.*

subject A word or word group that names who or what the sentence is about. In the following example, the complete subject (the simple subject and all of its modifiers) is italicized: *The devastating effects of famine* can last for many years. The simple subject is *effects*. Also see *subject after verb*; *understood subject*.

subject after verb Although the subject normally precedes the verb, sentences are sometimes inverted. In the following example, the subject *the sleepy child* comes after the verb *sat*: Under the table *sat the sleepy child*. When a sentence begins with the expletive *there* or *it,* the subject always follows the verb. See also *expletive*.

subject complement A word or word group that follows a linking verb and either renames or describes the subject of the sentence. If the subject complement renames the subject, it is a noun or a noun equivalent: That signature may be *a forgery*. If it describes the subject, it is an adjective: Love is *blind*.

subjunctive mood See section 11c.

subordinate clause A word group containing a subject and a verb that cannot stand alone as a sentence. Subordinate clauses function within sentences as adjectives, adverbs, or nouns. They begin with subordinating conjunctions such as *although, because, if,* and *until* or with relative pronouns such as *who, which,* and *that*. See *adjective clause*; *adverb clause*; *independent clause*; *noun clause*.

subordinating conjunction A word that introduces a subordinate clause and indicates the relation of the clause to the rest of the sentence. The most common subordinating conjunctions are *after, although, as, as if, because, before, even though, if, since, so that, than, that, though, unless, until, when, where, whether,* and *while*. Note: The relative pronouns *who, whom, whose, which,* and *that* also introduce subordinate clauses.

tenses See section 11b.

transitive and intransitive verbs Transitive verbs take direct objects, nouns or noun equivalents that receive the action. In the following example, the transitive verb *wrote* takes the direct object *a story*: Each student *wrote* a story. Intransitive verbs do not take direct objects: The audience *laughed*. If any words follow an intransitive verb, they are adverbs or word groups functioning as adverbs: The audience *laughed* at the talking parrot.

understood subject   The subject *you* when it is understood but not actually present in the sentence. Understood subjects occur in sentences that issue commands or advice: [*You*] Put your clothes in the hamper.

verb   A word that expresses action (*jump, think*) or being (*is, was*). A sentence's verb is composed of a main verb possibly preceded by one or more helping verbs: The band *practiced* every day. The report *was* not *completed* on schedule. Verbs have five forms: the base form, or dictionary form (*walk, ride*); the past-tense form (*walked, rode*); the past participle (*walked, ridden*); the present participle (*walking, riding*); and the -*s* form (*walks, rides*).

verbal phrase   See *gerund phrase; infinitive phrase; participial phrase.*

Acknowledgments

Academic OneFile, screen shot of David L. Kranz, "Tracking the Sounds of Franco Zeffirelli's *The Taming of the Shrew*." October 28, 2009. Reprinted with permission of Gale/Cengage Learning.

Louise Bogan, excerpt from "Women" from *The Blue Estuaries: Poems 1923–1968*. Copyright © 1968 by Louise Bogan. Reprinted with permission of Farrar, Straus & Giroux, LLC.

EBSCO Information Services, screen shots from *Centro Journal* 11.1 (1999): 10 and *Journal of Macromarketing* 27.4 (December 2007). Reprinted with permission of EBSCO Information Services.

Thomas Friedman, title page and copyright page from *Hot, Flat, and Crowded*. Copyright © 2008 by Thomas Friedman. Used with permission of Farrar, Straus & Giroux, a division of Macmillan Publishing.

Robert Frost, excerpt from "Fire and Ice," from *The Poetry of Robert Frost*, edited by Edward Connery Lathem. Copyright © 1916, 1936, 1942, 1944, 1951, 1956, 1958 by Robert Frost. Copyright © 1964, 1967, 1970, 1975 by Lesley Frost Ballantine. Copyright © 1916, 1923, 1928, 1930, 1939, 1947, 1969 by Henry Holt and Co., Ltd. Reprinted with permission of Henry Holt, LLC, and Random House, Ltd.

Shirley Geok-lin Lim, title page from *Asian-American Literature: An Anthology*. Copyright © 2000 by NTC/Contemporary Publishing Group, Inc. Reprinted with permission of the McGraw-Hill Companies.

Phil McKenna, "The Cyber-Bullies Are Always with You . . ." from *New Scientist* (July 2007): 26–27. Reprinted with permission of Reed Business Information.

Jack McLaughlin, ed., title page, copyright page, and pages 60–61 from *To His Excellency Thomas Jefferson: Letters to a President*. Copryght © 1991. Reprinted with permission of Avon Books, a division of HarperCollins Publishers, and W. W. Norton, Inc., original publisher of the hardcover edition.

Lydia Yuri Minatoya, first page of selection from "Transformation" from *Talking to High Monks in the Snow*. Copyright © 1992 by Lydia Yuri Minatoya. Reproduced with permission of HarperCollins Publishers, Inc.

The New Bedford Whaling Museum & Old Dartmouth Historical Society, screen shot of "Overview of American Whaling." October 27, 2009. Reprinted with permission of The New Bedford Whaling Museum & Old Dartmouth Historical Society.

Constance M. Ruzich, cover and first page of "For the Love of Joe: The Language of Starbucks" from *The Journal of Popular Culture* 41.3 (2008). Copyright © The Authors. Journal Compilation © 2008 Blackwell Publishing, Inc. Reprinted with permission of Blackwell Publishing, Inc.

Laurel Thatcher Ulrich, title page and copyright page from *A Midwife's Tale: The Life of Martha Ballard, Based on Her Diary, 1785–1812*. Copyright © 1991. Used with permission of Vintage Books, a division of Random House, Inc.

Brenda Wineapple, copyright page and title page from *White Heat: The Friendship of Emily Dickinson and Thomas Wentworth Higginson*. Copyright © 2008. Reprinted with permission of Alfred A. Knopf, a division of Random House, Inc.

Vivian H. Wright et al., "Cyberbullying: Using Virtual Scenarios to Educate and Raise Awareness" from the *Journal of Computing in Teacher Education* 26.1 (2009): 35–42. Reprinted with permission of the publisher.

Index

Documentation Directories

Directory to MLA works cited models

Continued >

Directory to MLA works cited models
(*Continued*)

Directory to APA reference list models

Continued >

Directory to *Chicago*-style notes and bibliography entries *(Continued)*

Directory to CSE reference list models

Charts and Lists for Quick Reference

Checklist for Global Revision

Focus

▶ Is your thesis stated clearly enough? Is it placed where readers will notice it?

▶ Does each idea support the thesis?

Organization

▶ Can readers easily follow the structure? Would headings help?

▶ Do topic sentences signal new ideas?

▶ Do you present ideas in a logical order?

Content

▶ Are your supporting ideas persuasive?

▶ Do you fully develop important ideas?

▶ Is the draft concise enough — free of irrelevant or repetitious material?

Style

▶ Is your tone appropriate — not too stuffy, not too casual?

▶ Are your sentences clear, direct, and varied?

Use of sources

▶ Which sources inform, support, or extend your argument?

▶ Have you varied the function of sources — to provide background, explain concepts, lend authority, and counter objections? Do you introduce sources with signal phrases that indicate these functions?

▶ Is it clear how your sources relate to your argument?

▶ Do you analyze sources in your own words?

▶ Is your own argument easy to identify and to understand, with or without your sources?

▶ Is the draft free of plagiarism? Are summaries and paraphrases in your own words? Is quoted material enclosed in quotation marks or set off from the text?

▶ Have you documented source material that is not common knowledge?

List of Excerpts from Student Papers

For full texts of these and other student papers, including annotated bibliographies and papers in CSE style, visit **hackerhandbooks.com/pocket** and click on Model papers.

Visiting the Writing Center

Step 1: Gather your materials.

▶ Gather materials your instructor has provided: the assignment, sample papers, your syllabus.

▶ Gather your own materials: a copy of your draft, copies of texts you have cited in your paper, previous papers with instructor comments.

Step 2: Organize your materials and prepare questions.

▶ Reread the assignment. If you are confused, ask your instructor to clarify the assignment before you visit the writing center.

▶ Look at previous papers with instructor comments. Can those comments help you think about your current paper?

▶ Create a list of specific questions to focus your writing center conversation.

Step 3: Visit the writing center.

▶ Be on time and treat your tutor or consultant with courtesy and respect.

▶ Participate actively by asking questions and taking notes.

▶ Understand the limitations of your visit. Be prepared to cover one or two major issues.

▶ Understand the purpose of your visit. Most writing center staff are trained to give you suggestions and feedback, but they will not write or edit your paper for you.

Step 4: Reflect on your visit.

▶ As soon as possible after your visit, make sure you understand your notes from the session and add anything you didn't have time to write during your visit.

▶ As you revise, apply your notes to your entire paper. Don't focus only on the parts of your paper you looked at in the session.

▶ Do not feel obligated to follow advice that you disagree with. Writing center staff are trained to provide helpful feedback, but you are the author; you decide which changes will help you best express your meaning.

▶ As you revise, keep track of questions or goals for your next writing center visit.

Revision Symbols

abbr	abbreviation **23a**	" "	quotation marks **20**
adj/adv	adjective or adverb **13**	.	period **21a**
add	add needed word **4**	?	question mark **21b**
agr	agreement **10, 12a**	!	exclamation point **21c**
appr	inappropriate language **9**	—	dash **21d**
art	article **16b**	( )	parentheses **21e**
awk	awkward	[ ]	brackets **21f**
cap	capital letter **22**	. . .	ellipsis mark **21g**
case	case **12c, 12d**	/	slash **21h**
cliché	cliché **9b**	*pass*	ineffective passive **2b**
cs	comma splice **15**	*pn agr*	pronoun agreement **12a**
dm	dangling modifier **7c**	*ref*	pronoun reference **12b**
-ed	*-ed* ending **11a**	*run-on*	run-on sentence **15**
ESL	English as a second language/multi-lingual writers **16**	*-s*	*-s* ending on verb **10, 16a**
frag	sentence fragment **14**	*sexist*	sexist language **9d, 12a**
fs	fused sentence **15**	*shift*	confusing shift **5**
hyph	hyphen **24b**	*sl*	slang **9c**
irreg	irregular verb **11a**	*sp*	misspelled word **24a**
ital	italics **23c**	*sv agr*	subject-verb agreement **10**
jarg	jargon **9a**	*t*	verb tense **11b**
lc	use lowercase letter **22**	*usage*	see glossary of usage
mix	mixed construction **6**	*v*	voice **2**
mm	misplaced modifier **7a–b, 7d**	*var*	sentence variety **8**
mood	mood **11c**	*vb*	problem with verb **11, 16a**
num	numbers **23b**	*w*	wordy **1**
om	omitted word **4, 16c**	//	faulty parallelism **3**
p	punctuation	^	insert
ˆ,	comma **17a–i**	*x*	obvious error
no ,	no comma **17j**	#	insert space
;	semicolon **18a**	‿	close up space
:	colon **18b**		
ˀ,	apostrophe **19**		

Detailed Menu